The
Secret
Life
of the
Modern
House

To Faith

The Secret Life of the Modern House

The evolution of the way we live now

Dominic Bradbury   **ilex**

Contents

Introduction

Charles Gwathmey – Gwathmey Residence and Studio,
Amagansett, Long Island, New York, United States, 1965

House and home represents the point where architecture and design impact most prominently upon our lives.

Our homes are our most precious safe havens. In good times, they offer the focal point for so many of our personal pleasures and delights. In more difficult times, they become refuges and one of our greatest sources of reassurance. Given this central position in our day-to-day lives, the importance of house and home can hardly be overstated. For the fortunate, 'home' becomes a silent but beloved member of the family, which plays an important part in so many daily experiences and routines. In this respect, house and home represents the point where architecture and design impact most prominently upon our lives.

So when our homes evolve, this has real resonance for us all. Since the beginning of the 20th century, houses and apartments have changed radically, within a gentle revolution that has gradually shaped and altered the manner in which we live. Over this period we have begun to pay more and more attention to the way that our homes are designed, arranged and ordered, while at the same time architects and interior designers have introduced ideas that have transformed patterns of living.

From the late 19th century through to the present, this quiet revolution has seen a move away from traditional, cellular and formal rooms towards a more relaxed, fluid and interconnected collection of living spaces. From the Victorian ideal of reception rooms, a dining room and back-of-houses spaces, including the kitchen, we have shifted increasingly towards open-plan living with combined spaces for living, eating and often cooking as well. Reacting against the restrictions of box-like rooms, architects have created 'universal spaces' or 'great rooms' with a more generous sense of scale, volume and light. Banks of glass within non-supporting 'curtain walls' have also helped to dissolve the boundaries between inside and outside space, connecting us to terraces, outdoor rooms and gardens.

While such changes may have been pioneered by architects designing and building new, modern houses, these ideas have also filtered into many period properties, where rooms have been combined and opened up to create more open and sociable living spaces. Extensions and additions to Victorian or Georgian homes might provide family rooms, perhaps with open kitchens, and links to the outdoors and possibly even the landscape beyond.

This home revolution has not just been about space and light, but has also embraced new technologies and engineering. Over the course of 150 years, electricity has – of course – transformed the way that we all live, with electric lighting taking over from gas lighting and candlelight, while new generations of domestic appliances have made their way into the heart of most houses and apartments. During a similar span of time, bathrooms came into their own, combining 'water closets', bathing and pleasure in one fresh space, and becoming ever more sophisticated and luxurious over the decades. In addition, many houses and apartments now offer space for working from home, while in recent decades the whole idea of leisure time has seen the introduction of home gyms, dens and media rooms. If we add all of these things together, we start to see that homes have been transformed and we have hardly even begun, yet, to talk about aesthetics and style.

From the Arts & Crafts movement, via Art Nouveau and Art Deco, 20th-century architecture and design began to embrace Modernism, followed by Post-Modernism and then something more eclectic and 'contemporary'. There was an ongoing struggle between minimalism and maximalism, between those who favoured rational functionalism and those who argued for vibrant self-expression. All of these movements and approaches helped, as we will see over the following chapters, to influence or inspire the character of our homes.

The personality of a home

The notion of 'character' in relation to our houses and apartments is an important one. Every home has a character, or personality. When we talk of a house that has little personality, we are generally being critical, given that the idea of character has such powerful allure. This sense of character comes from so many different ingredients, including the location and setting; the period and provenance of the building in question; the architectural and interior approach; the selection of materials; the choice of furniture, furnishings, art and books, as well as more personal treasures and curiosities. Our homes can be seen as echoes of our own personalities, yet they also have intrinsic individual characteristics that go well beyond us.

When we discuss character, we are soon reminded that the concept of house and home encompasses so many different roles, functions and possibilities, which overlap with architecture and design but also take us far beyond them. At the most simplistic level, a house is a shelter. Yet, as the writer and philosopher Gaston Bachelard puts it:

> Our house is our corner of the world. As has often been said, it is our first universe, a real cosmos in every sense of the word. If we look at it intimately, the humblest dwelling has beauty.[1]

A cabin or hut has this kind of simple charm and delight, at least in our imaginations. And yet we also talk of the 'House of God', or the 'Houses of Parliament' or the 'House of Representatives' and apply the concept of house and home to some of the most crucial, important and central institutions within our societies and cultures. Even in the absence of organized religion, most villages will have a 'meeting house' of some kind that plays a pivotal part in the social make-up of the community. The way that we use the word 'house' suggests that it's not just a shelter, but also a spiritual or emotional focal point for many people. It's the place most attuned to our own personal experiences, to our family lives and our relationships, while serving as a repository of memories. Even the most ardent Modernist architects, such as Le Corbusier, not only spoke of the house as a functional 'machine for living in' but also referred to the beauty, poetry and spirituality of the home:

> To build one's own house is very much like making one's will…When the time does arrive for building this house, it is not the mason's nor the craftsman's moment, but the moment in which every man makes one *poem*, at any rate, in his life.[2]

The focus on the poetic reminds us that the home is a crucial place of self-expression for the individual, as well as for the architect or designer. We all want to be able to express our own tastes and aesthetic ideas within our homes and write our own individual 'poem'. Part of the pleasure of having a home of one's own is the freedom to make such aesthetic and poetic choices for ourselves.

Many artists and designers have treated their houses as a particular kind of canvas for their own work. During the 1880s, the Swedish artist

Carl Larsson famously decorated his country house, Little Hyttnäs, at Sundborn, in a way that echoed his own painting style and then recorded the results – and his family life at home – in his watercolours. Similarly, the British painters and designers Duncan Grant and Vanessa Bell used the walls, doors and surfaces of their East Sussex farmhouse, Charleston, as a canvas for their decorative painting. For artists and architects from Jean Cocteau to Luis Barragán, a wall offered a surface to be filled with images and colour.

The home in the arts and philosophy

In his book *The Poetics of Space*, Gaston Bachelard explores how the concept of house and home has such a powerful place in art, poetry, literature and our own dreams and imaginations. This connects, also, with the idea of a house as a character in itself and with invented literary houses such as Austen's Pemberley, Dickens's Satis House and du Maurier's Manderley, which feel almost as vivid and 'real' as any iconic work of architecture. As Gaston Bachelard says:

> Through poems, perhaps more than through recollections, we touch the ultimate poetic depth of the space of a house. This being the case, if I were asked to name the chief benefit of the house, I should say: the house shelters daydreaming, the house protects the dreamer, the house allows one to dream in peace.[3]

Bachelard examines the importance of the house in art, yet also the personal resonance of, for instance, the house in which we were born or where we grew up and how we then carry this with us in our imaginations and memories. His book also serves to underline the importance of house and home within philosophy, as well as art and architecture.

For the writer and philosopher Henry David Thoreau, the cabin that he built for himself near Walden Pond in New England, where he lived for just over two years during the 1840s, represented a thoughtful escape from the pressures of work, commerce and society. It was a self-made escape, or 'poem', where he sought to reconnect with nature and the seasons, while trying to concentrate upon his own ideas and 'spiritual truths'. Part of

Thoreau's resulting book, *Walden*, looks at the importance of the whole idea of shelter and the value of simplicity:

> I went to the woods because I wished to live deliberately, to front only the essential facts of life, and see if I could not learn what it had to teach, and not, when I came to die, discover I had not lived… I wanted to live deep and suck out all the marrow of life, to live so sturdily and Spartan-like as to put to rout all that was not life.[4]

The German philosopher Martin Heidegger, similarly, preferred to work and write in a simple three-room cabin, known as 'Heidegger's Hut', in the Black Forest mountains. Again, part of the attraction for Heidegger was the combination of simplicity and solitude, which allowed him to focus on the essentials of living and the patterns of his own thoughts. 'On a deep winter's night when a wild, pounding snowstorm rages around the cabin and veils and covers everything, that is the perfect time for philosophy,' Heidegger wrote. 'Then its questions become simple and essential.'[5]

The philosopher Ludwig Wittgenstein, however, took a very different view of architectural simplicity (see page 45). Asked by his sister, Margaret, to help design her new family home in Vienna, Wittgenstein famously took charge of the project while developing an obsessive eye for detail and precision. The philosopher took a particular interest in the engineering and mechanical systems, while stripping away any decorative ornament or pattern in favour of minimalist purity and austerity.

Thoreau, Heidegger and Wittgenstein were all looking for their own version of domestic simplicity. Yet, as the architect, professor of urbanism and writer Witold Rybczynski has argued, the other great driver of the evolution of the home is comfort. An often underrated quality in architectural circles, comfort is – for most people – an essential requirement for house and home.

In his 1986 book *Home: A Short History of an Idea*, Rybczynski argues that the quest for comfort rather than technology or engineering has driven the development of the modern home, helping to explain – for example – the importance and relevance of key advances such as gaslight and a fully fledged bathroom. He is critical, though, of the modern interior and the way that it has – in his view – created 'a rupture in the evolution of domestic comfort' and goes on to say:

> Its emphasis on space has caused it to ignore privacy, just as its interest in industrial-looking materials and objects has led it away from domesticity. Austerity, both visual and tactile, has replaced delight.[6]

Just as there has been a long battle since the beginning of the 20th century between minimalism and maximalism, there has also been a philosophical struggle, or dialectic, between the desire for simplicity in the home and the desire for comfort, which Rybczynski tends to equate with a nostalgic love of tradition and the past. The good news is that, although our houses and apartments are shaped to a significant extent by shifts in modern architecture and design, we still have plenty of choices about whether we embrace a simpler way of living or opt for maximum comfort.

Designing for oneself and for family and friends

As well as being places of philosophical enquiry and self-expression, for architects houses are also essential laboratories of design. This is especially true of their own homes, many of which are described in this book, and which serve as vital places of experimentation and key drivers for new and original ideas. Here, without the constant demands of a client, architects and designers are liberated to either make their own mistakes or invent the future.

Architects' homes have often sat at the junction of new movements or stylistic shifts and changes, including the two very different houses that Otto Wagner built for himself in Vienna around the turn of the 19th–20th centuries (see page 35), or the pioneering modern house and studio that Charles and Ray Eames built for themselves in California (see page 110), Philip Johnson's Glass House in Connecticut (see page 146) and Oscar Niemeyer's Casa das Canoas (see page 208). These were architectural manifestos made real.

Similarly, the famous familial commission gifted by generous parents to a young architect who just happened to be their own child has generated some extraordinary and highly inventive houses. Chief among these are

Robert Venturi's house for his mother, Vanna Venturi, on the edge of Philadelphia (see page 252) and Charles Gwathmey's house on Long Island for his own parents (see pages 6 and 257).

Such projects offered ways and means to progress new thinking and to experiment with fresh materials, engineering and technology. Yet the same was also true of many enlightened and adventurous patrons of architecture and design, who were prepared to take risks in the pursuit of the creation of homes that were original, bespoke, modern and different. High among them was Edgar Kaufmann and his family, who asked Frank Lloyd Wright to design and build Fallingwater in Pennsylvania (see page 93) and then asked Richard Neutra to create another landmark 20th-century house in the form of the Kaufmann House in Palm Springs (see page 107).

There were also inadvertent, or reluctant, revolutionaries such as Dr Edith Farnsworth. Having commissioned master architect Ludwig Mies van der Rohe to design a weekend escape for her next to the Fox River, near Plano, Illinois, she found herself living in one of the most radical and experimental homes of the post-war period. A see-through house made of glass with a universal, open-plan living space, it was not quite what she expected (see page 140).

A gentle revolution

Importantly, as this book will hopefully convey as it traverses the course of the 20th and early 21st centuries, houses don't stay still. Our homes are in motion, always evolving and changing, little by little. Architecture and design are, in themselves, part of a complex continuum that allows houses and buildings the scope to evolve.

During the 20th century, architects explored reinforced concrete, steel frames and curtain walls while pioneering open-plan living, inside–outside connectivity and 'upside-down houses', where living spaces on the upper level could take advantage of the best of the views. Some experimented with prefabrication and factory-made houses, as they looked for ways to make good design more affordable and democratic. Gradually, we all learned more about architecture and the various component parts that contributed to modern patterns of living, while balancing the desire for simplicity with the need for both comfort and self-expression.

Looking forward, deep into the 21st century, we already have some idea of where the continuum is going to take us next and a sense of the key themes and preoccupations that will shape our houses and apartments. The green imperative and the need to play our part in the struggle against climate change are already seeing a much greater focus upon sustainability within both the design of our homes and the way that we live in them (see page 314). Architecturally, there is an increasing concentration on renewable materials, as well as ways of conserving energy in the home. More generally, a mixture of low-tech and high-tech ideas and systems means that we can lower our own carbon footprints while also moving towards net zero or even opting to take ourselves off the grid. Sustainability will be at the core of the next gentle revolution in residential architecture and design, offering all sorts of advantages. Whatever these changes may be, our houses and homes will remain our most precious and personal havens.

Arts & Crafts
The Thoughtful Home

1

Charles Rennie Mackintosh – Hill House, Helensburgh,
Argyll and Bute, Scotland, 1903

Philip Webb and
William Morris
Red House,
Bexleyheath, Kent,
England, 1860

Charles Voysey
The Homestead
Frinton-on-Sea, Essex,
England, 1905

Edward Prior
Voewood
Holt, Norfolk, England, 1905

Greene & Greene
Gamble House
Pasadena, California, United
States, 1908

Charles Rennie Mackintosh
Hill House
Helensburgh, Argyll and Bute,
Scotland, 1903

Edwin Lutyens
Castle Drogo
Drewsteignton, Devon,
England, 1930

L ike the two-faced Roman god, Janus, the architects and designers of the Arts & Crafts movement had the rare advantage of being able to look forwards to the future and backwards to the past at the same time. The Arts & Crafts pioneers of the late 19th and early 20th centuries represented an important period of transition between the old and the new. Architects and designers such as Edwin Lutyens, Charles and Henry Greene, Charles Voysey, Edward Prior and Charles Rennie Mackintosh were precursors – or outriders – for the modern age of architecture and aesthetics that was to come, playing a particularly important role in the evolution of attitudes and approaches to the turn-of-the-century home.

The gods and giants of the Arts & Crafts era, which spanned many different countries and contexts, could be described as romantic progressives. On the one hand, they took particular inspiration from a pre-industrial age, before the rise of the factories and mass production, with a nostalgic appreciation for what they saw as a golden age of artisanal beauty and achievement. There was a particular fascination with the Middle Ages, which Arts & Crafts thinkers revered for the essential simplicity and 'honesty' of its architecture and interiors – whether it was a village church or a farmstead. The Middle Ages also offered a marked point of contrast to the growing decorative excesses of the Victorian age, fuelled by the growth of an army of commercial tradesmen and the rise of the factory system.

> Time was when the mystery and wonder of handicrafts were well acknowledged by the world, when imagination and fancy mingled with all things made by man; and in those days all handicraftsmen were artists, as we should now call them.

So said one of the founding fathers of the Arts & Crafts movement, William Morris, in a famous lecture of 1877 originally entitled 'The Decorative Arts'.[1] Morris and his disciples argued for the vital reconnection of art and craft, of decoration and design, and for a resurgence of the skilled artisan, whose talent would be truly respected and valued once again. They praised the noble beauty of the applied arts, contrasting such passionate pursuits with the soul-destroying conditions of the factories.

Yet, on the other hand, Morris and many of his followers were avant-garde radicals and adventurers. They wanted the world to be a better and more beautiful place, and saw both design and the decorative arts as a way of making this possible. They rejected the prevailing grandeur of neo-classicism in favour of a more modest but original approach, drawing inspiration from vernacular architecture, including farmhouses, cottages and barns, and there were romantic references to medievalism along with Gothic flourishes now and again. But Arts & Crafts architects also took an innovative approach to spatial planning, adopting more relaxed, fluid and free-flowing plans and layouts than might usually be seen in Georgian and Victorian houses. Architects such as Edward Prior were among the first architects to explore the structural use of concrete for residential commissions, combined with more natural and familiar Arts & Crafts materials such as timber, brick and stone. Greene & Greene in the United States and Charles Rennie Mackintosh in Scotland embraced electricity and electric lighting for their house projects while the technology was still in its infancy, seeing no contradiction between such a distinctly modern medium and a design philosophy that promoted the importance of nature and the hand-made. These Arts & Crafts houses, like their designers, looked forwards and backwards at the very same time.

Red House, a slice of utopia

One of the foundation stones of the Arts & Crafts movement was William Morris's own home, Red House, completed in 1860. The house was designed by Morris and his friend and colleague the architect Philip Webb: the two first met while they were both working in the London architectural office of George Edmund Street. In 1859 Morris married Jane Burden, a muse and model to Pre-Raphaelite painter Dante Gabriel Rossetti, as well as to Morris himself, whose multiple, overlapping talents embraced the art of painting, textile design, poetry and other writing, including novels and translations. Morris wanted to build a new family home for himself and Jane but also wanted to step away from London's Bloomsbury district, where he had been living since 1856. He settled on Bexleyheath, long before it was swallowed up by the suburbs of southeast London. Back in the early 1860s, the setting was still bucolic, with orchards forming part of the grounds and fields beyond.

Philip Webb and William Morris – Red House, Bexleyheath, Kent, England, 1860

Here, Morris and Webb designed a new farmhouse, using brick, timber and tile, which helped to generate a vibrant organic character, also expressed in the close synergy between the building and the surrounding gardens.

From today's perspective, Red House may not appear very 'modern'. There were no fully functioning bathrooms in the way we think of them today (although indoor toilets were included) and there was a semi-traditional pattern of service spaces and servants' quarters within the L-shaped, two-storey house. But as the architect and architectural critic Sir Hugh Casson once wrote, 'at the time it was built…it represented a quiet revolution'.[2]

Morris and Webb placed two of the largest and most significant rooms upstairs, which was otherwise occupied by the bedrooms. Here were Morris's spacious study and also the drawing room: a generous space, with a vaulted ceiling and a large brick fireplace, which Morris wanted to be 'the most beautiful room in the world'.[3] Light and open, with the feel of a chapel, the room was beautifully detailed with an integrated settle and shelving unit at one end, topped by a miniature minstrels' gallery and flanked by paintings by Rossetti and fellow Pre-Raphaelite Edward Burne-Jones.

The house featured many integrated, custom-made elements and highly crafted pieces designed by Morris, Webb and others, including stained glass windows, a dresser in the dining room and textiles by William and Jane Morris. The house was a spur to Morris's own creativity, helping to inspire the beginnings of the decorative arts company that eventually became Morris & Co. There was an order and cohesion to the house that came from this rounded, all-encompassing vision that emanated from Morris himself and his devotion to the bespoke and the handmade. The house adopted multiple layers of character, which held together seamlessly but also modestly, with a degree of restraint throughout that allows the beautifully expressed detailing and the natural charm of the materials to shine through.

Red House represented a kind of romantic dream, or utopian ideal, and certainly there was a strong utopian theme to Morris's work as a whole and his notion of creating an 'earthly paradise'. But, like many dreams, it had to come to an end. Despite the couple having two children together, the relationship between William and Jane Morris became increasingly strained, partly because of her close connection and ongoing affair with Rossetti. Just five years later, in 1865, Morris felt the dream had ended and he sold his small slice of utopia. But that did not stop the house, nor Morris himself, becoming key points of reference in the development of the Arts & Crafts movement both in Britain and abroad.

For the celebrated writer and critic Nikolaus Pevsner, part of the importance of Morris and his work was the way in which he focused attention on house and home, rather than on a mansion or a country estate. 'We owe it to him that an ordinary man's dwelling-house has once more become worthy of the architect's thought, and a chair, a wallpaper, or a vase a worthy object of the artist's imagination.'[4] Other leading figures in the Arts & Crafts movement, such as Charles Voysey and Greene & Greene, similarly devoted themselves largely to the domestic sphere, helping to create a 'school' of architecture and design that was focused on the residential world above all, while adopting key ideas and principles eloquently laid down by Morris.

Today, we tend to celebrate Morris as a pattern designer and the creator of seductive and sinuous floral wallpapers produced by Morris & Co., which are still highly popular. But Morris was one of the first designers and cultural commentators to begin to question the place of applied ornament in the home, arguing that it needed to have a sense of connection to its setting rather than simply being superficial:

> True it is that in many or most cases we have got so used to this ornament, that we look upon it as if it had grown of itself, and note it no more than the mosses on the dry sticks with which we light our fires. So much the worse! For there *is* the decoration, or some pretence of it, and it has, or ought to have, a use and a meaning.[5]

Morris argued that ornament had to have relevance and beauty. He believed that decoration offered possibilities for pleasure, both for the user and the maker, but only when it had some meaning. For him, that meaning came from an 'alliance with nature'. For Arts & Crafts architects and designers, the natural beauty of the materials themselves, especially timber and stone, often was enough and could be simply made to shine through craftsmanship. There is a degree of restraint as well as modesty to many Arts & Crafts homes, beginning with Red House, where the intrinsic character of these materials was just as important as the considered, meaningful use of pattern and decoration. The same was true of Arts & Crafts furniture, which tended to be simpler, plainer and lighter in tone than much of the work of Victorian makers and upholsterers, with the joints, techniques and methodology exposed and seen as part of the whole rather than hidden away.

Understated beauty in The Homestead

This sense of restraint, order, modesty and cohesion shines through in the work of architects such as Charles Voysey and Mackay Hugh Baillie Scott, who were designing houses and interiors in the early years of the 20th century. Voysey's houses, such as The Homestead (completed 1905) in Frinton-on-Sea, have a calm sense of beauty, where everything is, of course, beautifully made but also thoughtfully conceived with an eye upon the whole, from the overall architecture down to small details like the hand-made timber door latches. Like Morris, Voysey was a wallpaper and textile designer, with a love of motifs drawn from nature such as birds and trees,

Charles Voysey – The Homestead, Frinton-on-Sea, Essex, England, 1905

yet at The Homestead – designed for a bachelor in the insurance industry – the interiors are beautifully rounded and understated. Voysey explained the benefits of his approach:

> Try the effect of a well-proportioned room, with white washed walls, plain carpet and simple oak furniture, and nothing in it but necessary articles of use, and one pure ornament in the form of a simple vase of flowers, not a cosmopolitan crowd of all sorts, but one or two sprays of one kind, and you will then find reflections begin to dance on your brain; each object will be received on the retina, and understood, classified and dismissed from the mind, and you will be free as a bird to wander in the sunshine or storm of your own thoughts.[6]

The Homestead, like so many of Voysey's houses, has many charms and playful touches, such as an occasional porthole window facing the garden in the sitting room and its welcoming inglenook fireplace – the hearth was always a key focal point in Arts & Crafts houses. Yet Voysey, like Morris, took a careful and considered approach to pattern and ornament so that it would never be overwhelming. There was as much pleasure in the simple brick arch over the inglenook as in the few small birds punctuating the white tiles around the fireside, in a living space that was warm and welcoming and offered the feeling of liberation that Voysey thought so important and valuable.

Voewood, a foretaste of open-plan living

In the early years of the 20th century, Arts & Crafts architects began to explore ideas and techniques that we now associate with modern architecture and modern living. A prime example is Edward Prior's Voewood in Holt, Norfolk, completed in 1905, which was one of the first houses in Britain built using reinforced concrete, even if there were few outward signs of it, given that the exterior was finished with brick and local flint.

Voewood (which was also known as Home Place for many years) was commissioned by the Reverend Percy Lloyd, who hoped that the rural setting, not far from the coast, would be of benefit to his wife, who was in poor health. Prior designed the house to connect to the gardens, providing terraces and two integrated verandahs, or 'cloisters', where the Lloyds could enjoy the fresh air. The sunken gardens in front of the house were created as Prior's workmen excavated the flint and aggregates used to build Voewood, lending it a highly organic, contextual charm.

For the three-storey house, Prior used an innovative butterfly floor plan (which has two or more wings at angles of about 45 degrees to the house's core), with the two wings pushing outwards towards the sunken garden. It was a plan favoured by Prior, together with a number of other Edwardian architects, as it allowed him to maximize the sense of light and the connections with the surroundings. It also created the opportunity to create a double-height 'great room' at the very heart of the house.

Partly inspired by the idea of the medieval great hall, this fluid, open-plan living space was another big favourite among Arts & Crafts architects. Prior's generously proportioned great room offered drama, light, volume and open space. There was a vast inglenook fireplace to one side and an open-sided gallery to the other, at first-floor level. The mezzanine gallery doubled as a landing connecting the bedrooms in the wings and as a modern

Edward Prior – Voewood, Holt, Norfolk, England, 1905

take on the minstrels' lookout. The great room looked to the past, yet was also a foretaste of open-plan living and the idea of a living space suited to many different uses.

Like Voysey, Prior was determined to allow the crafted character of the materials to shine through, both within and without. Flint is a commonly used material in north Norfolk, and Prior used it to great effect, combining it with candy-twist chimneys made of brick with a gentle spiral pattern. Inside, the staircase, floors and doors are largely in timber, highly crafted and simply expressed.

Looking at Voewood and its gardens today, it seems extraordinary that Mrs Lloyd was not enamoured by it. Yet she was reluctant to spend time here and the Lloyds soon rented out the house, which became successively a boys' school, a cottage hospital and a retirement home until it was eventually restored by rare-book dealer Simon Finch, who carefully turned it back into a home.

Arts & Crafts on the international stage

Importantly, Arts & Crafts was a movement with an international resonance that spread far and wide, becoming one of the first of many cross-border cultural and design movements that spanned the 20th century. There was a strong Arts & Crafts strand in parts of Europe, particularly in Finland and Hungary, while it was also one of the influences that played upon architects of the Vienna Secession (see page 34). In addition, parallels have been drawn with a revitalized craft tradition in Japan at around the same time.

But it was in North America that Arts & Crafts, or Craftsman Style, truly flourished. There was an English influence, particularly from Morris, but American Arts & Crafts architects and designers soon began to develop their own unique version of the aesthetic, which resonated widely with an American audience. This was, in part, because it fitted in with a growing desire to create a new kind of home that was distinctively American in character, rather than a variant of Mediterranean, Tudor, Spanish Revival or other styles largely imported from Europe. Towards the end of the 19th century and into the early 20th, American architects, including Frank Lloyd Wright (see page 84), saw a way of combining ideas promoted by Morris and others with their own outlook and their heartfelt ambition to create a style well rooted in American contexts and landscapes. With its thoughtful modesty, the Arts & Crafts ethos sat well with American architects and designers who wanted to create a more authentic, democratic aesthetic for the home while drawing on indigenous, local, natural materials that helped reinforce the bonds with land and location.

Furniture manufacturer Gustav Stickley promoted the Arts & Crafts design philosophy in his work while also, in 1901, launching a magazine called *The Craftsman*, which became a vehicle for spreading the gospel across North America. Within a few years, the highly ambitious Stickley had launched a 'Home Builders' Club' for subscribers and had begun making architectural plans for houses available to his readers.

Gamble House, a handcrafted original

On the West Coast, the most famous proponents of the Arts & Crafts style were Charles and Henry Greene, and their most accomplished achievement was the Gamble House (completed 1908) in a district of Pasadena known as 'Little Switzerland'. The house was designed for David Gamble, the wealthy son of the co-founder of the Cincinnati-based Procter & Gamble soap and tallow company, and his wife, Mary. The Gambles commissioned Greene & Greene to design a winter residence in Pasadena for themselves, their three children and Mary's sister, Aunt Julia. The generous budget available offered the Greenes the opportunity to create a home that was more ambitious, sophisticated and cutting-edge than anything they had done before but that was still infused with an Arts & Crafts, or Craftsman, ethos. In 1907, nearly two years before the completion of the Gamble House, Charles Greene wrote:

> Let us begin all over again. We have got to have bricks and stone and wood and plaster: common, homely, cheap materials, every one of them. Leave them as they are…why disguise them? The noblest work of art is to make these common things beautiful.[7]

The Gamble House was not exactly cheap, but the sentiments expressed chimed with those put forward by Morris and Voysey. The Gambles' home is elegantly made, but much of the intrinsic warmth comes from the

Greene & Greene –
Gamble House,
Pasadena, California,
United States, 1908

careful use of timber rather than applied ornament. There's something of a Japanese or Asian influence, particularly within the design of the branch-and-blossom stained glass in the hallway and dining room, as well as a touch of the American–Swiss-chalet style that permeates part of Pasadena, but the Greenes' work is a true handcrafted original.

The shingle-coated building is arranged over two principal floors and was designed to promote strong synergy with the outdoors and the fresh air. Terraces around the house, plus sleeping porches on the upper storey alongside three of the larger bedrooms, offer open-sided retreats on warm nights and for daytime escapism. Like so many Arts & Crafts houses in England, the architecture and interiors were designed by the same authors, lending clarity and purity to the results. A range of woods (including oak, cedar, ash, redwood, mahogany, maple and walnut) has been used for walls, floors, ceilings and a great deal of integrated furniture, including the fitted benches by the inglenook in the living room. Much of the joinery features rounded edges, which subtly soften the interiors throughout.

But the Gambles also wanted a 'modern' house. There was an internal intercom system and electric lighting, or lanterns, throughout. Electricity in the home was still something of a rarity in the early years of the 20th century and was treated by many with worry and suspicion, particularly concerning its potential impact on health and eyesight. Yet many Arts & Crafts makers, including Louis Comfort Tiffany, embraced electric lighting even if they did take a more expressive approach to its design, which stepped into the more ornate realm of Art Nouveau (see page 34). Electric lighting was, in itself, a new medium that was to rapidly transform the home over the following years in ways that are hard to imagine from the perspective of the 21st century.

On the cusp of change at Hill House

In Scotland, Charles Rennie Mackintosh famously combined elements of Arts & Crafts, Art Nouveau and Scottish vernacular to create a fusion style all of his own. He shared many ideals and interests with Arts & Crafts architects but also had a particular passion for Japanese craft, an awareness of shifting aesthetic styles (particularly Art Nouveau) on the European continent and a deep-rooted understanding of Scottish vernacular. All of these interests came together in his work, tied up with the idea of creating something fresh, original and new fitted to the turn of the century.

In the residential realm, one of the fullest examples of Mackintosh's convergent style was Hill House in Helensburgh (see page 16). Around 40km (25 miles) west of Glasgow, this house was built for the publisher Walter W Blackie and his wife, Anna. The exterior of the house, which was completed in 1903, has the feel of a reinvented Scottish baronial castle. A rendered sandstone façade lends a sculptural quality to the building, with its towering chimneys and an extraordinary semi-cylindrical drum to one side holding the main staircase, reminiscent of a submarine's conning tower. It's a building that feels on the cusp of change, somewhere between tradition and modernity.

From the outside the house looks almost austere, with nothing – at Blackie's request – in the way of 'adventitious ornament'. But Mackintosh and his wife and design partner, Margaret Macdonald, were given control over almost every aspect of the interiors, including much of the furniture and the distinctive gas lighting designs. There are highly romantic and uplifting spaces full of light, such as the drawing room, with its fitted window seat overlooking the garden, wall stencils and fireplace with a mosaic tile surround, or the master bedroom with its vaulted ceiling, rose stencils on the walls and fitted wardrobes. There are also more masculine, traditional rooms like Mr Blackie's library and the dining room, where the family introduced some of their own furniture. Such contrasts add to the intriguing complexities of a house sitting upon the boundary between two different worlds.

Castle Drogo, an inspirational folly

If we are searching for the end of the Arts & Crafts era, then we could carry on through to 1930 and consider the completion of Sir Edwin Lutyens's Castle Drogo in Devon. Often described as England's 'last castle', Drogo was another hybrid that spoke of the past and the future. The castle was commissioned in 1910 by Julius Drewe, who had made a fortune at a young age after co-founding the Home & Colonial Stores retail business. With both time and money to play with, Drewe became fascinated by his own family history and saw Drogo as an opportunity to create a new family seat. In the end, the project would take nearly 20 years to complete, at a vast cost way beyond the £60,000 originally anticipated.

Drewe turned to Lutyens, who was to become one of England's greatest architects and was at the height of a career that eventually spanned six decades and hundreds of projects. Among Lutyens's own heroes were Webb and Morris and, while Lutyens also explored neo-classicism, much of his work embraced Arts & Crafts thinking, along with multiple close collaborations with the celebrated garden designer Gertrude Jekyll. One of Lutyens's most delightful early houses in an Arts & Crafts style was Goddards (1900) in Surrey, complete with a butterfly floor plan, a central 'great room', and an indoor skittle (ninepins) alley in one of the two wings.

Drogo was on another scale entirely, originally conceived of as a vast Y-shaped building with two projecting wings and an epic great hall at the centre. Over time, the original plans were radically scaled back, but the house still retains an epic monumentality that spans the medieval and the modern. The castellated granite exterior, using stone from a nearby

Edwin Lutyens –
Castle Drogo,
Drewsteignton, Devon,
England, 1930

quarry, is pared down to create an almost abstract, unadorned outline, with
the bands of stone echoing geological strata; elements like the small chapel
alongside the main house look like sculptures or maquettes (preliminary
models). Circulation spaces are almost minimalist in character but are
juxtaposed with more colourful family spaces such as the panelled drawing
room. The semi-subterranean kitchen is a wonder in itself, top-lit by a
domed lantern window, and reads as an echo of the Middle Ages, yet the
house also had its own lifts and its own electric power supply from two
hydroelectric turbines. The craftsmanship throughout is exquisitely, and
expensively, done even if the asphalt-coated roof soon began to leak.

After Julius Drewe lost his eldest son in World War I, the feeling that
Drogo was a folly gathered pace and the house was only completed a year
before Drewe himself passed away. But the last castle was a glorious folly,
a decidedly immodest dream space encapsulating different times, centuries
and styles. It was an enigmatic epitaph to the Arts & Crafts era, but so
unique and varied in itself that it was also a rich source of inspiration for
Post-Modernists such as Robert Venturi (see page 250), who found much to
admire in Castle Drogo's complex fusion of forms and wonders.

Ornament & Crime
Vienna & Beyond

2

Otto Wagner – Villa Wagner I, Vienna, Austria, 1886

Otto Wagner
Villa Wagner I and II
Vienna, Austria, 1886/1912

Adolf Loos
Steiner House
Vienna, Austria, 1910

Josef Hoffmann
Palais Stoclet
Brussels, Belgium, 1911

Ludwig Wittgenstein
and Paul Engelmann
Haus Wittgenstein
Vienna, Austria, 1928

O ver the course of around 20 years, spanning the late 19th and early 20th centuries, Vienna saw a miniature revolution that carried the city all the way from traditional architecture and design through to the brink of Modernism itself and a whole new way of living. During this time, Viennese architects and artists shifted away from traditional historicism and plunged headlong into Art Nouveau – known in Vienna as the Wiener Secession ('Vienna Secession') – before questioning this movement's undeniable passion for ornamental excess and declaring it close to aesthetically bankrupt. It was a rollercoaster journey through a broad spectrum of very different aesthetics, offering an extraordinary microcosm of a wider, global debate around the role of decoration in design compared with the need for an emphasis on logic and function. This story was told in Vienna, as elsewhere, in the form of a sequence of ground-breaking houses.

Art Nouveau was, in itself, a complex and glorious mass of contradictions. On paper, Art Nouveau architects and designers had a good deal in common with their brothers and sisters in the Arts & Crafts movement, championed by William Morris and his followers (see page 18). They shared a suspicion of industrialization and mass production, arguing in favour of the skilled maker and the bespoke. They largely agreed on the need for change, the idea of making the world (and the home) a better place through design and the principle that each age must produce a design philosophy that would hold a mirror to the times. Some architects, such as Charles Rennie Mackintosh (see page 29) of the Glasgow School and the Finnish architect Eliel Saarinen (see page 53), managed to work successfully across the borders of both Arts & Crafts and Art Nouveau without getting too confused. Yet in other ways, the two movements were like chalk and cheese.

Many Art Nouveau, or Secessionist, architects and designers saw a good deal to admire in Morris's work and his focus upon the individual crafts- manship of the skilled artisan rather than machine age mass production. But while Morris and his disciples took inspiration from the pre-industrial age, the Secessionists wanted to break with the past; this was 'Art Nouveau', after all, and represented a new beginning. While Arts & Crafts designers believed in the example and influence of nature and the natural world, they also gravitated towards a simplicity of form and the honest, unadorned celebration of the character of natural materials. This often put them at odds with Art Nouveau designers, who saw mother nature as the richest source of pattern, colour and exuberant decoration. Arts & Crafts interiors tended to be calm and quiet, while Art Nouveau was, in comparison, an exotic aesthetic riot.

Art Nouveau was embraced by the French, in particular, with the name thought to be derived from a Parisian art gallery called Maison de l'Art Nouveau, opened in 1895 by the dealer Siegfried Bing. The movement was popularized by the Paris Exposition Universelle ('Universal Exhibition') of 1900 and spread its tendrils to many major European cities. A focal point was the city of Nancy, where furniture designer Louis Majorelle famously collaborated with architect Henri Sauvage on the design of his own house, Villa Majorelle (1902) – a flamboyant dream home full of sinuous curves, floral patterns and applied ornament, which was even used to great effect on the guttering. Other hot spots included Brussels, where architect Victor Horta made a strong impression, and Barcelona, which was the playground of Antoni Gaudí, the leading proponent of Modernisme, as the Catalans preferred to label their own version of Art Nouveau. And then there was the Vienna Secession, which connected in various ways with the lives and work of three highly influential proto-Modernist architects: Otto Wagner, Josef Hoffmann and Adolf Loos.

The Vienna Secession began in 1897, after a group of Viennese artists and architects split from the Association of Austrian Artists and the Vienna Academy of Fine Arts. The Secessionists wanted to veer away from the traditional historicism of the Academy and create a more inclusive collective, which embraced many different aspects of art, architecture and the decorative arts, while also connecting with like-minded groups internationally. Early members of the group included Wagner, Hoffmann and the painters Gustav Klimt and Egon Schiele, with the Secessionists creating their own exhibition space – the Secession Building (1898) – at the centre of the city, which was designed by Joseph Maria Olbrich, a student of Wagner.

Villa Wagner I and II: from neo-classical to visionary

Wagner designed two houses for himself in Vienna, more than a quarter of a century apart, which suggest in themselves how far the architect travelled from an establishment figure grounded in neo-classicism to something approaching a radical and, for some, a visionary. Villa Wagner I (see page 32) was completed in 1886, five years after his second marriage, to Louise Stiffel, who was eighteen years younger. By this time Wagner was already a respected figure, who had designed apartment buildings and the Austrian Länderbank offices (1884) in Vienna. His new house was described as an 'Italian dream', situated on the edge of parkland and surrounded by formal gardens. A hymn to historicism, this was essentially a neo-classical villa in the Palladian style (a 17th–18th-century style based on the architecture of the 16th-century Italian architect Palladio). Steps ascended to a dramatic colonnaded portico (a porch with the roof supported by columns) around a grand entrance that led into the *piano nobile* – an elevated principal storey in the Italian manner. Two subservient pergolas projected outwards, one at each end of the villa. In 1899, at the height of the Secession, Wagner converted one of these into a studio and the other into a garden room with ornate Art Nouveau stained glass windows, both designed by artist Adolf Böhm.

By 1912, when Wagner built Villa Wagner II in the same street, everything had changed. Increasingly, Wagner had begun to question the meaning of modernity and, in 1894, during an address at the Academy of Fine Arts, where he had been made a professor, he spoke of the need for architecture that was truly contemporary:

> Art and artists should and must represent their times. Our future salvation cannot consist in mimicking all the stylistic tendencies that occurred during the last decades…Art in its nascence must be imbued by the realism of our times.[1]

Two years later, in 1896, Wagner published the first edition of his book *Modern Architecture*, just before the formation of the Secession and his own break from the Academy. During the late 1890s and early 1900s Wagner's work embraced the Art Nouveau Secessionist style, as seen in – for example – the ornate façades and interiors of the three Linke Wienzeile apartment buildings, completed in 1898. Yet not long after that, Wagner moved towards a more functional and pared-down approach, as seen in the Döblergasse apartment building, built in 1909–11, when he was in his late 60s.

Otto Wagner – Villa Wagner II, Vienna, Austria, 1912

By the time that Villa Wagner II was finished, in 1912, Wagner had arrived at something close to early Modernism, with a crisp, linear outline, a rhythmic, repeating pattern of geometric windows, and decorative restraint, which he explained in his notes on the house:

> What was decisive for the ground plan was the desire for a strong conveyance of light within the rooms combined with its functional and individualised layout, the simplicity and durability of the construction, and the utilisation of those materials which industry had recently put at our disposal (patent plaster, sheet glass, marble décor, reinforced concrete, asphalt, fibre cement, glass mosaic, aluminium, magnalium, etc).[2]

As Wagner says, the house made the most of what were then new and modern materials, which help to define its character. The windows, for instance, use large sheets of glass rather than multiple glazing bars, and the house is neatly rendered, with a relatively simple band of blue glass panels punctuating the white façade. This simplicity creates a vivid contrast with Villa Wagner I and the architect's high Secession buildings in the Art Nouveau style. The scale of the house itself is modest, given that Wagner originally thought of it as a 'widow's residence' for his much younger wife, for use after his death – although, in the end, it was Louise who passed away before him, in 1915. The architect could not bear to live in the house alone and moved into an apartment in the Döblergasse building.

Palais Stoclet, a total work of art

Wagner's rapid architectural journey through style and aesthetics was echoed in the voyage taken by his former student, Josef Hoffmann. One of the founders of the Secession, Hoffmann had studied with Wagner at the Academy of Fine Arts and worked in his professor's architectural practice for a time. He was one of the most active protagonists in the early years of the Secession, designing a number of key exhibitions at the Secession Building. These included an 1899 show of work by Charles Rennie Mackintosh, whose designs Hoffmann greatly admired. Hoffmann was also active within the workshops and ateliers of the Wiener Werkstätte ('Vienna Workshops'), an influential cooperative of architects, artists and designers that he had co-founded in 1903. Like Wagner, Hoffmann argued that art and architecture needed to hold a mirror to the age and reflect the new century, while 'repeatedly searching our souls for our own forms, and finally by pushing away from ourselves with force the last strains of an obsolete, inebriated mix-up of styles'.[3]

During the early years of the 20th century, Hoffmann became a Viennese 'starchitect', developing a growing portfolio of commissions, including the Purkersdorf Sanatorium (1905) on the outskirts of Vienna. Built with reinforced concrete, this marked a key step on Hoffmann's own path towards modernity, encompassing a rigorous approach to geometry, symmetry, form and function. The interiors and furnishings were by either Hoffmann or his associates at the Wiener Werkstätte. The same was true of a series of increasingly ambitious and luxurious residences that Hoffmann designed in and around Vienna over the following years, including the Ast Residence (1911) for the wealthy building contractor Eduard Ast and the Skywa-Primavesi Residence (1915) for the industrialist Robert Primavesi.

Hoffmann was especially committed to the idea of a Gesamtkunstwerk, or 'total work of art', which became intimately connected with the Art Nouveau/Secessionist style and its architects. For the design of houses, the ideal of totality meant that the architect assumed overall responsibility for everything: architecture, interiors, furniture and furnishings. This represented an important alternative to the teamwork approach, where a house would be put together by a collection of tradesmen, suppliers and guildsmen, each with a particular area of expertise. The teamwork approach was usual during the 19th and early 20th centuries, with each trade jealously guarding its own territory, but architects like Hoffmann pushed the Gesamtkunstwerk as a way of achieving a more harmonious, cohesive result, where each strand of the design was part of one clear vision. The idea of totality pioneered by Hoffmann and others was to play a key part in the evolution of modern architecture and especially the home, as architects increasingly made a 'landgrab' for control, while pushing for unity of purpose and connectivity of passion and prose.

For Hoffmann, one of the greatest examples of a residential Gesamtkunstwerk was Palais Stoclet (1911), which was not actually in Vienna at all, but in Brussels. Adolphe Stoclet was from a wealthy Belgian banking family and settled in Vienna for a time after marrying Suzanne Stevens, the daughter of a Parisian art dealer. In Vienna, the young couple immersed themselves in the world of the Secession and met Josef Hoffmann, whom they first approached with the intention of asking him to design a new house for them in the city. But after the death of Adolphe's father, the Stoclets needed to return to Brussels, taking the idea of a Hoffmann Gesamtkunstwerk with them.

The result was a modern palace, three storeys high, which has been described as one of the most influential buildings of the 20th century, partly for the purity and cohesion of the design, which included architecture, interiors and furniture as well as spacious gardens and multiple terraces – Hoffmann even designed the silver-plated guestbook. From the outside, the Palais has the look of a transitional building somewhere between tradition and modernity. There is the sense of scale and grandeur that one expects of a luxurious period residence, with the entire Palais coated in marble, yet there is also a largely linear, almost cubist quality to much of the house, even if this is subtly subverted at times. The tower that crowns the

Josef Hoffmann – Palais Stoclet, Brussels, Belgium, 1911

building steps upwards like a ziggurat, topped with German sculptor Franz Metzner's four bronze figures, looking out across the city. The windows are generous, bringing in a rich quality of light, while Hoffmann also accentuated the relationship between house and garden, using the terraces as a happy border between them, as well as adding a rooftop conservatory.

Inside, the opulence continued but remained within the always coherent context of Hoffmann's vision for the project. A double-height great hall served as the main salon, pushing out into a large bay window and bordered by a gallery, while the dining room features murals by fellow Secessionist Gustav Klimt. The sense of luxury carries through to the bathrooms, which had become places of indulgence in themselves, presaging the opulent spa-like sanctuaries of the Art Deco era (see page 50). The Stoclet's own spacious bathroom featured a vast marble bathtub, which could also be used for showering, and a choice of comfortable seating. Even the kitchen was part of the Gesamtkunstwerk, with its striking fitted, glass-fronted cupboards and pendant ceiling lights; in many ways, this rational, functional, pared-down space was one of the most truly modern elements in the house, even if it was largely the preserve of servants and staff. The choice of materials was carefully considered, with a profusion of marble, teak and palisander (a type of rosewood), and there was an emphasis throughout upon the bespoke and the unique.

Palais Stoclet is considered Hoffmann's masterpiece. It helped to carry his reputation (and by extension those of the Secession and the Wiener Werkstätte) well beyond Vienna, with the house resonating in Belgium, Germany, Czechoslovakia and other parts of Europe, as Hoffmann picked up fresh commissions across the Continent. Yet he remained focused upon Vienna, marrying a Weiner Werkstätte fashion model, Karla Schmatz, in 1925, designing Wagner's memorial in 1929 and eventually, in 1948, becoming President of the revived Vienna Secession.

Adolf Loos's assault on ornament and the Steiner House

Hoffmann's buildings spoke of opulence and indulgence, which set him at odds with an influential contemporary in Vienna: Adolf Loos. Hoffmann and Loos had little in common apart from location and a respectful love for Otto Wagner. Beyond this, they represented two opposing forces. Hoffmann concentrated on the multilayered intricacies of the Secessionist style. Loos, however, established himself in opposition to what he regarded as the ornamental excesses of the Secession, while focusing on a more rational approach to function and experimenting with form, space and volume.

For Loos, ornament and decoration were very much secondary concerns rather than a vital component of architectural design. A prime example is a simple ceiling light, or chandelier, that Loos designed with exposed and bare light bulbs. Functionally it was more than fit for purpose, but aesthetically it was a world away from the Art Nouveau style of Hoffmann and his associates, who would do everything they could to disguise the bulb in a composition full of colour and pattern, so that it became something else entirely.

Such superfluous decoration became anathema to Loos, who went to war with the Secessionists. He was not only a successful, if controversial, architect, but also a polemicist who captured the public imagination with, above all, a lecture in 1910 called 'Ornament and Crime' (see page 66), which was published a few years later. Railing against ornament in turn-of-the-century Vienna was like shouting at the lions from inside their den, but Loos carried on making noise. In applied ornament he saw wasted time, energy and labour, with the innate risk that superficial decoration tied to fashion and ephemeral shifting trends could render a useful design irrelevant and outmoded in just a few years: 'I have made the following discovery and given it to the world,' said Loos. '*The evolution of culture comes to the same thing as the removal of ornament from functional objects.*'[4]

'Ornament does not enhance my joy in life, nor does it that of any cultured person,' Loos also said in the lecture. 'If I want to eat a piece of gingerbread, I choose a piece that is quite smooth, not a piece depicting a heart or a babe in swaddling or a knight covered from head to toe in ornaments.'[5]

Taking aim at the romantic nostalgia of Arts & Crafts architects, Loos argued for modernity itself and a definitive break with the past. 'The lack of ornament is a sign of intellectual power,' he concluded. 'Modern man uses the ornaments of former and foreign cultures on a whim, as he sees fit. His own inventiveness is concentrated on other things.'[6]

When it came to the design of the home, Loos made a particular distinction between the exterior and the interior. For the façade, he believed in pure, unadorned surfaces, coated in stucco, and without any decoration, which allowed the composition and form of the house to dominate, without distraction. The crisp, linear outlines of Loos's Scheu House (1913), in Vienna, Villa Moller (1928), also in Vienna, and Villa Müller (1930), in Prague, are distinctly Modernist in their outward appearance and profiles. But inside was a rather different matter. Here, Loos still argued for restraint but he saw the interior realm of a house as private rather than public, allowing for greater freedom of expression. A careful, modest attitude to decoration and pattern did not preclude fine and natural materials, such as marble or timber panelling, with Loos insisting on high standards of craftsmanship and positively favouring quality in his sophisticated approach to materials.

The most famous and original of Loos's early houses was the Steiner House (1910) in Vienna – it became a key reference point for generations of architects to come. Designed for the painter and illustrator Lilly Steiner and her husband, Hugo, the house featured plain stucco walls, yet in every other way it was radical. Planning restrictions suggested that the façade facing the street should only be one storey above ground level, so Loos cheated, tucking a basement level under the house and 'hiding' a third storey behind a curving, copper-coated, semi-vaulted roof, which softens an otherwise linear composition. Seen from the rear garden, the house has more of the geometric symmetrical purity that we associate with later Modernists, such as Mies van der Rohe and Walter Gropius (see pages 78 and 124).

Inside, the timber panelling, brick fireplace, parquet floors, rugs and English dining room furniture disguised the extraordinary spatial adventurousness that Loos was beginning to develop. He created a fresh hierarchy of rooms and spaces, based on their functions, and he played with volume, height and light to design spaces that were fluid and flexible. In doing so, Loos – far more than his contemporaries – began to move away from the conventional pattern of 19th-century houses and to develop a more 'modern' way of living. This was modelled on connectivity between spaces rather than their separation into a series of self-contained compartments. At the Steiner House, for example, Loos created a variant on the 'great room' at the back of the house, overlooking the garden, with a dining area to one side and a seating area (and hearth) to the other. These spaces also connected with a rear terrace, which then stepped down to the garden. Loos's spatial and volumetric dexterity, just as much as his attitude to ornament (and crime), set him apart and sat well with his instruction that 'we must learn a new way of dwelling'.[7]

ORNAMENT & CRIME

Adolf Loos – Steiner House, Vienna, Austria, 1910

Divisive, irreverent, avant-garde, experimental – Loos was a complex figure, a progressive hero for some and a debauched villain for others. He became an 'architect's architect', offering a key reference point for those fascinated by his approach to space and volume, functionality and rationality, materiality and personality, as well as the way in which he built on the foundations of classicism (symmetry, scale, proportion, order) while inventing something that was completely new. In doing so, he set himself firmly against the forces of conservatism.

Later projects included two extraordinary Parisian houses: an unbuilt project with a black-and-white striped façade, designed for the American singer Josephine Baker, and an intriguing home for Tristan Tzara, the founder of the Dada surrealists. In the Tzara house, completed in 1926, Loos created a powerful, monumental, enigmatic façade and then punctuated it with a series of inset apertures, windows and balconies, subverting – from the outside at least – all expectation of what a traditional house should look like.

Haus Wittgenstein and the austerity of minimalism

One more house in Vienna that we really should drop in on is Haus Wittgenstein (1928), where the assault on ornament was taken to a whole new extreme. The Wittgensteins were a wealthy Viennese family of industrialists, who played the part of patrons for a number of Austrian architects and designers. Karl Wittgenstein, the head of the family, had commissioned Josef Hoffmann to design a hunting lodge near Hohenberg (1906), following in the steps of his brother who had also commissioned a Hoffmann house. In 1925 one of Karl's children, Margaret 'Gretl' Stonborough-Wittgenstein, asked architect Paul Engelmann, who had been a student of Adolf Loos, to design a new house for her in Vienna.

Engelmann made the mistake of discussing the house with Margaret's brother, Ludwig Wittgenstein, who was (eventually) to become one of the 20th century's most famous philosophers. At that time, the impatient, tempestuous Wittgenstein was at something of a loose end following an incident when he had hit one of his pupils, who then collapsed, thus ending Wittgenstein's brief career as a schoolteacher.

He gradually became obsessed with his sister's new house, which Engelmann had already designed. One of Wittgenstein's first loves was engineering, particularly aeronautics, which he had studied in Berlin, Germany, and Manchester, England. Here was an opportunity to translate this early passion into the reality of a Viennese town house, which he began to redesign to the point that Engelmann distanced himself from the project, suggesting that the finished building was ultimately more representative of Ludwig Wittgenstein than it was of Engelmann himself.

Margaret granted her brother a free hand, and Wittgenstein ended up moving into a project office set up alongside the site. His obsessive interest encompassed both the exterior and the interior, especially the mechanical services and systems. Outside, he stripped away any embellishment or decoration to create a pure, stucco-coated cubist composition, which included the roofline. The form was not especially symmetrical, but it was highly ordered. Inside, Wittgenstein went way beyond Loos, who at least took a more liberal approach to expression in the private realm. In Haus Wittgenstein, the focus on purity, proportion, scale and order was carried right through the house, as Wittgenstein erased any trace of ornament left by Engelmann within the building as well. Even the skirting boards and architraves were edited out, and Wittgenstein himself designed many of the small details, including light switches and door handles, with an obsessive attitude to everything he saw, as another sister, Hermine, testified:

> Ludwig designed every window, door, window-bar and radiator in the noblest proportions and with such exactitude that they might have been precision instruments. Then he forged ahead with his uncompromising energy, so that everything was exactly manufactured with the same exactness. I can still hear the locksmith, who asked him with regard to a keyhole, 'Tell me, Herr Ingenieur, is a millimetre here really that important for you?' and even before he had finished the sentence, the loud, energetic 'Ja,' that almost startled him.[8]

Hermine Wittgenstein talked of the high logic that pervaded this 'dwelling house for the gods' but, like many others, suggested that the house lacked something, which we might call 'character' or 'personality' or 'soul'. 'Even though I admired the house very much, I always knew that I neither wanted to, nor could live in it myself,' she said.[9] By outdoing Loos, by taking logic and order to an extreme, Ludwig Wittgenstein had created an important, innovative, intriguing but perhaps rather sterile house, where a sense of character had been smothered by the austerity of minimalism.

His biographer, Ray Monk, suggested that Ludwig Wittgenstein himself recognized that something was missing from the house: 'The house I built for Gretl is the product of a decidedly sensitive ear and good manners, and expression of great understanding…But primordial life, wild life striving to erupt into the open – that is lacking.'[10]

Wittgenstein left Vienna for a fellowship at Cambridge University, England, in 1929, and Haus Wittgenstein is now home to the Bulgarian Cultural Institute. Perhaps the building was always best suited to serving as an institution of some kind, rather than as a home. Wittgenstein's house took the idea that 'ornament is crime' further than ever before, but at the expense of the wild life.

Ludwig Wittgenstein and Paul Engelmann – Haus Wittgenstein,
Vienna, Austria, 1928

Deco by Design
Gods of the Machine

3

Seely & Paget – Eltham Palace, Eltham,
London, England, 1936

Cedric Gibbons
Del Río House
Santa Monica, California,
United States, 1931

Eliel Saarinen
Saarinen House
Bloomfield Hills, Michigan,
United States, 1930

Seely & Paget
Eltham Palace
Eltham, London, England, 1936

Robert Mallet-Stevens
Villa Noailles
Hyères, France, 1933

Eileen Gray
E-1027
Roquebrune-Cap-Martin,
France, 1929

Glamorous, opulent and exotic, the Art Deco style was also distinctively modern and international. Art Deco offered a seductive aesthetic approach that transcended borders and boundaries, encapsulated by the great transatlantic ocean liners of the Jazz Age such as SS *Normandie* and RMS *Queen Mary*, as well as the streamlined locomotives of the Twenties and Thirties. The extraordinary lingua franca of Deco connected Paris and New York, London and Los Angeles, and was expressed in the form of cinemas, hotels, department stores and skyscrapers such as William Van Alen's iconic Chrysler Building (1930) in Manhattan. The Deco style carried through to glassware, ceramics, lighting and furniture, along with the paintings of Tamara de Lempicka and the enticing advertising posters of Cassandre, which helped to promote this new, modern world of travel and adventure. The movement was also to play an important part in the evolution of the 20th-century home.

The sheer exuberance and optimism of the aesthetic ensured that the Deco style travelled the globe in the space of just a few years during the late Twenties, making its way into countless houses and apartments. Art Deco took its name from a key exhibition, the Exposition Internationale des Arts Décoratifs et Industriels Modernes ('International Exhibition of Modern Decorative and Industrial Arts'), which was held in Paris in 1925 and captured global attention. The message was carried by newspapers, magazines and especially by Hollywood, which embraced the Deco style with a particular passion. For Hollywood film-makers and producers of the Twenties, Art Deco was the perfect gift for the post-war years, translated into lavish filmsets that spoke of escapism and a golden future, as well as the interiors of dream homes, both imaginary and real.

The Jazz Age charms of Del Río House

One of the many visitors who made their way to Paris for the 1925 Expo was the legendary Hollywood set designer and art director Cedric Gibbons. At the time, the Irish American creative impresario had just started working with Louis B Mayer at the MGM studios, marking the start of a 30-year career. Gibbons is also credited with the Deco-inspired design of the award statuettes for the Oscars; his own Academy Awards, for art direction, included *The Bridge of San Luis Rey* and *The Merry Widow* plus nominations

Cedric Gibbons – Del Río House, Santa Monica, California, United States, 1931

for *Romeo and Juliet*, *The Great Ziegfeld* and *The Wizard of Oz*. In 1930 he married the Hollywood actress Dolores del Río, one of the cinematic icons of the Jazz Age, and decided to build a new house for the two of them in the Art Deco style.

Del Río, also known as the 'Princess of Mexico' after her first career back in her homeland, hit the Hollywood big time in 1926 with her role in the film *What Price Glory?* followed by *Resurrection*, *The Loves of Carmen* and *Ramona*, while her first 'talkie' was *The Bad One*, released in 1930. She met Cedric Gibbons at a Hearst Castle party and they became one of the great Hollywood power couples, as well as the focal point for a social circle centred upon the charms of the Del Río House (1931) in Santa Monica.

Gibbons designed the house himself, in collaboration with architect Douglas Honnold, and naturally embraced Art Deco, or the Moderne style, as it was sometimes called in the United States. The son of an architect, Gibbons had worked in his father's architectural practice as a junior draughtsman but was not an architect himself. He designed a crisply rendered, linear house that is relatively closed to the street but opens up dramatically to the rear garden and terraces. From here, the clean lines of the white house stand out vividly against the greenery of the trees, while large banks of steel-framed glass punctuate the rear façade, with balconies on the upper level reminiscent of the decks of those transatlantic liners.

Within, there is a striking sense of openness and light. Gibbons contrasted dark linoleum floors with white walls and crisp, pared-down detailing for the fireplaces and coffered ceilings, which were also in a linear, geometric style. The same was true of the long brushed-steel staircase linking the two levels, which allowed del Río to make a suitably dramatic entrance. The layout was beautifully conceived for entertaining, with a liberating flow of interconnected spaces on the ground floor and a spacious sitting room upstairs, overlooking the gardens. Such a fluid plan was the opposite of the traditional box-like rooms of the past, creating a home that was truly dynamic in its character, as well as decidedly avant-garde for the times.

One contemporary black-and-white photograph of the house shows del Río reclining in a Deco lounge chair in front of the super-sized windows, with the trees silhouetted outside, as Gibbons perches upon one of the armrests. This image, its elegantly dressed subjects and the house itself all speak of Jazz Age Hollywood and the romantic ideal of the 'Moderne', with its fresh new mode of living. Guests at the many house parties here included Errol Flynn, Greta Garbo and Clark Gable.

In 1940, ten years after their marriage, del Río began an affair with Orson Welles, who once mentioned that he was greatly impressed by – among other things – her lingerie, which was handmade in France by nuns. Unfortunately, this put an end to her marriage to Gibbons and fairy-tale life in their Deco dream house. In more recent years, the house has been sensitively updated and restored a number of times by designers such as Michael S Smith and Madeline Stuart.

A unique bridge

Art Deco living was not simply about luxury and glamour. There was a more intellectual and experimental ethos to Deco houses and apartment buildings, as well as to the aesthetic as a whole, along with vital points of difference that set the movement apart from anything that had gone before. In common with Art Nouveau (see page 34) there was still an emphasis on craftsmanship and the use of fine, characterful materials, yet, while Art Nouveau looked to nature as its greatest source of inspiration for ornamental flamboyance, Deco was the style of the machine age. It took its cue from motorcars, liners, planes and airships, with their rounded, streamlined forms that embraced the energetic rush of speed. Deco architects and designers adopted a simpler and more restrained approach towards decoration, together with an open-minded attitude to new and semi-industrial materials, such as Bakelite and chrome. But, on the other hand, Deco disciples retained a special affection for luxe materials, including exotic hardwoods, shagreen, leather and lacquered finishes. The result offered a unique bridge between, on the one hand, a *fin de siècle* focus on craft and materials and, on the other hand, the progressive futurism of the early Modernists, which began to take hold in the Thirties. This notion of a 'bridging' movement, or transitional style, is encapsulated within a number of important houses from the Twenties and Thirties.

Saarinen House, connecting tradition and modernity

One of the most handsome and rounded of these transitional houses was Saarinen House, architect Eliel Saarinen's own family home on the Cranbrook Academy of Art campus at Bloomfield Hills, Michigan. From the outside, this 1930 brick-built and ivy-covered house has the elegant look and feel of an Arts & Crafts building, while a courtyard at the rear is partly enclosed and sheltered by a studio to one side and a long porch to the other, creating a protective U-shaped formation. But, stepping inside, the interiors are a hymn to high Deco, with expressive and crafted materials set in the context of a flexible floor plan.

Eliel Saarinen began his career as an architect in Finland, where he became much respected for his early work infused with an Arts & Crafts flavour, including Helsinki's Central Railway Station and its National Museum of Finland. He entered an international competition to design a new skyscraper for the *Chicago Tribune*, which also attracted entries from Adolf Loos (see page 41) and the eventual winners, John Howells and Raymond Hood. Even though Saarinen did not win, his work caught the eye of American newspaper baron George Gough Booth, who had turned his attention to philanthropy and decided to create a new educational

Eliel Saarinen – Saarinen House, Bloomfield Hills, Michigan, United States, 1930

community in Bloomfield Hills, around 32km (20 miles) northwest of Detroit. Booth invited Saarinen to masterplan the campus, design a number of key buildings and, eventually, serve as the first president of the Cranbrook Academy of Art.

Sitting within the campus itself, Saarinen House (1930) was designed not only for Saarinen and his family but also for the future use of subsequent Academy presidents. As such, it was a showcase home, representative of Saarinen's own design philosophy as well as of the talents of a number of resident craftsmen and tutors from the Academy workshops. These included Saarinen's wife, Loja, who ran the weaving and textile design atelier and created many of the rugs for the house, and Swedish master craftsman Tor Berglund, who headed the cabinet-making workshop and made much of the furniture in the house to designs by Saarinen.

The key spaces on the ground floor include a spacious living room with one of Loja's rug designs leading the eye towards a focal point fireplace, designed by Saarinen, with a Deco-style tiled surround. This vibrant room flows into a library alcove to one side and connects – via a double-width opening featuring a draw-across curtain – with the timber-panelled dining room, in which the furniture and lighting were by Saarinen. The living room also feeds into a spacious studio to the rear of the house, which offers another generous, adaptable space. This atelier was used as an open study and office, yet was large enough to be used as a venue for parties and Academy events, when the drafting and drawing tables would be tucked away; there was also a 'cosy corner' at one end, which provided a more intimate and relaxed seating zone. Upstairs, the tiled master bathroom offered an elegant example of hygienic Deco luxe, while much of the furniture in the master bedroom was designed by the Saarinens' son, Eero, who was to become one of America's most famous and innovative mid-century architects and designers (see page 126).

Another Finnish master architect, Alvar Aalto (see pages 97 and 164), described Eliel Saarinen as a 'bridge builder', who was able to connect past and present, tradition and modernity. This can be seen in Saarinen House but also in his work as an educator and the way in which he helped shape the ethos of the Cranbrook Academy, enticing there and encouraging original talents such as Charles and Ray Eames, Harry Bertoia and Florence Knoll, all of whom also became highly influential and multifaceted designers during the post-war period.

Eltham Palace, a new level of sophistication

In southeast London, another 'bridging' house plays host to the most extraordinary Art Deco interiors in Britain. Eltham Palace, near Greenwich and Blackheath, was once a royal household, where Henry VIII spent part of his childhood. After the English Civil War Eltham Palace was largely abandoned and began to fall apart, with the Great Hall – the one part of the palace that had survived through the centuries – used as a barn. But, eventually, during the late Twenties, it caught the attention of Stephen and Virginia Courtauld, who decided to revive Eltham and turn it into their own palatial home (see page 48).

Stephen Courtauld's family made its fortune in the textile business, and his brother, Samuel, founded the Courtauld Institute of Art. Stephen Courtauld's own interests were varied, but included art collecting, gardening and mountaineering. He was awarded a Military Cross in World War I, sponsored a British expedition to the Arctic, helped to establish the Ealing Studios in west London and was part of the team that mastered the Innominata face of Mont Blanc in 1919 – the same year that he first met Virginia, or 'Ginie', as she was known to her family and friends. The daughter of Italian-Hungarian parents, Ginie was as gregarious as her husband was reserved, with an eye for fashion, style and interior design, as well as an elegant snake tattoo.

The Courtaulds restored the Great Hall as a music room for concerts and recitals, while commissioning architects John Seely and Paul Paget to design a spacious new house (1936) alongside it in a semi-traditional 'Wrenaissance' style (the nickname for a late 17th-century revival style that had been popular around 1890–1914). Yet the true drama was inside, where the Courtaulds created an opulent Deco home with echoes of the ocean liner interiors with which they would have been very familiar. For these, they turned to Peter Malacrida, also known as Marchese Piero Luigi Malacrida de Saint-August. Like Ginie, Malacrida had an Italian heritage, was a great socialite and had married an English partner, the radio broadcaster, aviatrix and racing driver Nadja Malacrida.

For Malacrida himself, who had also designed interiors for Samuel Courtauld, as well as a family yacht christened the *Virginia*, Eltham Palace became a magnum opus, encapsulating an extraordinary sense of theatre and drama, but also threaded through with state-of-the-art technology and layered with the richest materials and the most captivating craftsmanship. The rooms were served by every convenience and a wave of up-to-the-minute gadgets, with underfloor heating, internal telephones, an integrated vacuum-cleaning system, along with centrally piped music and built-in speakers.

The scene was set from the start by the entrance hall: one of London's finest rooms, topped by a circular dome perforated by repeating discs of glass. It was surrounded by timber panels of Australian blackbean veneer, inlaid with marquetry depicting figures, landscapes and scenes, created by the Swedish designer Rolf Engströmer and the Swedish master craftsman Jerk Werkmäster. In the dining room, Malacrida's design featured bird's-eye maple veneer on the walls, black and silver lacquered doors featuring a menagerie of animal motifs, and an aluminium-leaf ceiling. The quality of the finishes, the fineness of the materials and the level of detailing were of the highest order throughout. Built-in furniture added to the cohesion of spaces, as in Stephen Courtauld's study and the bedrooms, including the oval master suite with its own timber-panelled walls. There was even a specially designed and muralled cage room for the Courtaulds' pet lemur, Mah-Jongg, accessed by a bamboo ladder.

Malacrida excelled himself in the design of the Eltham bathrooms. During the Art Deco period, the bathroom truly came of age, becoming a key space in itself rather than a functional afterthought or an incidental amenity. For the many long centuries between the sophistication of Roman bathing and the Victorian predilection for piped hot water, the bathroom itself was a rarity. Intimate rituals were reduced down to a washstand in the bedroom, perhaps a freestanding tub somewhere in the house for an occasional dip with water heated piecemeal on a stove, and a chamber pot tucked discreetly under the bed. The development of plumbing during the 19th century, along with greater concern for health and hygiene, helped usher in a more refined approach to such matters and the gradual appearance, in more affluent households at least, of a dedicated 'bath room'.

Virginia Courtauld's own personal sanctuary takes the whole notion of such a space to a new level of sophistication. It has the luxurious quality of a hotel bathroom, or spa, with an onyx bathtub sitting against an arched alcove lined with gold mosaic tiles, while a statue of the goddess Psyche watches carefully over the water spilling from the gold-plated taps. There's enough space for a large integrated vanity unit, while a heated radiator keeps the towels nice and warm. At Eltham Palace, the bathroom has become a space for indulgence, for true pleasure, as much as private or personal functions.

For Peter Malacrida, Eltham turned out to be not only his magnum opus but also his swansong. His wife Nadja's love of speed and fast cars ended in tragedy when her car came off the road one night in 1934 and she died instantly. Her heartbroken husband devoted himself to finishing Eltham but then retreated from public life. His clients lived there happily until 1944, when the Courtaulds moved to Scotland and from there to Southern Rhodesia, where they settled.

Robert Mallet-Stevens
– Villa Noailles,
Hyères, France, 1933

Villa Noailles and 'the reign of reason'

In France, which was the spiritual birthplace of Art Deco, one of the most fascinating Deco houses was the Villa Noailles (1933) at Hyères, on the Mediterranean coast between Toulon and Saint-Tropez. Rather like Eltham Palace, this unique holiday villa was commissioned by wealthy patrons of the arts: the Vicomte and Vicomtesse de Noailles. As well as being great collectors of modern art between the wars, Charles and Marie-Laure de Noailles financed a series of famous experimental films, including Jean Cocteau's *Le Sang d'un Poète*, the 'scandalous' *L'Âge d'Or* by Salvador Dalí and Luis Buñuel, as well as Man Ray's *Les Mystères du Château de Dé*, which was partly filmed at the Villa Noailles.

The couple had commissioned the celebrated Deco interior designer Jean-Michel Frank to design the rooms of their Parisian mansion, and they were determined to create something truly modern and exceptional on the parcel of land that Charles de Noailles was given by his mother on the Provençal coast. They considered a number of architects for the project, including Le Corbusier and Mies van der Rohe (see pages 68 and 78), until a friend recommended the French architect Robert Mallet-Stevens. He was working on a series of new Deco-inspired villas in Paris upon a street in the 16th arrondissement now known as Rue Mallet-Stevens, including a house for himself and another for the sculptors Jöel and Jan Martel. The architect was committed to a new approach to architecture and design, as he explained:

> Rational, the home of tomorrow will be comfortable, healthy and light, because that is where its real duty lies. We will build simply and cleanly, the edifices will be well suited to their functions, there will no longer be the need for pastiche. The new architecture will re-establish the reign of reason.[1]

Mallet-Stevens's houses featured characteristic Art Deco flourishes, including decks, terraces, sculptural staircases, fine materials and integrated furniture. But he was also preoccupied by performance and hygiene, with houses such as his Villa Cavrois (1932) in Normandy exhibiting a particular focus on more functional spaces. For example, the master bathroom featured a Carrara marble-clad tub, vanity and shower cubicle complete with massage jets. Mallet-Stevens was a master of modern luxe and the perfect choice for Charles and Marie-Laure de Noailles.

The villa at Hyères began as a relatively modest commission for a five-bedroomed house, completed around 1925. Made of reinforced and rendered concrete with large windows at regular intervals, the house was composed of ascending rectangular blocks, creating a distinctive ziggurat formation. Yet, almost straightaway, the Viscount and his wife began making new requests, and the villa began to grow and grow. Over the next eight years, up until 1933, Mallet-Stevens added a series of extra bedrooms, taking the total up to fifteen, plus *en suite* bathrooms, along with a squash court, a gym, an indoor swimming pool, a hairdressing salon and an extensive collection of terraces and outdoor rooms. The garden was like a vast room in itself, complete with protective walls punctuated by large rectangular 'windows' framing the view.

Other Deco artists and designers were brought into the project, including Louis Barillet who created a stained glass skylight in the 'pink salon', and Gabriel Guévrékian, who designed a cubist-inspired formal garden. Pierre Chareau, creator of the early Modernist Maison de Verre in Paris (see page 73), designed a glass room on one of the terraces: a crisp, rectangular conservatory that could be opened up to connect with the terrace itself. There were artworks by the Martels, Alberto Giacometti, Piet Mondrian and Constantin Brancusi, creating a powerful fusion of art and architecture united by a love of straight lines and the southern sunlight. During its Thirties heyday the house became a creative hub, drawing in artists and film-makers, even as the owners' own tempestuous relationship began to crumble. Beyond their shared love of the arts, it seems as though the couple had very little in common, with personal tastes that took them in radically different directions. The always outgoing and occasionally eccentric Vicomtesse preferred the bright lights and sociable salons of Paris, while the Vicomte was much happier in the countryside where he indulged his own great love: gardening.

For Mallet-Stevens, the great 'cubist chateau', with its campus of intersecting squares and rectangles, became a career-defining project, taking his work to a new height of ambition. But his approach, with his own interest in functionality, rationality and the relationship between inside and outside living, as seen upon the decks of Villa Noailles, was also indicative of the evolution of Modernist architecture itself. There was a significant degree of overlap between architectural Art Deco and early Modernism, especially in terms of form, function, fluid living-space layouts and the use of 'modern' materials like reinforced concrete and sheets of glass – even if there were also important points of difference and divergence, particularly the continued focus upon decorative ornament and the luxurious, crafted finishes seen within Deco design and interiors.

E-1027, a house with emotional depth

Coincidentally, another of the great 'bridging' houses between Art Deco and early Modernism was situated just along the French Mediterranean coast on the Côte d'Azur: Eileen Gray's E-1027, which was completed in 1929. Perched upon a hillside, looking over the waters of the bay below, it picks up on a nautical theme and has often been compared to a white liner waiting to set sail. The house conforms to many of the architectural principles set out by influential early Modernists, especially Le Corbusier, yet it is also the work of a designer rooted in Art Deco who felt that a home was much more than a machine.

Eileen Gray was born into an aristocratic Irish family in County Wexford and studied fine arts at the Slade School of Fine Art in London. During the early years of the new century, she settled in Paris and began collaborating with a Japanese lacquer master, Seizo Sugawara, and designing early pieces of furniture and textiles. After World War I, during which Gray served as an ambulance driver, she opened a gallery in Paris selling her own furniture, alongside pieces by other designers. Many of these early Eileen Gray pieces, along with the apartment interiors she designed in Paris, were Deco in style and modern in feel. They included finely lacquered screens and sculptural sofas and armchairs, exhibiting her fondness for texture and pattern, as well as new, semi-industrial materials such as chrome-plated tubular steel.

During the Twenties, Gray became increasingly interested in architecture and effectively trained herself rather than taking any formal courses. She was encouraged to pursue this new passion by her lover, Jean Badovici, a Romanian-born architect and journalist who launched the magazine *L'Architecture Vivante* in Paris in 1923. Badovici was right at the heart of the French architectural avant-garde, counting Le Corbusier among his friends, while pushing Gray to explore new ideas and embrace Modernist thinking. Eventually he commissioned her to build a house by the sea at Roquebrune-Cap-Martin, a project that would be her first major building and would also become her most important.

Gray embraced the challenge wholeheartedly. She found the site for the house, which offered spectacular open views of the Mediterranean but could only be accessed down a narrow pathway, meaning that all of the building materials had to be brought in by wheelbarrow or trolley cart. Moving into a flat nearby, Gray oversaw the project herself from beginning to end, spending the best part of three years working on a house that she eventually christened 'E-1027'. The name feels like the identification number for a sailing yacht but actually is code for the combined initials of Gray and Badovici (with E for Eileen, followed by numbers representing the tenth, second and seventh letters of the alphabet, J, B and G).

Eileen Gray – E-1027, Roquebrune-Cap-Martin, France, 1929

Responding to the site and setting, Gray raised the majority of the concrete house on a series of pillars and placed all of the main living spaces on the upper level, while the undercroft (below the house) served as a shaded terrace. She created an open-plan living space with a long sequence of folding, floor-to-ceiling glass windows (designed by Badovici), which open out onto a long balcony while framing the vista of the sea. This multi-functional room included a day bed that could also be used by guests at night, as well as a dining area, while there was a separate master bedroom, bathroom and kitchen. Gray designed all of the integrated furniture in the house, as well as loose pieces, such as her famous Transat armchair, named after the deckchairs used on the ocean-going liners, the Bibendum armchair (with upholstered bands of leather like the rings of Bibendum, the mascot of the Michelin tyre company) and her circular glass and chrome E-1027 adjustable table. While the exteriors were painted white, Gray used colour and pattern extensively within the house.

'A house is not a machine to live in,' Gray declared, taking aim at Le Corbusier's famous dictum (see page 69), which argued that a house was exactly that. 'It is the shell of man, his extension, his release, his spiritual emanation.'[2] As such, there was an emotional character and depth to E-1027, which was – after all – a very personal and intimate project for both Gray and Badovici, who expressed his own delight in the pages of his magazine:

> This very small house thus has, concentrated in a very small space, all that might be useful for comfort and to help indulge in *joie de vivre*. In no part has a line or a form been sought for its own sake; everywhere one has thought of *man*, of his sensibilities and needs.[3]

This focus on *joie de vivre* and the spiritual character of the home helped to set E-1027 apart from Gray's other work. There were so many layers of depth to this fully bespoke home, tailored to Badovici himself and the surroundings. It must have been traumatic, then, when Le Corbusier tried to lay claim to the house and this special, private place that Gray had first discovered. The relationship between Gray and Badovici had begun to fall apart on account of his multiple affairs with other women, provoking her to move out of E-1027. Later, during one of his many visits to the house, Le Corbusier painted a series of murals upon the walls of the house, using it as a 'canvas'. For Gray, this was an act of vandalism, yet it also seems like an animalistic act of territorialism as much as creative expression: a famous photograph showed Le Corbusier painting the pictures naked. Gray asked Badovici to have the murals removed, but he refused, which must have seemed like a final betrayal.

Le Corbusier became rather obsessed with Roquebrune-Cap-Martin, building a small cabin here for his own use, along with a tiny drawing studio, declaring himself 'at home' here more than anywhere else in the world. He died, of a heart attack, while swimming in the bay in 1965. E-1027 itself also suffered, with one of the subsequent owners murdered here by an itinerant gardener and the house then falling into semi-dereliction.It took many years for the township itself to buy the building and, eventually, restore E-1027 and its interiors much as Gray had intended them to be. This transitional house between Art Deco and mainstream Modernism is, above all, a monument to Eileen Gray and her work, even if the master's murals are still in place.

Make it New
The Birth of Modernism

4   Le Corbusier – Villa Savoye, Poissy, France, 1931

Le Corbusier
Villa Savoye
Poissy, France, 1931

Gerrit Rietveld
Schröder House
Utrecht, Netherlands, 1924

Pierre Chareau
Maison de Verre
Paris, France, 1932

Ludwig Mies van der Rohe
Villa Tugendhat
Brno, Czech Republic, 1930

Patrick Gwynne
The Homewood
Esher, Surrey, England, 1938

T he pioneering Modernists believed that they could create a better world by design. They were dreamers and schemers, artists and artisans, who agreed wholeheartedly with the instruction 'make it new' and actively searched for a new beginning. Early Modernist architects and designers saw in this 'newness' a way of living that they believed was better in almost every sense of the word.

They dreamed of modern, ordered and interconnected cities, laid out in grids and punctuated with high-rise apartment buildings. They drew linear houses, defined by order and function, in which a wealth of space, light and air would bring health and pleasure to their inhabitants. And they drew inspiration from a new generation of machines, which promised to improve lives and liberate us from the tyranny of time-choking chores, freeing up more time to spend enjoying and appreciating these 20th-century spaces. This was a true revolution, but one focused not so much on politics as on a way of life.

Aesthetically, Modernist architecture and design famously rejected ornamentation in favour of purity. Its followers sought to strip away excess and decoration for its own sake in favour of simpler, cleaner lines. The Austrian proto-Modernist architect and designer Adolf Loos summed up his thinking in a 1910 lecture entitled 'Ornament and Crime' at the Academic Association for Literature and Music in Vienna (the lecture was published as an essay in 1913). It was excessive decoration that Loos really objected to and the idea of ornament for its own sake. He argued that applied and superfluous ornament might soon make something as useful as a teapot, or a kettle, redundant simply because the decoration upon it was part of a transient fashion.

'Ornament means squandered manpower and thus squandered health,' said Loos. 'It has always been so. But today it also means squandered material and both together mean squandered capital.'[1] It was this wastefulness that so upset Loos, who freely admitted in the same breath that he demanded work of great quality and made with the finest materials. He also argued, like a fervent preacher, in favour of aesthetic modernity itself as a reflection of the new century:

Behold, this is what constitutes the greatness of our age, that it is not capable of producing a new ornament. We have overcome ornament, we have fought our way through to ornamentlessness. Behold, our time is at hand. Fulfilment awaits us. Soon the streets of the cities will gleam like white walls![2]

'Ornament is crime', as Loos's ideas were summed up, serves as one of the three great slogans of early Modernist architecture and design. To this, let's add architect Ludwig Mies van der Rohe's masterfulmaxim 'less is more' to the triptych. For Mies, fine and characterful materials were also vitally important, as one finds in the Barcelona Pavilion (see also page 142), created by Mies and the designer Lilly Reich for the 1929 Barcelona International Exposition, or Expo 1929, and officially known as 'The Pavilion of German Representation'.

The Pavilion – which has a residential scale yet also the atmospheric purity of a temple – features walls of marble and onyx, as well as floor-to-ceiling walls of glass. Yet these materials are allowed to simply express themselves without the need for added layers of ornament, which would subvert the intrinsic value and beauty of the materials themselves. 'Less is more' suggests a level of restraint and a recognition of not only the value of materials, but also the beauty of detailing and execution within a building.

Last, but by no means least, we should also remember that 'form follows function'. The phrase set out by the Chicago architect Louis Sullivan, in an 1896 essay, was actually 'form ever follows function', which appeared in this comment from the essay:

It is the pervading law of all things organic and inorganic, of all things physical and metaphysical, of all things human and all things superhuman, of all true manifestations of the head, of the heart, of the soul, that the life is recognizable in its expression, that form ever follows function. This is the law.[3]

Sullivan was another influential proto-Modernist, playing a key part in the evolution of steel-framed skyscrapers in turn-of-the-century Chicago, as well as serving as Frank Lloyd Wright's patient employer, before Wright went on to follow his own path (see page 84). 'Form follows function' became the third law of the Modernists, reinforcing Loos's message that applied ornament should be largely redundant, but also pointing to the vital importance of functionality within Modernist architecture and design. A house, for example, was a complex combination of aesthetics and performance, yet the form and structure of the building had to be the result of a pragmatic approach to its function. In other words, the house had to work well and work hard, enabling its occupants to live an ordered and rewarding daily life. The building needed to fully serve the needs of its owners, rather than simply be an artistic statement.

Following on from this focus on function is Le Corbusier's idea that 'a house is a machine for living in' ('*une machine à habiter*'). It's a statement that is often quoted by critics of Modernism as evidence of the cold, calculating design philosophy of its leading proponents, such as the great Corbusier. Yet we should also remember that he and his disciples thought of cars and ocean liners as inventions of particular beauty and accomplishment. As new machines, they certainly embodied modernity and the future, but they were also highly engineered, intelligently conceived and elegantly crafted. So when Le Corbusier talks of machines, as he often does in his landmark book, *Towards a New Architecture* (first published in French in 1923 and translated into English in 1931), then he's discussing something that embodies both beauty and function, like a transatlantic liner such as SS *Normandie*.

Arguably the single most influential architect of the 20th century, Le Corbusier became a figurehead of the Modernist movement. As well as being an architect, he was an artist, a painter, a furniture designer, a writer and a polemicist campaigning for a new way of living. He was gifted and egotistical, original and controversial, and even the name Le Corbusier was an invention, or a design. Born in Switzerland as Charles-Édouard Jeanneret, he eventually became a French citizen in 1930 and adopted the name Le Corbusier, often shortened by friends and colleagues to 'Corbu', close to the French word *corbeau*, meaning 'raven'.

With his distinctive look, bow tie and round glasses, he was certainly an extraordinary thinker and a powerful personality, who remains, for many architects, the true master.

Villa Savoye, a temple to Modernism

Le Corbusier's most famous house is often cited as the ultimate example of 'a machine for living in'. This is Villa Savoye (see page 64). The house is situated in Poissy, an area that felt semi-rural back in the Twenties and early Thirties but has now been all but consumed by greater Paris, and feels largely suburban. A place of pilgrimage for architectural aficionados, the house sits within about 7 hectares (17 acres) of grounds and gardens, which still allows for a processional approach towards the villa itself. Visitors leave the busy streetscape and begin a journey through the trees until the house finally reveals itself – a crisp composition within a clearing in the woods. It's a largely linear building, painted white, and partially elevated upon a series of structural pillars, known as piloti. Floating upon a meadow of green grassland and framed by the trees, this white building also has the feel of a chapel or honoured building, given space and prominence.

For Le Corbusier, certainly, a house was not just a machine but also a place of spiritual and emotional importance. He talked of 'making the home the temple of the family' in which the family itself is sacred, and he described the home as follows:

> First, it is a machine for living in, which means a machine designed to make our daily work as rapid and simple as possible, and to look after our bodily needs attentively providing comfort. It also provides surroundings where meditation can take place, and a place in which beauty brings the repose of spirit which is so indispensable.[4]

The family consisted of Pierre Savoye – an insurance company director – his wife, Eugénie, and their young son. They asked Le Corbusier to design a weekend retreat in Poissy, easily accessible by car from their main residence in Paris itself. The architect described the Savoyes as open-minded, which allowed him the creative freedom to explore some of the ideas that were uppermost in his mind.

The form of the house itself allows for a continuation of the processional journey, or *promenade architecturale*, down the driveway, through the trees and into the meadow. For those arriving by car, the elevated structure of the house creates an undercroft accommodating a sheltered carport, the main entrance and also a discreet garage, along with quarters for a chauffeur and house staff. From the beginning, there is a choice of circulation routes through the house, offered by the spiral staircase and a separate ramp, which also winds its way upwards.

All of the principal living spaces are at mid-level, which serves as an elevated *piano nobile* – or principal storey – looking down upon the garden and into the trees. This part of the house holds the family bedrooms, a bathroom, a small kitchen and a large, multipurpose living space with a fitted fireplace. The living room connects, via a sliding wall of floor-to-ceiling glass, to a large and sheltered terrace, contained within the outline of the building itself. To one side of the terrace, the ramp continues upwards to a modestly sized upper level, holding a sundeck, partially shaded by protective walls to two sides.

Built with a steel framework in combination with reinforced concrete, the Villa Savoye manages to explore a whole range of ideas in a single building. There is movement here, along with the *promenade architecturale*, and a blurring of indoor and outdoor space, as seen in the way the main living room connects with the elevated terrace. There is a surprising amount of colour within the interiors, including pale blue tiles for the bespoke bathtub and a darker mosaic for the fitted, tiled recliner alongside it.

It's a shame, perhaps, that the house feels so empty now, lacking much in the way of furniture that might help bring the spaces to life. All family treasures and artworks are long gone, and for the Savoyes the house – which was completed in 1931 – was not a complete success. Construction problems and experimental engineering led to a series of leaks and dampness, prompting understandable complaints from the Savoyes, whose son already suffered health problems that were only made worse by the conditions in the house. Letters looking for solutions to these problems passed from client to architect throughout the Thirties, until the family finally abandoned their temple on the meadow. The house was later requisitioned by the occupying German army during World War II and then by American forces. Later still, there was talk of replacing the house with a school, and it was only in the Sixties that the house was given protected status and restoration work began.

For all these faults, and the reservations of the Savoyes themselves, the house has become one of the great exemplars of Modernism, as well as an icon within Le Corbusier's extraordinary canon of work. One of the many reasons for this is that Villa Savoye neatly encapsulates so many of the key characteristics of early Modernist houses. It is linear, crisp and white but also follows very succinctly Le Corbusier's 'Five Points of Architecture', making it in itself a Modernist manifesto in miniature.

Le Corbusier's Five Points of Architecture

The Five Points include the use of piloti, which help to elevate the main body of the building, providing a floating *piano nobile*. The use of long, horizontal ribbon windows is a second element. Then there are two key structural and organizational principles: the 'free façade' and the 'free plan'. Given the use of a steel and concrete frame, the exterior walls are no longer load-bearing, so they are liberated from any structural function, and this 'free façade' can be punctured with windows and banks of glazing. The internal walls are not load-bearing either, allowing areas like the multi-purpose sitting room to become 'universal spaces', fluid and free to be used in a variety of ways, blessed with an open sense of proportion and scale in this 'free plan'. Finally, the integrated roof garden, which helps blur the boundaries between inside and outside space, is the fifth element.

The Villa Savoye summed up, in clear and solid form, these Five Points plus a good deal more. Even in an age of manifestos and grand declarations of intent coming from all quarters, the Five Points could be clearly understood, and now there was also a building – which happened to be the Savoyes' home – to illustrate them in concrete form.

A number of other architects applied the Five Points to their own work in the years that followed. For example, Giuseppe Terragni's Casa del Floricoltore, in Rebbio, Italy, completed in 1937, used the Five Points, many of which were also explored in his Villa Bianca, in Seveso, Italy, that same year. Colin Lucas's 66 Frognal in Hampstead, London – a Modernist house that architect and client had to fight tooth and nail to get past the planners – was completed in 1938. Harry Seidler's 1950 house for his mother, Rose, in Wahroonga, near Sydney, incorporated the Five Points (plus a neat ramp) in an Australian setting and launched Seidler's career as one of the country's most influential Modernists (see page 134).

The multilayered Maison de Verre

Just one year after the completion of the Villa Savoye, another French architect finished work on a second key exemplar of the Modernist movement, but in a very different context and setting. This was architect and designer Pierre Chareau's 1932 Maison de Verre – or 'The House of Glass' – in Paris, not far from the Musée d'Orsay. Chareau was approached by Dr Jean Dalsace and his wife, Annie, who wanted to create both a new home and a consulting room within a hidden courtyard. One of the greatest challenges offered by the site was that it was already occupied by an 18th-century town house, including, in an apartment at the top of the building, a sitting tenant who refused to move.

Chareau's solution was both startling and imaginative. He promised to keep the top portion of the stone town house and slot the new home and surgery underneath it. A framework of steel columns to support the old and the new elements liberated the façade, which became a 'curtain wall' (a non-structural external wall). Here, Chareau produced his famous wall of glass, using translucent bricks.

Like the Villa Savoye, the Maison de Verre was revolutionary. The translucent walls introduced a rich quality of light within the house and turned the building into a vast, glowing lantern at night. The revolution carried on within the house, where Chareau looked after every detail of the interiors. On the ground floor, the architect created a series of spaces for Dalsace and his patients, with an emphasis on function and, of course, hygiene. A curving screen to one side helped to shelter the main staircase from his clients, with a clear distinction made between the public and private realms.

As with the Villa Savoye, the family living spaces were elevated to the floors above. And here, too, there is a 'great room', or 'universal space': a dramatic, double-height living area and library, illuminated by the glass-block walls and punctuated by the structural steel pillars. 'The great room

Pierre Chareau – Maison de Verre, Paris, France, 1932

Patrick Gwynne – The Homewood, Esher, Surrey, England, 1938

is a beating heart,' says Annie Dalsace's granddaughter, Dominique Vellay. 'It is like a modern cathedral.'[5]

The house feels 'modern' in so many different ways and not just because of the glass and steel. The combination of a clinical work space and the Dalsaces' own home within one building is striking in itself, with many ingenious high-tech elements and solutions in both realms, including dumbwaiters, ventilation systems and sliding screens. This ingenuity carries through into the spatial planning, with contrasts between high, open spaces like the 'great room' and more intimate retreats such as Annie Dalsace's private sitting room. The Maison de Verre is highly engineered for the times, with the exposed steel lending a semi-industrial flavour to the building, yet this is also a layered home of books, art and furniture.

The Homewood, a true original

Crossing the Channel, we find another layered, rounded and accomplished home of the same period in England. This was not always an easy place to be a Modernist, yet many significant Modernist houses and buildings were designed and built in Britain during the Twenties and Thirties. One of the most delightful of these, The Homewood by Patrick Gwynne, is now in the safe hands of the National Trust, representing (along with Ernö Goldfinger's 1939 house at 2 Willow Road, Hampstead, London) one of the very few Modernist houses in its care.

Completed in 1938 in Esher, Surrey, The Homewood owes an acknowledged debt to the Villa Savoye and embraces Le Corbusier's Five Points. The house was actually built for Gwynne's parents, who were unhappy with the growing noise of the traffic along the road close to their existing country home. Their son, a young architect, managed to persuade them to build a new and bespoke building on a quieter spot within the 3 hectares (8 acres) of land owned by the family. His parents raised some money, and Gwynne, still in his 20s, was handed the definitive commission of his career.

Here, again, the main living spaces are raised on piloti to create a *piano nobile* looking out into the woods, while the undercroft was used for parking. A spiral staircase winds upwards, leading through to another 'universal space' – an open and expansive area with maple floors and a dramatic sequence of floor-to-ceiling windows looking across the landscape. A folding screen could be used to lightly separate a dining area at one end from the seating area at the other, while timber-panelled walls and a marble fireplace added textural depth. Service spaces were pushed to the rear and the bedrooms were in an adjoining wing. New technologies featured throughout, including glow-in-the-dark electric light switches and a concealed cinema screen. Gwynne's friend and fellow architect Denys Lasdun designed an oval swimming pool in the garden.

Beautifully detailed and elegantly sited, The Homewood was a true original that also conformed to many of the key Modernist principles: it was linear, geometric and flat-roofed, featuring curtain walls with banks of glass that brought in light and framed the view, while it also explored a more informal and fluid living pattern internally. As such, it represented a new kind of English country house, in which the architectural solution helped to enhance nature and the landscape rather than being an imposition upon it. Unfortunately, Gwynne's parents had little time to enjoy it, with both passing away by the end of World War II, leaving The Homewood to its architect, who lived here until his death.

De Stijl, Schröder House, and breaking free of excess

Patrick Gwynne could be described as one of the many disciples of the great Corbu. Yet Modernism was a broad church and admitted many worshippers, along with the Corbusians. There were Russian Constructivists, Italian Futurists, Rationalists, Purists and Expressionists. In the Netherlands, Modernism was associated with De Stijl – or 'The Style' – which embraced art, architecture, graphics and furniture within an all-encompassing design philosophy focused on the new.

De Stijl was, famously, a movement not only of modernity but of rich, primary colours, presented as evidence to refute accusations that Modernist design was an all white and grey affair. Artist Piet Mondrian was one of the leading lights of the Dutch movement, along with the graphic designer, typographer and editor Theo van Doesburg, often described as the group's 'ambassador'.

The most significant De Stijl architect and designer was Gerrit Rietveld, another multitalented master, who designed not only houses and buildings but also furniture, lighting, interiors and more. Rietveld distilled De Stijl in

Gerrit Rietveld – Schröder House, Utrecht, Netherlands, 1924

the form of a chair and a house. The Red & Blue chair, originally designed in 1918, was a manifesto in itself, with its tall, bright red back and blue seat that were contained in a geometric lattice of black timber with vivid yellow detailing.

And then there was Gerrit Rietveld's Schröder House of 1924, in Utrecht. As with Gwynne's The Homewood, the project was career-defining in architectural terms. It was, in a way, a lifeline, as his client – Truus Schröder – became his collaborator, partner and lover, and Rietveld returned to the house in his later years, also making it his own home.

Truus Schröder first met Rietveld in 1921. She was a young widow, who had been married to a lawyer, and had three children. The house in Utrecht represented a new beginning for her but also for Rietveld, as he explained:

> The building of this house is an attempt to break free of the humdrum excesses, which around 1920…still influenced the architecture. We used solely primary forms, shapes and colours because these are so elementary and because they are free of association.[6]

The house is free from traditional associations with period architecture, like the pitched roof and gable ends. Such elements have been swept away in favour of radical geometry and an experimental use of form within an abstract composition of slab walls – made of rendered brick – and irregular windows and balconies. Inside, the house is equally radical, with Schröder and Rietveld dispensing with the familiar hierarchy of rooms and spaces.

The ground floor is dominated by an open-plan living room – encompassing living, cooking and dining – with a separate master bedroom, study, reading room and studio. Upstairs, Rietveld designed a dynamic and fluid space for the children, using a flexible system of sliding screens, which meant the whole level could be opened out or separated at will. Conventions that suggested a dedicated dining room, a kitchen, a sitting room and private, cellular bedrooms were discarded by Schröder and by her architect, who layered the house with furniture and lighting of his own design. The Schröder House is, therefore, as much about the use of space and the function of those spaces as it is about colour and geometry.

Villa Tugendhat, a Modernist icon

In Germany, it was – above all – the Bauhaus that became the great epicentre of Modernist art and design, first in Weimar and then in Dessau (and finally, briefly, in Berlin), initially under Walter Gropius and later under Mies van der Rohe. Embracing a variety of disciplines and a range of 'masters' (tutors), the ambition of the art school was – in its own way – to change the world. Its most influential director, Walter Gropius (see page 124), championed the idea that good design certainly could transform lives for the better and wanted to see that philosophy applied in a broad, almost democratic way. He encouraged both the masters and their pupils to think about how they could translate their furniture, ceramics or textiles into mass-produced and affordable products for a broad audience. There was not an architectural workshop as such at the Bauhaus, yet many of the masters – Gropius, Mies van der Rohe, Marcel Breuer – were architects or architectural designers who carried the school's ethos with them.

Ludwig Mies van der Rohe became director of the Bauhaus Dessau in 1930, but in 1933 the Bauhaus was shut down by the National Socialist,

Ludwig Mies van der Rohe – Villa Tugendhat, Brno, Czech Republic, 1930

or Nazi, authorities. The National Socialists and their German fascist supporters saw the Bauhaus and the Modernists as decadent leftists and began agitating against them, while Hitler's architect, Albert Speer, embraced a grandiose version of neo-classicism for the buildings of the Third Reich. In Italy, Mussolini dabbled with Modernism in general and machine age Futurism in particular, before also veering towards neo-classicism.

Like the Bauhaus, Mies van der Rohe's most famous European house itself became a victim of politics and the shift towards the far right that would eventually lead to a world war. Villa Tugendhat in Brno was completed in 1930, the same year that Mies became the last director of the Bauhaus. By this time, his reputation was well established and the previous year had seen him enjoy the success of the Barcelona Pavilion (see pages 67 and 142).

Grete Löw-Beer initially saw Mies's work in Germany but after her first marriage broke down she returned to her native Czechoslovakia, where her family were wealthy industrialists in the textile business. She married Fritz Tugendhat, and Grete's father gifted her a piece of land on a steep hillside overlooking the city of Brno. Here, the Tugendhats decided to build a new house and, naturally, they turned to Mies. 'I truly longed for a modern spacious house with clear and simple shapes,' Grete said.[7] Mies obliged, creating a contextual house (one that is appropriate to the site) on the hill. The villa is accessed from the rear and on the upper level, where the site connects with the street; a separate pavilion holding a garage and staff accommodation sits nearby. The entrance hallway and bedrooms are all on this upper level, and it's only as you descend that the house opens up to the view of the city and also spatially.

A structural steel framework for the house allowed Mies to create a curtain wall with a vast ribbon of glass that connects the main living area with this open vista. Two sections of glass drop down into the floor mechanically, dissolving the boundary between inside and outside, where there is an adjoining terrace. A slim conservatory alongside, holding a winter garden, adds another natural element. The structural steel columns are disguised in sheets of glimmering chrome, while a crafted onyx screen (an echo of the Barcelona Pavilion) lightly separates the library from this main space. A semicircular enclosure made of Macassar ebony helps protect and define the dining area, which is also part of this 'universal space'. Working with the designer Lilly Reich, Mies designed much of the furniture in the house, creating a cohesive and truly modern work of art, tailored to the needs of the Tugendhat family, who fully embraced their new home, as Grete attested:

> From the first moment we truly loved the house. When we were on our own we would sit in the library, while with friends we would prefer to spend evenings in front of the glass wall lit up from the rear with its subtle and gentle light. We enjoyed the house even more during the spring and summer. When the children were small, we were constantly with them on the terrace. They had a tub there for splashing as well as a polygon crate with sand in the shade. They would ride along the entire terrace in their skates and children's cars.[8]

But within just a few years the whole political landscape of Germany, Czechoslovakia and the wider region had shifted again. In 1938 Mies left Europe for America. That same year, the Tugendhats lost the house they loved and, as Jewish émigrés, the family moved to Switzerland and, later, on to South America. The next year, Villa Tugendhat was occupied by the Gestapo. The story of the house is elegantly explored in Simon Mawer's poignant novel *The Glass Room* (2009).

Houses, as well as their owners and architects, can become the victims of extreme politics and war. Yet Mies and the pioneer Modernists had already laid the foundations for a new way of life and a fresh way of living that spliced form and function, while also suggesting that less might be more. There was no turning back.

The Organic Home
The World According to Frank

5   Alden B Dow – Alden B Dow Home and Studio,
Midland, Michigan, United States, 1941

Frank Lloyd Wright
Robie House
Chicago, Illinois,
United States, 1909

Frank Lloyd Wright
Hollyhock House
Los Angeles, California,
United States, 1921

Frank Lloyd Wright
Fallingwater
Bear Run, Pennsylvania,
United States, 1937

Alden B Dow
**Alden B Dow Home
and Studio**
Midland, Michigan,
United States, 1936/1941

Alvar Aalto
Villa Mairea
Noormarkku, Finland, 1939

One of the giants of 20th-century architecture and design, Frank Lloyd Wright was certainly a larger-than-life character. During his professional career he designed and built hundreds of houses and other buildings, becoming – arguably – the most famous and influential architect of his generation, even if Le Corbusier might beg to differ. His personal life was worthy of a film script, with a flamboyant lifestyle, constant money worries and a sequence of intense personal relationships punctuated by tragedy and destruction. All this made Wright a subject of fascination, not just within the architectural community but for newspapers and the wider world. In this sense, he was the first celebrity architect, or 'starchitect', whose reputation burst out of his homeland of Wisconsin and Illinois and spread nationally and then internationally, taking his unique design philosophy along with it – particularly the ideal of the 'organic home'.

Over the many phases of a very long career, Frank Lloyd Wright invented a unique approach to Modernism and modern living. More than this, Wright was looking for nothing less than the new American house: a fresh architectural and design aesthetic that was uniquely suited to America and the new century. Rather than looking to Europe for inspiration, as had so often been the case with architects of the past, Wright looked to the landscape around him and embraced a more informal, relaxed and even radical attitude to the internal order of the home, which spliced architecture and interiors within one cohesive, unified design. He emphasized the importance of context, setting and surroundings, seeking a deep-rooted connection with the land and the *genius loci* (spirit of a place), yet at the same time he was always willing to experiment with form, composition, engineering and materials. Over the years Wright embraced steel-framed structures, concrete blocks, sculptural forms made of cement and expanses of glass that framed the landscape. One of his last buildings was the beloved Solomon R Guggenheim Museum (1959) in New York, completed in the year that he died, and it was also one of Wright's most innovative and unexpected buildings, suggesting that his energetic creative spirit never wavered.

Wright was always particularly committed to the architecture of house and home, with residential commissions forming the majority of his extraordinary and original portfolio. Even as a child, he would use his set of

Fröbel geometrical building blocks, which his mother – a schoolteacher – had bought for him, to assemble his very first structures and compositions. He became a gifted draughtsman and eventually joined the Chicago architectural firm of Adler & Sullivan, starting as an apprentice but quickly rising through the ranks. Wright's mentor, Louis Sullivan, was the 'father of the skyscraper', who pioneered steel-framed, high-rise buildings in Chicago and coined the famous phrase 'form follows function' (see page 67). Sullivan encouraged and supported Wright, even lending him the money to build his first family home, in the Chicago suburb of Oak Park, for himself and his wife, Kitty (or Catherine). Before long, Wright was Sullivan's head draughtsman but was also moonlighting on the side and designing his earliest houses, which had a strong Arts & Crafts influence. When Sullivan spotted one of these houses, the two friends fell out and didn't speak for twelve years. Wright established his own practice and eventually, in 1898, moved into his first studio, built alongside the family home in Oak Park.

As the century turned, Wright devoted himself to building a fresh way of life. There was a whole series of houses in and around Oak Park, many of which can be seen from the street following a tour of the Frank Lloyd Wright Home and Studio, which is now open to the public. Wright gradually began to move away from the traditionalism that some of his early clients demanded and to create a style tailored to the landscape of Illinois. These distinctive Frank Lloyd Wright houses from the 1900s were known as 'prairie houses' and the style as Prairie style, named after the flatlands of outer Chicago and beyond. Typically they were low-slung, as though hugging the ground, with shallow pitched roofs and a strong sense of the horizontal, forming a series of parallel lines with the ground plane arranged over one, two or three levels. One of the most accomplished and ambitious of these Prairie-style homes was the Robie House of 1909.

Robie House, custom-designed in the Prairie style

Frederick Robie was an engineer and an inventor, working in the family firm, Excelsior, which manufactured bicycles and parts for the nascent car industry. From the start, Robie, who was a car owner himself and a technologist, wanted a modern home and so he turned to Wright. 'I

Frank Lloyd Wright – Robie House, Chicago, Illinois, United States, 1909

contacted him and from the first we had a definite community of thought,' said Robie. 'When I talked in mechanical terms, he talked in architectural terms. I thought, well, he was in my world.'[1]

Robie acquired a parcel of land in the neighbourhood of Hyde Park, a southern suburb of Chicago that is now dominated by the campus of the University of Chicago. A corner site at the junction of two roads, it created challenges in terms of privacy, so the house is protected from the public domain by brick boundary walls. Behind these the building spreads itself out, arranged over three levels, while Wright also created a semi-separate mews house at one end for Robie's automobiles, with staff accommodation above. The brickwork is beautifully detailed using 'tuckpointing', which has brick-coloured mortar on the vertical joints (with cream-coloured mortar used for the horizontal joints), allowing the surface of the walls to read as a plane of terracotta. There are long bands of windows, with crafted leadwork and stained glass details, while the slender pitch of the roof projects outwards to protect terraces and balconies, emphasizing the horizontality of the composition. These various levels read as stacked strata, hovering above the streetscape within a rigid geological geometry.

Yet much of the ingenuity and originality of the Robie House lies within. Robie and his family did not want to live in a conventional manner, in which their lives would be dictated by the familiar formal hierarchy of entrance hall, reception rooms, ancillary spaces and service spaces, with bedrooms beyond. Entering the Robie House is a more enigmatic process, with the 'front door' leading into a hallway and ground storey that feel almost subterranean, with limited ceiling heights. This lowermost level holds spaces such as the billiard room, a playroom and other service rooms, meaning that one climbs the stairs to a modern *piano nobile* (elevated principal storey) largely devoted to the family living spaces. The middle level of the house is dominated by what is essentially one long, fluid space with a spacious seating area at one end and the dining area at the other. A brick fireplace partially separates the two but not completely, so that one can walk freely around the fireplace to the space beyond. A long run of windows facing the street introduces a wealth of light and enhances the sense of openness and space. Wright also designed the lighting and much of the furniture, including many integrated pieces. This provides a unity to the house in the manner of a Gesamtkunstwerk, or complete work of art, a concept pioneered and promoted at around the same time by European architects such as Otto Wagner and Josef Hoffmann (see pages 35 and 38). The family bedrooms and bathrooms were positioned on the top floor, which has a smaller footprint than the levels beneath and forms a tower, framing the best of the views.

Spatially the Robie House was pioneering, while technically, or mechanically, it was also finely tuned. As well as the custom electric lighting designed by Wright, the heating system was ingeniously tucked away from view, with, for example, concealed radiators underneath the windows in the long living room complemented by floor vents. Yet, for Wright, the fireplace and hearth remained a key focal point within a living room, offering a visual, social and emotional anchor without which a home would feel incomplete.

Unfortunately for Robie and his family, the delight of a custom-designed prairie house was short-lived. After the death of Frederick's father, the Robies' finances began to fail, not helped perhaps by the great cost of their new family home. They were forced to sell the house in 1911 and it is now in the care of the University of Chicago, having escaped the threat of demolition during the late Fifties.

For Wright, the Robie House could also be seen as a turning point. It was one of the last but also the greatest of the Prairie style projects and featured in the famous Wasmuth Portfolio, a collection of Wright's work published by Ernst Wasmuth in Germany in 1910. The Portfolio publicized Wright's work in Europe, earning him a fresh and devoted following, particularly among younger architects, who would begin beating a path to the master's door in the years that followed.

On a personal level, the years between 1909 and 1914 were also the most dramatic and traumatic of Wright's complicated life. He walked out on his wife and their children after starting an affair with Mamah Borthwick Cheney, the wife of one of his Chicago clients. After a trip to Europe, they settled down together at Taliesin, the new house and studio that Wright designed and built in 1911 at Spring Green in Wisconsin. In 1914 one of the household staff at Taliesin, cook and handyman Julian Carlton, murdered Mamah Borthwick and six others – including draughtsman Emil Brodelle – before setting fire to the house. Carlton tried to kill himself by drinking acid, but was eventually found hiding in a cold furnace among the ruins; he starved to death in prison seven weeks later.

Frank Lloyd Wright rebuilt Taliesin, which comes from a Welsh word meaning 'shining brow', although fire haunted him, with another blaze followed by reconstruction in 1925. Wright went on to form a tempestuous new relationship with Miriam Noel, who became his second wife, although their marriage lasted only three years. He eventually settled down with the dancer Olgivanna Hinzenberg, whom he married in 1928. The tangled and often harrowing story of these multiple relationships is explored in T C Boyle's 2009 novel, *The Women*.

There was so much drama in Frank Lloyd Wright's life during these years and yet, somehow, he found the energy and imagination to take on fresh challenges such as the Imperial Hotel in Tokyo, Japan, which was a seven-year project, while also opening a satellite office in Los Angeles. At the same time, Wright continued exploring new ideas, fresh materials and innovative ways of building, as well as exploring more expressive forms and compositions.

Hollyhock House, a piece of architectural theatre

One of the most theatrical of these innovative buildings was the Hollyhock House in Los Angeles, completed in 1921. It was commissioned by Aline Barnsdall, an independent and free-spirited woman who had travelled in Europe, had studied acting there and had a fortune of her own, stemming from her father's and grandfather's timely involvement in the Pennsylvanian oil boom of the late 19th century. Barnsdall came to Wright with the ambition of creating a campus of buildings that would include a theatre, a restaurant and residences for staff and visiting actors, along with a public garden. She bought 14 hectares (35 acres) of land between East Hollywood and Los Feliz, now known as the Barnsdall Art Park but at the time called Olive Hill on account of its olive groves. Wright described it as Barnsdall's 'little principality', and the first part of the project was her own home, known as the Hollyhock House after her favourite flower.

Frank Lloyd Wright – Hollyhock House, Los Angeles,
California, United States, 1921

Situated at the centre of the site, the house feels a world away from either Chicago or Taliesin. 'You will put your freest dreams into it, won't you!' Barnsdall asked her architect. 'For I believe so firmly in your genius that I want to make it the keynote of my work.'[2] Wright did not disappoint her, allowing his imagination to embrace a far older version of the architecture of the Americas, looking to the example of Mayan temples and Indian pueblos. The house was largely single storey, yet on the site it took on a monumental presence, with its dramatic roofline and blocks of 'cast stone' (precast concrete), with abstract hollyhock motifs and patterns.

Importantly, Wright decided to arrange the house around a central courtyard garden. This was, in itself, a reinterpretation of an old idea, seen in Roman villas and Moroccan riads, where living spaces are arranged around a central garden. The courtyard offers a private and protected outdoor room, a hidden oasis at the heart of a building, yet also helps to bring sunlight and fresh air into the rooms that surround it. The idea of the courtyard house has been revisited by many 20th- and 21st-century architects, including Wright. It has particular value in warm climates, where a quiet, shaded garden can be a delight, but also in cities, where the idea of a green, secluded sanctuary set apart from prying eyes also has great appeal and resonance. For Wright and Barnsdall, the courtyard offered all of these things, while becoming part of an integrated approach to the landscaping around the house, which included water pools and terraces.

Inside, Wright characteristically involved himself in every aspect of the interiors, including the lighting and furniture design. One of the most dramatic spaces is the generously scaled sitting room, arranged – again – around a focal point fireplace. Here, the concrete bas-relief above the hearth is said by some to depict Barnsdall herself as an abstract figure on Olive Hill, looking out across the plains to the distant mountains. Wright created a small water pool around the stone hearth and designed the integrated couches here, while also introducing decorative panelled screens on the walls, which reflect his lifelong love of Japanese art. For the interiors, he used wood extensively, introducing a sense of warmth while contrasting with the stonework and cement blocks.

In the end, Barnsdall appears to have been distracted from the idea of creating a campus devoted to the arts and only completed Hollyhock House and two other residential buildings; in 1927 she gifted the house and the park to the City of Los Angeles. Yet the Hollyhock House is, in itself, a piece of architectural theatre. As well as possessing an undeniable sense of drama within and without, the building is a kind of illusion or artifice, with many of the 'concrete' walls actually made of timber coated in stucco. Judging from Wright's own comments about the house, in which he implied that the building was made of poured concrete and concrete blocks, it seems as though he might have regretted not making greater use of concrete.

Buildings connected to their environment

For other Californian residential projects over the following years, such as the Alice Millard House in Pasadena and the Charles Ennis House in Los Feliz (both completed in 1924), Wright embraced 'textile block construction' more fully than ever before. Rather like a modern version of the Fröbel building blocks that Wright had loved as a child, his own idea offered a total construction system using cast units made in moulds that gave each one a textured surface or pattern, reinforced with steel bars that could be used not only to strengthen the blocks but also to lock them together on site. The material and Wright's approach to it spoke of modern engineering and innovative 20th-century tectonics, combined with a love of ornament inspired by the natural world. Wright explained his approach:

> We would take that despised outcast of the building industry – the concrete block…[and] find a hitherto unsuspected soul in it – make it live as a thing of beauty – textured like the trees. All we would have to do would be to educate the concrete block, refine it and knit it together with steel in the joints…The walls would thus become thin but solid reinforced slabs and tied to any desire for form imaginable.[3]

Even with such a systematic approach to construction, where the blocks could be prefabricated and brought on site for assembly, Wright was concerned about linking his ideas back to nature and context. The same was true of his attempt to create a more democratic, affordable and available version of the new American home, known as the 'Usonian house'.

For Wright, the word Usonian implied something uniquely American, and, starting in 1934, he began designing a sequence of residences that were intended to be a considered response to the landscape, climate and conditions of American communities.

These Usonian homes shared a set of common characteristics without being identical in the manner of a pattern book. They were modestly scaled and usually on one level, with flat rooflines and a significant overhang for the eaves to help protect the spaces inside. As in the prairie houses, there was an emphasis on horizontality and the use of indigenous materials. The Usonian homes tended to be relatively closed to the street, with a 'car port' usually provided to one side, but opened up to the rear gardens. They have been described as important precursors of the 'ranch houses' that became popular in the post-war period and beyond, which also have a uniquely American character to them.

The emphasis upon connecting inside and outside space was one of the key elements of Wright's whole philosophy of 'organic architecture'. For Wright the idea of organic design did not necessarily mean using natural materials, as we know already from his liberal use of materials such as concrete, steel and glass. Instead, it was more about creating contextual buildings that were a direct response to the site and surroundings, all of which should play a key part in shaping a specific design inspired by this unique set of circumstances and conditions. He described a building's relation to its context as if it had grown out of the ground:

> It is in the nature of any organic building to grow from its site, come out of the ground into the light – the ground itself held always as a component part of the building itself. And then we have primarily the new ideal of building as organic. A building dignified as a tree in the midst of nature.[4]

Wright talked of the integration of the house with the environment and the natural world, but also of the integration of materials, of inside and outside space, and even of 'integral ornament', in the sense of 'the developed sense of the building as a whole, or the manifest *abstract pattern of structure itself*'.[5] In arguing in favour of this integrated, organic architecture,

Wright set himself apart from 'internationalist' or 'modernistic' design, which he saw as essentially 'superficial' or – at best – 'sterile' given the absence of a 'truly sentient' approach.

Fallingwater, Wright's masterpiece

The most rounded example of what Wright meant by organic architecture is Fallingwater (1937), often described as the architect's masterpiece and certainly one of the most original houses of the 20th century. Here, the integration of the natural and the artificial reaches a fresh level of accomplishment, with the house woven into the contours of the landscape and sitting gently among the trees, while seeming to float above the sonorous waters of the all-important stream as they freely tumble down the hillside.

It was the stream of Bear Run that first mesmerized the landowner and Wright's client, Edgar Kaufmann, who owned a small cabin in the Allegheny Mountains. A Pittsburgh department store owner as well as a patron of the arts, Kaufmann wanted to build a more substantial weekend house among the woods. Frank Lloyd Wright was recommended to him by his son, Edgar Kaufmann Jr, who had worked for the architect as an apprentice at Taliesin and went on to become the director of the Industrial Design Department at the Museum of Modern Art in New York. Wright described the motivation for the house's design:

> There was a rock ledge bank beside the waterfall and the natural thing seemed to be to cantilever the house from the bank over the fall. He [Kaufmann] loved the site where the house was built and liked to listen to the waterfall. So that was the prime motive in the design…At least it's there, and he lives intimately with the thing he loves.[6]

Looking to fund his often extravagant lifestyle, Wright repeatedly took on too much work, and Kaufmann eventually grew impatient to see the designs for his new house. After another chasing phone call from his client, Wright finally told him the designs were ready to see, even though he had yet to put pencil to paper. Famously, the architect sketched out the building that was to become Fallingwater in just two hours, and the resulting design was much to his client's delight.

Frank Lloyd Wright – Fallingwater, Bear Run, Pennsylvania, United States, 1937

Wright used a series of reinforced horizontal concrete slabs to push the three-storey house out over the stream itself, contrasting these distinctive planes with vertical stack walls and chimneys made of local stone. Following the principles of integration, the architect sought constant synergy between the interiors of the house and the landscape beyond, making extensive use of bands of glass windows to frame the views of the creek and the woods, but also creating a series of terraces that offer a halfway point between the two realms. Here, boundaries between house and landscape are so blurred that the two constantly intersect, overlap and intertwine, meeting in the form of plunge pools, walkways, bridges and viewing points.

At ground level, Wright created a version of the 'great room': a large, open-plan space with the all-important fireplace and links to the adjoining terraces. Boulders push up from the stone floor by the hearth, helping to anchor the fireplace visually, while integrated sofas designed by Wright run just below the line of the windows. Family bedrooms are positioned on the two floors above, forming a kind of tower or observation post, with the mid-level used by Edgar Kaufmann himself and the bedroom at the top of the house used by his son. This was the private realm of the family. Wright also designed and built a separate guesthouse nearby, with a winding, covered walkway connecting this satellite back to the master building.

Completed in 1937, Fallingwater offered an immersive experience that stimulated the senses to the full. The colours of the landscape and the quality of the light shift and change according to the seasons, gently shaping the experience of being in the house, but the one constant is the sound of the waterfalls, offering a steady, soothing backdrop whatever the time of year.

Fallingwater embodies the ideal of 'organic Modernism', stepping well away from the idea of a building as 'a machine for living in' (see page 69). By emphasizing the importance of 'sentient architecture', achieved through integration, Wright reminded us that modern architecture – like any kind of architecture – is about fostering the emotions through feeling and perception as much as dealing with spatial planning, mechanics and engineering. It is, perhaps, Wright's commitment to the emotional and experiential aspects of architecture, combined with such a vital and heartfelt respect for nature, that helps him stand apart from other modern masters within the pantheon of 20th-century design.

Alden B Dow Home and Studio, an organic retreat

Certainly, Wright had no shortage of disciples. There was a long roll call of younger architects who took inspiration from him and his work, many of whom either worked in his practice or became apprentices under the master's Taliesin Fellowship programme. These included architects such as Rudolph Schindler, Richard Neutra and John Lautner (see pages 103,105 and 117) who went on to give shape to mid-century architecture in America and beyond, adopting their own interpretations of organic architecture and creating variants upon it. One of Wright's most faithful followers, in terms of residential work, was Alden B Dow, who became a member of the Taliesin Fellowship after studying architecture at Columbia University. At first, it seemed likely that Dow would join the fast-growing family firm, Dow Chemical, which his father had established in Midland, Michigan. But Alden B Dow had other ideas and, following on from Taliesin, returned to Midland in 1933, full of inspiration. One of his earliest projects was his own studio, built on a parcel of land on the edge of the town. Over the following years he went on to create a family house and garden alongside the atelier (see page 82), while embracing the principles of organic architecture.

Dow gently embedded the interconnected house and atelier into the landscape, with water providing a key element within it, rather like Fallingwater. The building sits alongside a large pond, which creates a frame for the architecture but also serves as a reflecting pool, mirroring the trees and sky while casting dappled light into the building. In the atelier the 'Submarine Room', which was used for meetings with clients, sits just above the water line, while in the house the cantilevered porch off the dining room 'floats' above the pond itself, serving as a seductive observatory looking out across the trees.

The complex floor plan of Dow's unique retreat follows the shape and contours of the land, with a constant interplay between inside and outside and between private and 'public' space. The main drafting room in the atelier is reminiscent of Taliesin, while Dow used his patented Unit Blocks to build the structure itself. An evolution of Wright's textile block system, the blocks featured sculpted edges and were painted white, standing out against the greenery of the trees and woven into abstract shapes, such as the twisting chimney stacks. They contrast with the expressive copper roof, which, with its green tones, blends into the surroundings. Dow also believed in an intimate relationship between architecture and landscape design, and he gave the gardens around the house and studio a Japanese flavour, as he had visited the country in 1923; his visit included a stay at Tokyo's Imperial Hotel designed by Wright. 'Nature relieves architecture,' said Dow. 'Architecture relieves nature. Gardens never end and buildings never begin.'[7]

Organic Modernism offered Dow and many others an alternative route, a kind of Third Way between pure Modernism and traditionalism, while the focus upon the importance of a considered contextual response to the site and surroundings was to have lasting relevance and resonance.

Aalto's 'warm' Modernism and Villa Mairea

Wright and his followers were not the only architects who were realizing the value of an integrated approach to architecture that recognized the importance of nature and the natural conditions of a setting. It was also true of a number of influential architects in other parts of the world, particularly Scandinavia, where Alvar Aalto was one of the great proponents of 'warm', or 'soft', Modernist architecture and design.

By the late Twenties and early Thirties, Aalto was aware of the work of European Modernists such as Le Corbusier, and also of Frank Lloyd Wright's 'integrated architecture'. The son of a land surveyor, Aalto often accompanied his father on his working trips across rural regions of Finland during his childhood and always cherished a love of the Finnish landscape and of natural as well as modern materials. As with Wright's buildings, Aalto's work showed an emotional sensitivity and a recognition of how important architecture and design could be to an individual's health, wellbeing and peace of mind.

Aalto famously explored these ideas with his designs for Finland's Paimio Sanatorium of 1933. Here, the architect began by placing the patients at the heart of the project and considering every detail in relation to what might make the residents' daily lives easier and more rewarding, as well as helping relieve the symptoms experienced by tuberculosis sufferers. His plywood Paimio chair, for instance, featured an ergonomic shape that helped patients breathe more easily. Aalto also created a series of integrated sundecks at the

Alvar Aalto – Villa Mairea, Noormarkku, Finland, 1939

sanatorium that allowed patients to enjoy the fresh air and the surrounding landscape without leaving the building.

It was a humanistic architectural approach, threaded through with empathy, which also carried through to the design of Aalto's houses, especially Villa Mairea (1939), in rural Noormarkku, where constant connectivity between architecture and nature was all-important. The house was named after Maire Gullichsen, the daughter of Finnish industrialist Walter Ahlström, who had built a highly successful family business centred upon forestry and timber. After the death of her father, the company was run by Harry Gullichsen, Maire's husband, and the couple shared a love of architecture, art and design. Among many other collaborations, the Gullichsens and Aalto co-founded the furniture company Artek. Naturally, they asked him to design their new summer house among the woodlands of the Ahlström estate.

Villa Mairea was fully tailored to the tastes, needs and desires of the Gullichsens, and, again, Aalto worked on every detail of the design, including architecture, interiors, furniture and lighting. But most important of all, in terms of warm, organic Modernism, was the way in which the house reflected and echoed its setting in the forest. There were windows, terraces and decks, along with a garden room, that offered a borderland space between indoors and out. More than this, the trees are constantly referenced and repeated within the design of the interiors, which feature crafted timber ceilings and joinery using pine, hornbeam and teak. Supporting columns are wrapped in rattan, echoing the tree trunks in the woods. The notion of a forest of protective timber reappears in the lattice of pillars around the staircase and again around the sinuous front porch, which pushes outwards into the landscape. Such elements soften the outline of the house itself, with crafted woodwork helping to bond the villa with its surroundings.

Warm Modernism, with an organic foundation, was to play an essential part in the evolution of mid-century modern architecture and design in Scandinavia. The characterful, considerate, empathetic design philosophy pioneered by Aalto, Arne Jacobsen, Jørn Utzon and other Nordic architects (see page 152) became an essential aspect of mid-century style during the Fifties and Sixties in particular. Organic, contextual design – with its integrated approach to architecture and landscape – continues to be profoundly important to contemporary architects looking at ways of building site-sensitive, eco-friendly homes that touch the earth as lightly and gently as possible.

California Dreaming
Let there be Light

6   Pierre Koenig – Case Study House #22, Los Angeles,
     California, United States, 1960

Rudolph Schindler
Schindler House
Los Angeles, California,
United States, 1922

Pierre Koenig
Case Study House #22
Los Angeles, California,
United States, 1960

Richard Neutra
Kaufmann House
Palm Springs, California,
United States, 1947

Craig Ellwood
Palevsky House
Palm Springs, California,
United States, 1969

Charles and Ray Eames
Eames House
Pacific Palisades, California,
United States, 1949

John Lautner
Elrod House
Palm Springs, California,
United States, 1968

The state of California has always been a promised land for architects and designers. In this way, they were no different from so many other dreamers of the early 20th century who saw the West Coast as a place of golden opportunity. Along with countless actors, movie-makers, artists and innovators, these architects viewed California as somewhere that fostered creativity and imagination. With the rise of Hollywood, Los Angeles became a powerful focal point for fashion, style and aesthetics with an international influence. Its art directors and cinematic icons played an important role in the evolution of key design movements such as Art Deco (see page 48) and also a particular version of pioneering modern architecture known as Desert Modernism.

California offered a number of advantages for such pioneers. There were, of course, many affluent and open-minded clients connected to the film industry and the early tech companies that began to emerge during the post-war years. Their ranks were bolstered by many incomers who loved the landscape and climate, looking for vacation houses along the coast and desert retreats in places like Palm Springs where they could overwinter in the sunshine. The benign, gentle climate of the state was, in itself, a gift for architects and designers looking to break down the old divisions between inside and outside while creating a more fluid and informal pattern of living. The whole idea of the 'outdoor room', for instance, became more realistic and more inviting in the context of the 'architecture of the sun' and was explored to the full by Modernists seeking a more intimate and direct sense of connection with the landscape and the open air. Many Desert Modern architects argued that an intelligently designed home, tied to the natural world, could make a huge difference to health and wellbeing.

Two of the most influential and inventive architects within West Coast Modernism were a pair of friends from Austria: Rudolph Schindler and Richard Neutra. They met in Vienna, where they were taught by architect Adolf Loos (see page 41), and both shared an admiration for the work of Frank Lloyd Wright (see page 84), of whom they became aware after the publication in 1910 of the Wasmuth Portfolio (see page 88), which celebrated the early residential work of the American master architect.

Schindler was the first to emigrate to America, in 1914, hoping to find work with Wright at his practice in Chicago. It took him four years to find an opening with Wright, but then Schindler rose quickly to a trusted position in Wright's Oak Park studio in Chicago. Wright had managed to hold on to it during the most dramatic years of his life, when he had left his wife, lost his mistress in tragic circumstances and spent a good deal of time in Japan working on the design and construction of the Imperial Hotel in Tokyo. Schindler helped to hold the fort in Chicago and then, in 1920, Wright asked him to launch a satellite office in Los Angeles and oversee the construction of the Hollyhock House at Olive Hill for Aline Barnsdall (see page 89).

Collective living in the innovative Schindler House

While he was working for Wright in LA, Schindler began designing a project for himself, his new wife – the art and music teacher Pauline Gibling – and two of their friends. This was one of the first truly modern houses in America. Schindler found inspiration for the idea of a more communal way of living on camping trips to Yosemite National Park, as well as visits to New Mexico, where he noted the ancient adobe pueblos. He started thinking about a house that would be designed not simply for himself and Pauline, but for a collective, which included Pauline's college friend Marian Chace and her husband, Clyde, who was a structural engineer and a skilled building contractor.

Schindler found a large and leafy site in West Hollywood and began designing a house that offered a completely different lifestyle compared with the traditional American home. He created a pinwheel plan composed of three distinct spokes, or wings. Two of these held pairings of studios creating flexible live–work spaces for each of the four residents of the house. The third wing held a guest bedroom and a garage, while a communal kitchen sat close to the central axis, yet there was no sign of a traditional sitting room or dining room or even a multifunctional 'great room'. Instead, everyone had their own private internal portion of the house, while also being encouraged to step outside and use the communal outdoor 'rooms' offered by the two patio gardens, complete with outdoor fireplaces. In this way, the design echoed the idea of camping out, which was reinforced by the creation of a series of 'sleeping baskets' up on the roof supported by a distinctive spider-leg timber framework that formed a kind of pergola. The

Rudolph Schindler – Schindler House, Los Angeles, California, United States, 1922

baskets offered the chance to sleep out under the stars on warmer nights. Schindler explained the design:

> The basic idea was to give each person his own room – instead of the usual distribution, and do most of the cooking right on the table, making it more a social 'campfire' affair than the disagreeable burden to one member of the family.[1]

The single-storey Schindler House – also known as the Kings Road House and completed in 1922 – was just as innovative tectonically as it was spatially. Working with Clyde Chace, Schindler used a new system called 'tilt-slab' or 'tilt-up' construction. The concrete is poured into wooden moulds on site and left to cure, and then, when the wall slabs are ready, the moulds are removed and the slabs levered into position one by one to create the structural outline of the building. But there were also a lot of windows, including sliding walls of timber-framed glass that could be drawn backwards to create a seamless flow between the studios and the garden.

With the Schindler House, Rudolph Schindler proposed an alternative living pattern that balanced the need for personal privacy, and the idea of an individual escape space, with sociable, communal living areas shifted from the inside to the outside. The patios, terraces, gardens and landscaping all became an essential part of the house itself, as the lines between them started to fall away. With its fresh paradigm, the house offered an example of a way of life that not only was 'modern' but also could have an impact upon health and happiness, by shifting the focus of day-to-day experience towards these inviting, welcoming and open outdoor spaces rather than closed, cellular units.

While the thinking behind the house was positive, in reality the idea of collective living was not a complete success. Marian and Clyde Chace moved on to Florida two years later and were, for a time, replaced by Richard Neutra and his wife, Dione, who arrived in the United States during the early Twenties. There were then a series of broken friendships, as the relationship between Schindler and Pauline became strained and the architect fell out with Wright and then Neutra. It took many years for these relationships to mend, although Schindler himself stayed on at the house right up until his death in 1953, while Pauline also moved back in eventually but lived in a separate part of the house.

Richard Neutra and biorealism

Schindler's friend Richard Neutra was, over time, able to explore some of the ideas developed in the Schindler House but with a great deal more in the way of praise and public attention. While Schindler was a little ahead of the curve, Neutra got his timing just right as far as California was concerned. A few years younger than Schindler, Neutra was caught up in the chaos of World War I, when he served as an artillery officer with the Austrian army and spent some time recovering from malaria and tuberculosis. He saw these years as a terrible waste of time and energy, while recognizing, as a patient, the importance to our health of the built environment and the design of the spaces around us. There was also, perhaps, a determination to make up for lost time.

Neutra had worked in Erich Mendelsohn's architectural practice in Berlin before, eventually, arriving in America in 1923. He spent some time with Frank Lloyd Wright at Taliesin (see page 88) and then in 1925 settled in Los Angeles, reconnecting with Schindler and collaborating with him on a number of projects. The project that made Neutra's reputation in America was the Lovell Health House, for the celebrated naturopath Philip Lovell – a client Neutra met through Schindler, which inevitably caused tensions between the two architects.

Lovell was a liberal-minded celebrity physician with a loyal following generated by his newspaper column. He believed in the power of natural healing and promoted regular exercise, fresh air, a vegetarian diet and nude sunbathing. He was a dream client. Lovell and his wife, Leah, wanted their new house in Los Angeles to enhance and facilitate this kind of lifestyle, with terraces, sleeping porches and space for exercise, as well as a swimming pool. Neutra used a steel framework, concrete foundations and a tension cable to fix the house to the side of a steep ravine, from which it stepped downwards to the pool terrace on the lowest level.

Full of public praise for his custom-made house, Lovell described it as a masterpiece on its completion in 1929, and proudly invited his readers to come over and visit. It was a project that opened countless other doors for Neutra, especially after it was chosen for inclusion – alongside work by Le Corbusier and Mies van der Rohe – in a key exhibition at New York's Museum of Modern Art in 1932 (see page 146).

The Lovell Health House, as it became known, was not just a catalyst for Neutra's American career, but also a vital stepping stone within his own design philosophy, which he called 'biorealism'. In some ways, biorealism echoed the ideals of 'organic architecture' promoted by Frank Lloyd Wright (see page 92), with its focus on contextual architecture inspired by the natural site and setting of a building. But Neutra took this a step further, examining the way that inside and outside space relate to one another and the impact of the architectural design of a building upon the daily lives of its inhabitants. As an architect, his approach to his clients and their needs has been compared to the doctor–patient relationship, with Neutra's 'prescription' opening the possibility of a better way of life encompassing health, hygiene and both physical and mental wellbeing. Along with many other influential Modernist architects, he believed that architecture and design could make the world a better place, especially when it came to the home, but Neutra took this idea forward within the Californian context where the sunshine and warmth was a liberating force for good. Unlike Vienna or Berlin, California was a place where inside–outside living was a real possibility, not just for a few months but almost all year round.

Inside–outside living at the Kaufmann House

The culmination of Californian biorealism came with Neutra's design of the Kaufmann House in Palm Springs, completed in 1947. The client was department store magnate and philanthropist Edgar J Kaufmann, the very same man who commissioned Frank Lloyd Wright to design Fallingwater in Pennsylvania (see page 93) just before World War II. This optimistic and original post-war family residence, which can be seen as one of the earliest mid-century modern homes, was a very different building in a very different setting.

For Kaufmann and his family, this was a January house. It was to be used as a vacation home at the start of the year, when the weather was certainly cold back in Pennsylvania but perfect in Palm Springs. The house next door was owned by the famous industrial designer Raymond Loewy, while the desert resort itself was just on the cusp of its transformation into a full-blown designer playground for the Hollywood elite.

Rather like the Schindler House, the Kaufmann House adopted a pinwheel design but with four spokes instead of three revolving around a central circulation point. The first arm consisted of a carport plus a breezeway – a covered but open-sided walkway – leading to the centre point of the house. Another breezeway led out to the semi-separate guest wing, while the third spoke held the kitchen, service spaces and staff quarters. The fourth held a multipurpose living and dining space, which also led through to the master suite.

This floor plan offered a great deal of flexibility. The master wing of the house functioned as a comfortable unit for Kaufmann and his wife, while guests had their own defined domain, allowing everyone to enjoy a sense of privacy while coming together at key moments. Yet it was the dissolution of the boundaries between interior and exterior space that was so dramatic.

Richard Neutra – Kaufmann House, Palm Springs, California, United States, 1947

Neutra used sandstone for retaining walls and for the chimneys, tying the building to the desert, and there were long walls of floor-to-ceiling glass that not only framed the landscape but also drew the surroundings deep into the house itself. Most extraordinary of all was the wall of glass that separated the living room from the pool terrace – it slid away so that the boundary between inside and outside space completely dissolved. The lightweight steel framework of the house, which supported the weight of the building, allowed Neutra to use these curtain walls to the full, while the use of the same stone flooring within and without allowed internal and external space to unite and read as one.

Local planning restrictions meant that the house was largely limited to a single storey. But Neutra managed to create, up on the roof, with open views across the landscape and towards San Jacinto Mountain, a gloriette, which was another take on the idea of an outdoor room. It was a roof terrace with a roof plus a *brise-soleil*, or sun screen, to one side made with adjustable aluminium louvres. The gloriette had its own fireplace and comfortable seating, making it the perfect elevated escape room.

The Kaufmann House represents a dream version of the modern Californian home. With its swimming pool, mountain backdrop and collection of indoor–outdoor spaces, it embodies a kind of fantasy of warm and wonderful Desert Modernism. But it was also part of an important push towards a new way of building houses, using curtain walls that enabled the glorious sense of transparency and the intoxicating quality of natural light, which made these buildings stand apart.

The 'sunshine' Modernists

Early Modernists like Le Corbusier, Eileen Gray and Walter Gropius embraced reinforced-concrete structural solutions, pillars and ribbon windows, together with the idea of a 'free façade' (see page 71). But there was still a tangible sense of mass to many pre-war Modernist houses, even if their gleaming walls were painted white and the entire building raised up on stilts. The Californian pioneers, including Neutra, took things further in the years after World War II.

These 'sunshine' Modernists began adopting lightweight steel frames for their houses. The frameworks offered a great deal of flexibility, enabling architects to create a whole range of buildings of all shapes and sizes where the majority of the weight load of the structure was carried not by the walls themselves but by the frame. The steelwork allowed for a degree of movement, which was especially important in an area of earthquake risk, but also created a malleable building that an architect could shape at will both externally and internally. Curtains of glass rather than brick or stone could be used to envelop a house, while the lack of internal supporting walls meant that the interiors were also liberated, with the possibility of large, open-plan living rooms. The result was fluid space, with a fresh sense of openness within the home and free-flowing links via the curtain walls and sliding banks of glass to the outside, including terraces, porches and verandahs.

Among the pioneers of this new approach were Charles and Ray Eames, the great power couple of mid-century modern design. Today, they are best known for their furniture designs, including their ground-breaking plywood and fibreglass chairs, which still sell like hotcakes. But the Eameses were truly multidisciplinary designers, whose work included not just furniture but graphics, photography, film-making, exhibition design and architecture.

Charles Eames trained as an architect and went on to become head of the Department of Industrial Design at the Cranbrook Academy of Art in Michigan, as well as working and collaborating with the Academy's first president, the Finnish architect Eliel Saarinen, and his son Eero (see pages 53 and 126). Here Eames met a student, Ray Kaiser, who became his second wife in 1941, the same year that the couple settled in Los Angeles, where they moved into an apartment building designed by Richard Neutra.

Eames House, home and studio to a power couple

As well as developing their early collections of plywood furniture and other projects, Charles Eames began working on ideas for a new house and studio for himself and his wife. From the start, he wanted to build the house using a prefabricated steel frame, but wartime restrictions on industrial materials meant a long wait; initial designs for the house were drawn in 1945 but the house was not completed until 1949. Over these years, the composition and shape of the Eames House changed radically, evolving from a floating, linear 'bridge house', raised above the ground, into a two-storey house and studio with a courtyard between them. This might have been because Eames saw a similar design by Mies van der Rohe featured in an exhibition, or it could have been more about the couple's wish to preserve a line of eucalyptus trees on the meadow in Pacific Palisades where they wanted to build the house. 'We'd got to love the meadow and the idea of putting a house in the middle of it seemed terrible at that moment,' said Ray Eames. 'So that's how it happened.'[2]

Tucked between the trees and the rise of a gentle hill, the steel skeleton of the house and studio went up in just two days, with the whole construction process taking only a few months. Looking at the house today, one sees how the trees have grown, forming a green sun screen in front of the building and helping to soften its impact on the site. Behind this natural *brise-soleil*, there is the linear façade of the building itself with a mixture of banks of glass and brightly coloured panels, which have been compared to a Mondrian painting – although Ray Eames, who is credited with this abstract pattern, disliked the reference.

The sequence of spaces began with the double-height work studio, which included a dark room and kitchenette plus a mezzanine level above, while

Charles and Ray Eames – Eames House, Pacific Palisades,
California, United States, 1949

the courtyard beyond created an important sense of separation between work and home. The house itself featured a two-storey section with a kitchen and a bedroom on the ground level and other bedrooms and bathrooms above, along with a spiral staircase linking the two. Right at the end of the sequence was a dramatic, double-height living room, which was the true heart of the house, layered with the Eameses' furniture, books and other treasures. Light, warm and open, the space feeds out onto an adjoining terrace, while the steel frame and corrugated steel roof are left exposed and visible, contrasting with the tallowwood (a type of eucalyptus) used for the panelling of the high wall to the rear. Charles Eames's daughter, Lucia Eames Demetrios, recalled her own experiences of the house:

> When one wakes in the morning, there is the most wonderful shadow play as light filters through the eucalyptus leaves onto the screens and walls. One takes a delighted look at the beautiful pattern of the living room, as seen from above, and then a wonderful spin down the spiral staircase and into the sudden openness of the living room before settling into the kitchen for breakfast.[3]

The Case Study House Program

For Charles and Ray Eames, the Eames House was, by definition, a very personal project. But it was one that they also shared with a wide audience through the Case Study House Program. The program was published and promoted by *Arts & Architecture* magazine, which was edited by John Entenza, a good friend of the Eameses; Ray Eames worked for the publication regularly during the Forties as a graphic designer and advisor. It was actually Entenza who had bought the 2-hectare (5-acre) meadow in Pacific Palisades, selling on part of the land to the Eameses to build the Eames House (which was also called Case Study House #8) and, right next door, building his own single-level house (Case Study House #9) to a design by Charles Eames and Eero Saarinen.

The idea behind Entenza's Case Study House Program was to provide inspiration. These were exemplars of architect-designed modern family houses, commissioned by private clients but endorsed and published by the magazine. The houses were one-offs, but at the same time they were presented as prototypical and relatively affordable, so ideas and principles set out within the projects might potentially be replicated elsewhere. As writer Esther McCoy put it in her book on the series, 'The Case Study program encouraged a body of work which it was hoped would turn the tide against the Anne Hathaway cottage and the salt box.'[4]

Many of the Case Study House architects – who included Richard Neutra, Pierre Koenig and Craig Ellwood – used lightweight linear steel frames, flat roofs, curtain walls and vivid indoor–outdoor connectivity. Unlike the Eames House, most were single-storey and the houses tended to be quite compact and modest in scale, while seeking to maximize every bit of potential living space and create a sense of synergy with the landscape or surroundings. Picture an archetypal Californian Case Study House and it could well be a residential pavilion designed by Koenig.

Pierre Koenig built his first house, for himself, while he was still an architectural student at the University of Southern California. It was a small home in Glendale, around 93 square metres (1,000 square feet) in size, and was constructed with a steel structural frame for $5,000. It was a delightful statement of intent: 'The home is light and spacious, with all the strength, durability, warmth, beauty and economy desired for modern living,' he said. 'And steel makes this possible.'[5]

As Koenig found, there was still a suspicion about using steelwork to build houses in the early Fifties. Steel was associated with industry, factories, warehouses and 'supersheds', rather than the home. Koenig and his Californian contemporaries set out to prove that it was not only relevant for house building but also revolutionary, helping to reduce costs and simplify the whole construction process, as well as creating a fluid and flexible modern home. This was combined with environmental concerns, with Koenig also exploring natural cooling techniques and energy conservation, while carefully designing and positioning his buildings to avoid overheating and the need for air conditioning.

Two of Koenig's most famous Los Angeles houses were part of the Case Study House Program. Case Study House #21, or the Bailey House (1958), for a psychologist and his wife, was an open-plan, steel-framed home designed to block the heat in the baking summer season and to capture the warmth of solar gain in the winter. Koenig created a vibrant indoor–outdoor relationship with terraces and an internal courtyard, while also using shallow water pools around the house, which provided evaporative cooling and reflected the Californian skies. Water was also circulated up to the roof and spilled back down into the ponds via elegant steel spouts.

Case Study House #22, breaking down barriers

Some called #21 Koenig's best and most inventive building. But the most famous was surely Case Study House #22 (see page 100), completed in 1960, and also known as the Stahl House. Designed for Clarence 'Buck' Stahl, and his wife, Carlotta, this was another highly engineered steel-framed pavilion, laid out on a distinctive L-shaped grid. But the house was lent an extraordinary sense of cinematic drama by its location on Wood Drive, West Hollywood, where it sat perched upon the edge of a cliff looking across to the Hollywood Hills and out over the open cityscape in the valley below. Koenig and his clients wanted to make the most of this powerful open vista, as he explained:

> The owner wanted a clear and unobstructed view of 270 degrees and this is the only way we could do it, the way I did it. It's all glass all the way around, except for the front which is solid...The house is supposed to fit in with the environment and relate to it. You don't see the house when you're in it, you see the view.[6]

Koenig used concrete piers embedded into the hillside to support the floor pad and the house itself, which pushes out over the edge of the hill towards the void. He devoted this part of the house, naturally, to the main living space: a long, glass-sided, multifunctional space holding the seating area, dining area and an open-plan kitchen, which became an important part of the whole social realm of the Stahls' home. The informality and sociability of Californian living offered the perfect setting for breaking down the old, traditional barriers between living spaces and service spaces such as the kitchen. Instead of being banished to the back of the house, the kitchen was now an integral, elegant and open part of the heart of the home. Bedrooms and bathrooms were pushed landwards, towards what Koenig called the 'front', but we might think of as the back, given that this is the only part of the house that feels more enclosed. The architect placed a swimming pool and terrace within the elbow of the L-shaped plan, while the overhanging eaves of the roof created shaded fresh-air retreats, as well as more open sundecks.

The drama and originality of the house were brilliantly captured by the photographer Julius Shulman, who famously enjoyed populating the homes he shot, to bring them to life. Shulman's familiar images of the cantilevered living room of the Stahl House at night, with the city lights spread out below and running away into the distance, caught the spirit of the house but also defined, for many, the dream of mid-century modern Californian living. The elegantly dressed gentleman at the window, looking out over the view, or the two ladies sitting and talking, while the epic cityscape unfolds beneath them, help us to imagine ourselves within this dreamland.

The perfect balance at Palevsky House

As far as architectural aesthetics and approach were concerned, one of Koenig's closest contemporaries was Craig Ellwood. After serving in the US Army Air Corps during World War II, Ellwood began working as a cost estimator in the construction industry while taking evening classes in architecture and engineering. He then set up his own design practice, becoming an expert in the design of highly engineered, steel-framed buildings. After meeting John Entenza, Ellwood went on to design and build three Case Study Houses during the Fifties in Bel Air and Beverly Hills.

One of Ellwood's most fascinating clients was Max Palevsky, who made his fortune as a computer-tech pioneer in California during the Fifties and Sixties. After working with Packard Bell, Palevsky co-founded a company called Scientific Data Systems (SDS), which was eventually sold to Xerox for nearly a billion dollars; later still, he played a part in founding the company that became Intel. Helped by his considerable fortune, Palevsky began collecting modern art, financing Hollywood films and pursuing his own personal interests, which included architecture.

The two men became good friends after the architect designed a production plant for SDS, so when Palevsky decided to build a desert escape in Palm Springs, Ellwood was the natural choice. By the late Sixties,

Craig Ellwood – Palevsky House, Palm Springs, California, United States, 1969

with Palm Springs becoming busier and busier, Palevsky was beginning to worry about his privacy, so for the Palevsky House (1969) Ellwood designed a walled compound, partially open at one end where it looked out towards the open landscape (see page 4). Within this compound the architect created not one but two single-storey glass and steel pavilions, which – rather like the Eames House – were separated by a courtyard. The first pavilion was a guesthouse with four bedrooms. The other held the master suite, a modest galley-style kitchen towards the centre and a large living area. Arranged around a big fireplace, this spacious room featured artworks by Roy Lichtenstein and Donald Judd, while the glass curtain walls connected with the courtyard to one side and the pool terrace to the other, complete with a large steel sculpture by Alexander Calder near the pool.

Here, Ellwood achieved the perfect balance between privacy and transparency, escapism and sociability, openness and order. The combination of the two pavilions meant that Palevsky could live comfortably in his own private realm or open up the compound and the secondary pavilion for entertaining. The walls around the house created the retreat that he wanted, while openings and apertures in the walls offered edited views and glimpses of the landscape.

Elrod House, a cinematic design

As a setting, Palm Springs and the Coachella Valley certainly offer beauty and drama. The Elrod House, designed by John Lautner and completed in 1968, brings out the best of both with a truly cinematic design that combines high engineering and a contextual response to its prominent hillside location. Like Schindler and Neutra, Lautner had worked with Frank Lloyd Wright, spending six years with him at Taliesin before striking out on his own. Lautner took with him a deep-rooted appreciation of an organic approach to architecture, with its focus on a contextual response to a site and its surroundings, but he fused this with a unique sense of theatre. With his designs for a collection of gravity-defying and dynamic, sculptural houses, John Lautner became the greatest showman of West Coast Modernism, and the Elrod House was one of his proudest productions.

Lautner's client, Arthur Elrod, was an interior designer with a Hollywood client list of his own. He designed the interiors of many houses in and around Palm Springs, including a 'Hollywood-Regency' style house for himself close to the centre of the city. But then Elrod bought a cliffside parcel of land up on Smoke Tree Mountain and asked Lautner to design a new house perched high above the city, looking down on the valley. Elrod wanted something 'architecturally exceptional' and Lautner duly obliged.

The centrepiece of the house is the circular living room, with its vast propeller-blade concrete roof floating above. Skylights sit between the 'blades', while one's eye is instantly drawn to a long band of glass framing an epic vista of the Coachella Valley. This curving window wall retracts at the touch of a button while crossing the surface of a kidney-shaped swimming pool that creeps into the house from the adjoining terrace. Rather like Wright's Fallingwater (see page 93), the rocks push into the house, thrusting up from the black slate floor of this church-like great hall. The boulders also make their presence felt in the adjoining master bedroom and the bathroom, where the integrated tub sits by the window, drawing the landscape inside. Stone, concrete and glass converge in a house folded into the hillside, with a guest wing positioned a little lower down the slope, at one remove from the master residence.

It is here, in the 1971 James Bond film *Diamonds Are Forever*, that business magnate Willard Whyte is imprisoned by the arch villain Ernst Stavro Blofeld. When Bond (Sean Connery) comes looking for Whyte (played by Jimmy Dean), he is met in the living room by Blofeld's energetic guards Bambi and Thumper. Bambi, played by Lola Larson, and Thumper, played by Trina Parks, are certainly a good match for Bond, who memorably struggles and ends up in the pool before finally gaining the upper hand and managing to free the engaging Jimmy Dean.

The Elrod House is, of course, the perfect Bond villain lair. The house feels almost impossible, like a fantasy in itself. The combination of the clifftop setting, the sense of theatrical tectonics and the scale make the main living space one of the greatest cinematic rooms. As an architect, Lautner brought something special to his residential work, which celebrated the idea of an inside–outside lifestyle, with its inviting informality and openness. But he added high drama, making the most of challenging West Coast situations like hillside and clifftops. In doing so, he became a favourite among not just movie-makers but also those looking for a more adventurous version of modern Californian living.

John Lautner – Elrod House, Palm Springs, California, United States, 1968

International Style
Crossing Continents

7   Eero Saarinen – Miller House, Columbus, Indiana, United States, 1957

Walter Gropius
Gropius House
Lincoln, Massachusetts,
United States, 1938

Eero Saarinen
Miller House
Columbus, Indiana
United States, 1957

Josep Lluís Sert
Sert residence
Cambridge, Massachusetts,
United States, 1958

Antonio Bonet Castellana
La Ricarda
Barcelona, Spain, 1963

Harry Seidler
Rose Seidler House
Sydney, New South Wales,
Australia, 1950

During the course of the 20th century the world became a much smaller place. Communication advanced and improved through multiple means, with journals and magazines, as well as radio and television, transmitting ideas and information as never before. Within the world of architecture especially, there was a rapid process of outreach and interconnectivity as fresh ways of working and innovative approaches to form, structure and space spread around the globe. Increasingly, as with so many other professions, architects and designers themselves travelled, communed and compared notes with each other. This important process of cross-pollination accelerated during the Thirties and then again during the Fifties, with the arrival of the Jet Age, and became a key element in the spread of the 'International Style' of architecture and the Modernist design philosophy, which was to have far-reaching consequences for the shape and style of the home in many different parts of the world.

During the late Twenties and Thirties, architects began to talk like never before. Modernist architects, particularly in Europe, realized that they had much in common, including the desire to make the world a better place through design. There was a shared interest in industrially made materials and building systems, a widely held belief that such systems could improve the lives and homes of countless people, and a passion for a matching modern aesthetic that broke away from the past. One of the most influential of the many new talking shops that sprang up during the interwar years was CIAM, or the Congrès Internationaux d'Architecture Moderne, founded in 1928.

CIAM's early members included many figureheads of the Modernist movement, such as Le Corbusier, Pierre Jeanneret (Le Corbusier's cousin and business partner), Pierre Chareau, Gerrit Rietveld, Walter Gropius, Alvar Aalto and Josep Lluís Sert. A series of CIAM conferences was held in Switzerland, Belgium, France and Germany, including a famous meeting in 1933, held aboard SS *Patris II* as it sailed from Marseille to Athens while the architects talked about how to reshape the modern city. They began to set down the principles of Modernist thinking, issuing the occasional manifesto or statement of intent, and also inspiring smaller groups and sub-groups. These included Britain's Modern Architectural Research (MARS) Group, established in 1933, with Wells Coates, Maxwell Fry and F R S Yorke among the founding members.

This dialogue about modern living crossed borders. The work of a number of CIAM participants – including Gropius, Le Corbusier and Aalto – fed into a landmark exhibition held at the Museum of Modern Art (MoMA) in New York in 1932. Entitled *Modern Architecture: International Exhibition*, it was curated by Henry-Russell Hitchcock, an architectural historian, and Philip Johnson, who later became a highly influential architect himself (see page 146). The exhibition also included the work of Johnson's architectural hero and mentor, Ludwig Mies van der Rohe. The show, which went on to tour the United States, featured exemplary modern homes such as Le Corbusier's Villa Savoye and Mies van der Rohe's Villa Tugendhat (see pages 69 and 78), completed in 1930 and 1931 respectively, along with Walter Gropius' designs for the Bauhaus School buildings at Dessau (1926). As well as an exhibition catalogue, there was an associated book, also by Hitchcock and Johnson, entitled *The International Style: Architecture Since 1922*, published by W W Norton & Co.

The MoMA exhibition, catalogue and book sought to define the common features of the International Style, including key elements like the curtain wall and open-plan space, as in this extract from the catalogue:

The effect of mass, of static solidity, hitherto the prime quality of architecture, has all but disappeared; in its place there is an effect of volume, or more accurately, of plane surfaces bounding a volume. The prime architectural symbol is no longer the dense brick, but the open box. Indeed, the great majority of buildings are in reality, as well as in effect, mere planes surrounding a volume.[1]

The houses and buildings of the International Style, then, were built with steel and concrete skeletons (frameworks) and curtain walls (external walls that were not load-bearing), allowing for large expanses of glass and long ribbon windows, which in turn forged a strong indoor–outdoor relationship. Internally, these homes featured open-plan living spaces of one kind or another, and aesthetically they tended to be linear and geometric, while ornament was stripped back in favour of a more rational and functional design approach. This was the essential core of the modern house according to the pioneer architects of the modern movement and the International Style.

The combination of such exhibitions, organizations like CIAM and MARS and many modern manifestos helped to promote internationally the ideas that lay behind Modernist architecture and design, as did the houses and buildings that circulated via architectural magazines, journals and books. The word was spreading widely even as the political world was changing and unravelling.

Within the space of just a few years, something that had begun as an essentially cultural movement was given a new impetus by the rise of radical politics and far-right extremism in parts of Europe, particularly Spain, Italy and Germany. The rise of Nazism was a very real threat to German Modernist architects, who were regarded by the Nazi party as left-wing socialists and avant-garde agitators. The Bauhaus School in Dessau was completely shut down in 1933, just 17 months after the MoMA exhibition in New York. Many leading German Modernist architects, who suddenly found themselves without work and under threat, began to leave Germany for other countries, especially Britain and the United States. They included the former director of the Bauhaus, Walter Gropius.

In 1934 Gropius and his family moved to London, where he established a new architectural office in partnership with fellow CIAM member and MARS co-founder Maxwell Fry. They worked on a small number of projects in England, including a house at 66 Old Church Street in London's Chelsea district (1936) and The Wood House, in Shipbourne, Kent (1937). But within just a few years of arriving in London, Gropius was offered a job he could not refuse and travelled across the Atlantic to become Chair of the Department of Architecture at Harvard University's new Graduate School of Design in Cambridge, Massachusetts.

As an educator, Gropius was to play an important part in the evolution of American mid-century Modernism, influencing architects such as Philip Johnson, John M Johansen and Eliot Noyes, all of whom studied architecture at Harvard. Along with other former Bauhaus émigrés, such as Mies van der Rohe, Gropius became a practising architect in the United States. He invited another key colleague and friend, Marcel Breuer, to join him at Harvard and become his partner in a fresh architectural firm. Along with other influential exiles, such as the artists and former Dessau tutors Josef and Anni Albers, Gropius and Breuer brought the Bauhaus ethos with them to the New World.

Gropius House, a unique fusion

Many of the early New England projects taken on by Gropius and Breuer during the Thirties and early Forties were residential. Of these, one of the most important was Walter Gropius' own family house in Lincoln, Massachusetts, built upon a parcel of land not far from Walden Pond, where Henry David Thoreau's famous cabin had been located. Gifted by a generous benefactor, the 1.6-hectare (4-acre) site was around 30km (20 miles) from the Harvard campus.

Completed in 1938, the Gropius House seems, at first, to conform to many of the ideas and principles common to the International Style. It is essentially a two-storey, linear house with ribbon windows, a flat roof and an integrated roof terrace. Painted a clean, crisp white, the building stands out brightly against the backdrop of the trees and grounds, while, inside, the main living spaces are partially open-plan, with a large interconnected sitting room and dining area. Gropius' study alongside is separate, yet the use of a translucent glass-block wall as the dividing line creates some sense of connection and allows the light to circulate. In the entrance hall, a twisting staircase with lightweight steel safety rails also allows the sunlight to percolate through. The tubular-steel furniture was designed by Breuer. Within the context of New England, the house was fresh, original and new. Gropius' daughter, Ati Gropius Johansen, recounted:

> To many of my friends, when I was growing up, this house was a curiosity. They loved to visit our unusual house which was so different from theirs. I remember a woman who once asked my mother, 'Mrs Gropius, don't you find it terribly exhausting to always live so far ahead of your time?'[2]

Yet in other ways Gropius purposefully tailored the house to the New England setting. The skeletal framework was actually made from timber, not steel, and the building is clapboarded in timber rather than rendered. He opted for a dramatic flying entrance porch with a roof canopy that projects outwards from the front of the house and a fly-screened terrace at the back, while there was also a brick chimney and fireplace. The

Walter Gropius – Gropius House, Lincoln, Massachusetts, United States, 1938

architect saw the house as a kind of test bed for a contextual New England home of a kind explored with Breuer over the following years, using local materials, such as wood and stone, and responding to each unique situation. It is perhaps not surprising that Gropius himself began to grow suspicious of the term 'International Style', given that it implied a universal approach to architecture and design. He wrote:

> When I built my first house in the USA, I made it a point to absorb into my own conception those features of the New England architectural tradition that I still found alive and adequate. The fusion of the regional spirit with a contemporary approach to design produced a house that I would never have built in Europe with its entirely different climatic, technical and psychological background.[3]

Softening the geometry of Miller House

One of the great American post-war, mid-century modern houses does manage to conform more closely to the precepts of the International Style, while its architect was also carried to the United States as a young man by transatlantic currents. Miller House in Columbus, Indiana (see page 120), was a relatively rare but highly influential residential project by architect Eero Saarinen, completed in 1957. He became famous for his corporate buildings for the likes of John Deere, General Motors and IBM, as well as commissions for more expressive and sculptural buildings such as churches, chapels and the TWA Flight Center at John F Kennedy International Airport (1962), the sculpted lines of which came to define the early years of the Jet Age itself.

Saarinen was born in Finland and was the son of architect Eliel Saarinen and textile designer Loja Saarinen. As a teenager, Saarinen moved with his family to the United States, where his father became the first president of the Cranbrook Academy of Art in Michigan, while also designing a series of buildings on the new campus (see page 53). The family maintained its links to Finland, often heading back for the summer months, while Eero Saarinen travelled extensively in Europe during the early Thirties, as well as studying architecture at Yale. Around 1936, he started working in his father's architectural practice, collaborating on a number of commissions, an arrangement that lasted through to 1950 when Eliel Saarinen died and his son took full charge of the practice.

The architect's relationship with Columbus, Indiana, and the Miller family was long and significant. The initial project here was the First Christian Church (1942), designed by both Eero and Eliel Saarinen, and one of the last was the sublime North Christian Church (1964), with its pencil-point spire sitting on top of a dramatic hexagonal roof. Between these projects, there was Miller House, completed in 1957 for Irwin and Xenia Miller.

Irwin Miller was an industrialist, a financier, a philanthropist and a patron of modern architecture and the arts. He transformed the family company, Cummins Corporation, into a major player in the field of commercial diesel engines but also became chairman of the Irwin Union Bank and president of the National Council of Churches. Through these various roles, Miller played a key part in commissioning a whole collection of Modernist buildings in Columbus and turning this small city into a hotspot of mid-century architecture and design. He was also someone who practised what he preached, commissioning a truly modern family home on the green edge of Columbus.

The house is a rectangular, single-storey building but on a significant scale. The flat roof extends outwards from the main body of the steel-framed building to shelter the entrance and protect the verandahs around the house. Together with the extensive use of floor-to-ceiling glass, which maximizes the views out across the extensive gardens and grounds, the verandahs help to break down the divisions between inside and outside. The house sits upon a landscaped plateau, planned by landscape architect Dan Kiley, while the land slips away westwards towards open meadows and woodland beyond. This creates a kind of plinth and formal framework for the house, which has often been compared to a temple floating in this semi-rural setting.

Inside, the organization of the house was truly innovative. Using the formal grid established by the steel-framed structure, Saarinen placed four self-contained units, or pavilions, at the corners of the building, and each of these had its own clear purpose. One held the master suite, including a study, while another held quarters for the children. The third hosted a large kitchen, with space enough for a large family breakfast table, and the fourth was devoted to garaging and a guest suite. Between these four pavilions, which featured internal walls clad in white marble, was a fluid, open-plan living space that looked out to the view while skylights added some extra sunshine. Working with interior designer Alexander Girard, Saarinen subtly 'zoned' this open space, positioning a dining area to one side, where a dining table and Tulip chairs designed by the architect were framed by a Girard rug 'floating' upon the travertine floor. There was a seating area arranged around a circular fireplace, vented by a flue in the shape of a drum suspended from the ceiling, and then there was a comfortable 'conversation pit' set into the floor, with a surround sofa and an assembly of colourful cushions.

Using the idea of zoning, Saarinen was able to preserve the expansive sense of openness while leading the eye outwards to the landscape. The shape and plan of the open room helped in lightly zoning these spaces, but just as important were the organization of rugs and furniture, the position of the fireplace, and the shifts in floor level as seen in the four steps down to the conversation pit. Saarinen and Girard also integrated many other pieces of furniture and storage, such as bookshelves and cupboards, tucked away along the internal walls and other parts of the house, and helping to preserve that all-important sense of open space and the free flow of light.

What is most remarkable, walking around Miller House today, is the way that the rigour, discipline and order of the International Style are complemented and softened by the characterful interiors of this family home. This was helped by the fact that Saarinen was, himself, a furniture designer and the author of classic pieces for Knoll like the Womb chair (1948) and the Tulip chair (1956). Yet Girard's contribution was also important, especially in the way that he layered the house with texture, colour and curiosities. What might have been a cold temple became a house of great character and delight.

Sert residence, a modern courtyard house

Another American exemplar of the International Style was the house that Spanish architect Josep Lluís Sert built for himself in Cambridge, Massachusetts, in 1958. Born in Barcelona, where he studied and worked for many years, Sert designed and built a number of apartment buildings and other projects in and around the city during the Thirties and became a leading light in the Spanish branch of CIAM. But he was forced to leave Barcelona in 1937 after the outbreak of the Spanish Civil War in the previous year, as the Nationalist rebels under General Franco began advancing across the country and pushing back the Republican government forces. Exiled in Paris, Sert designed the Spanish Republic's pavilion for the Paris Exposition of 1937. The pavilion exhibited Picasso's famous painting *Guernica*, depicting the Nationalist bombing of the Basque town using German air power.

In 1939 Sert moved from France to the United States and eventually, in 1953, he became Dean of the Harvard Graduate School of Design. Harvard offered Sert a modest corner site in Cambridge, Massachusetts, to build a new house for himself and his wife. The challenge with the Sert residence was to create a modern pavilion that felt open and generous, while offering the kind of privacy and protection demanded by this exposed urban setting. Sert's solution, completed in 1958, was a 20th-century version of the courtyard house.

The idea of courtyard houses stretches back to Roman times, when villas were often arranged around a central courtyard or patio. Traditional courtyard houses can also be seen in parts of Spain, France and especially North Africa, where Moroccan riads, for example, are organized around a central garden while the exterior walls are high and closed off to the city.

Sert recognized that courtyard houses are well suited to modern urban living, where the desire for outdoor space needs to be balanced with designs that offer protection from the cityscape and the gaze of countless eyes. Courtyards offered a way of creating a secret haven, as he explained:

> The scarcer and more expensive land becomes in urban zones, the more attention we should pay to the Mediterranean type of house with a patio. The motifs are simple: by putting fences almost on the boundaries of the plot, one can take more advantage of a piece of land that has become valuable. Both the interior and exterior spaces turn private and quiet. Each room can have pleasant views regardless of what is beyond the walls.[4]

Sert created an enclosure of brick and timber walls and then tucked the single-storey house behind the walls along with a patio garden at each end of the enclosure, plus the central courtyard. This arrangement meant that almost every internal room in the house looked onto an outdoor room of one kind or another, increasing the sense of space and maximizing the available light with banks of floor-to-ceiling glass. Sert positioned internal circulation routes to either side of the courtyard, linking the large open-plan living space at one end of the building with the bedrooms and ancillary spaces at the other.

The most dramatic space in the house was the living room, which formed an open pavilion blessed with high ceilings created by a butterfly roof, with wings that lifted to either side while providing clerestory windows (rows of windows at the upper part of walls) at the tips. Complete with a fireplace, a dining area and seating, this inviting room formed the heart of the house, which featured artworks by Sert's friends from home,

Josep Lluís Sert – Sert residence, Cambridge, Massachusetts, United States, 1958

including Picasso and Joan Miró.The Sert House managed to fuse, with great success, elements of the International Style – such as curtain walls, inside–outside connectivity and open-plan living spaces – with a concept of courtyard living that carried back to Sert's homeland.

Having relaunched his architectural practice in the mid-Fifties, Sert was able to balance work in America with projects that took him to Europe and eventually to Spain once again. Many of these projects connected to the world of art in one way or another, including the Fondation Maeght in Saint-Paul-de-Vence in France, a studio for Miró called the Taller Sert in Mallorca and the Fundació Joan Miró in Barcelona, which was completed in 1975, making it one of Sert's final projects.

La Ricarda, a new take on an old idea

The sequence of exile and homecoming experienced by Josep Lluís Sert was mirrored in some ways by his slightly younger countryman and former colleague, Antonio Bonet Castellana. An architect and furniture designer, Bonet studied at the Barcelona School of Architecture and joined Sert's practice in the mid-Thirties. Like his mentor, Bonet was forced into exile in Paris during the Spanish Civil War and worked with Sert on the design of the Spanish Republic's pavilion for the Paris Expo of 1937, before spending some time working in Le Corbusier's office.

Then, rather than heading to North America like Sert, Bonet went to South America. Largely based in Buenos Aires, he designed and built a number of houses in Argentina and Uruguay, as well as creating pieces of furniture, such as his famous Butterfly chair of 1938, designed with Jorge Ferrari Hardoy and Juan Kurchan, whom Bonet first met in Le Corbusier's atelier. Made with a leather or canvas sling seat over a lightweight tubular-steel frame, the Butterfly chair is now ubiquitous and widely imitated.

Bonet's South American projects of the Forties included a series of commissions in the Uruguayan coastal resort of Punta Ballena, such as a hotel and restaurant called the Hostería Solana del Mar (1945) and Casa Berlingieri (1947). Built in the dunes, facing the sea, the house is slotted into the coastal topography and features banks of floor-to-ceiling glass, integrated terraces and an undulating, wave-like roofline formed by a series of vaulted ceilings. These were created in conjunction with the much respected Uruguayan structural engineer Eladio Dieste, who was very fond of these thin, shell-like forms, yet they also echoed the traditional arched roofs seen back in Barcelona, known as 'Catalan vaults'.

During the early Fifties, Bonet was tempted back to Spain by a commission for another house, La Ricarda. The initial designs were finished by 1953, but it took until 1963 for the house to be finished. For much of that time Bonet was supervising the construction at long distance from South America, but he did eventually return to Spain.

Engineer Ricardo Gomis and his wife Inés Bertrand Mata wanted to build a new home for themselves and their six children on a family estate on the outskirts of Barcelona, not far from the sea, a lagoon and a small airfield, which eventually became the city's international hub, El Prat. The Gomis family had a strong interest in modern architecture, art and music and waited patiently while Bonet shuttled backwards and forwards between Spain and South America.

For La Ricarda, which was completed in 1963, Bonet developed a new take on the idea of a compound house composed of a series of interlinked

Antonio Bonet Castellana – La Ricarda, Barcelona, Spain, 1963

pavilions, or modules. Rather like the notion of a courtyard house, this was a reinterpretation of an old idea but in a very modern form. It created a kind of farmstead formation composed of a small collection of complementary structures rather than one large super-house. Bonet identified some of the factors involved:

> The central concept of the design came from the landscape, which is why I decided to build it as single storey, in spite of the large scale of the project. The needs of a large family had to be considered along with the ability of the parents, great music lovers, to separate themselves and have the option of using the living room for holding concerts.[5]

The use of a modular layout helped to reduce La Ricarda's visual and physical impact upon the setting, while allowing the pavilions to sit gently among the trees. One of these miniature houses held the parents' bedroom and bathroom, another was devoted to the children and another hosted the main living spaces. Each one was crowned by Bonet's vaulted ceilings, which increased the height and drama of the space. Covered walkways linked the units, while an empty, open-sided pavilion served as a kind of communal gazebo.

There was a great deal of ingenuity to the design of the units, especially when it came to controlling light and heat. The bedroom pavilions featured folding, timber shutters while Bonet also used latticed ceramic screens in various parts of the house, sometimes in combination with translucent glass blocks and discs of colourful stained glass. Much of the furniture throughout the house was also designed by the architect, including the double-sided sofas arranged around the fireplace in the master pavilion.

The ambition and success of La Ricarda convinced Bonet to return to Spain full time. He went on to design a number of other innovative houses in Catalonia, including Casa Cruylles near Girona (1968), which – rather like Sert's later work in Spain – spliced the principles of Modernism and the International Style with vernacular references and local materials.

Rose Seidler House, an impressive debut

One of the most remarkable architectural journeys was surely the one taken by a young architect from Vienna called Harry Seidler. He was one of the many European émigrés who left Austria and Germany during the late Thirties, arriving in England with his family as a teenager. From England, Seidler moved to Canada, where he studied architecture at the University of Manitoba, graduating in 1944. He continued his education at Harvard Graduate School of Design under Walter Gropius and Marcel Breuer, followed by a design course at Black Mountain College under Josef Albers, another of the former Bauhaus masters.

After finishing his studies, Seidler went to work for Alvar Aalto's American office in Cambridge, Massachusetts, where Aalto was a professor at MIT. Seidler then became an assistant at Breuer's practice in New York, before eventually responding to an invitation from his parents to join them in their adopted country, Australia. Rose and Max Seidler wanted their son to design a new home for them, and so, among other things, Seidler took with him ideas for a house that he had already designed and drawn while

Harry Seidler – Rose Seidler House, Sydney, New South Wales, Australia, 1950

working with Breuer. There was a stopover in Brazil, where he spent three months with the Brazilian master architect Oscar Niemeyer (see page 208), and finally in 1948, at the age of 24, Seidler arrived in Sydney.

His parents had bought a 2-hectare (5-acre) site at Wahroonga, north of Sydney and on the edge of the Ku-ring-gai Chase National Park. Making allowances for the site and situation, Seidler created his own take on the International Style with a building that is remarkably sophisticated and accomplished for a young architect's debut. The house was tucked gently against the slope of a hillside, backed by eucalyptus trees, with the main level of the building raised up on steel columns and sandstone walls. There was a sheltered entrance and carport at ground level, with a Corbusian-style ramp to one side that offered an alternative route into the house via a semi-sheltered roof terrace that was integrated into the overall outline of the building. Partially shaded with a sun screen and decorated with a colourful wall mural by Harry Seidler, this deck created an elevated courtyard, offering an outdoor room, an observatory and a vivid sense of integration with the main living room within the house via a floor-to-ceiling wall of glass.

Inside, the spatial arrangement was dynamic. Seidler devoted around half of the building to an open-plan seating and dining area, along with a partially connected galley-style kitchen. Rather than installing a solid partition between these spaces, Seidler created a flexible dividing line using kitchen units and cupboards, with a long serving hatch positioned between them. Opaque sliding glass panels could be used to close this hatch as desired, but even with the sliders in place, light still filtered through and offered some relationship between the kitchen and dining area alongside. This was an inventive variant on open-plan living, ensuring that the kitchen – and those within it – felt connected to the heart of the house, yet also offering degrees of separation if, for example, the family wanted to hide away the pots and pans while they ate together or entertained at the dining table.

Harry Seidler specified almost every detail of the house, including furniture by Charles and Ray Eames, Eero Saarinen and Bonet, with the latter's Butterfly chairs on the terrace. Seidler commented on the choice of furnishings:

There can be no more captive client than a mother. Mother agreed to sell all her Viennese furniture, but refused to part with her elaborately decorated silver cutlery. Whenever I came to dinner, only the Russel Wright flatware I brought from New York was allowed to be seen.[6]

Completed in 1950, the Rose Seidler House was followed by a house for the architect's uncle, Marcus Seidler, a year later on the same family compound. There was also a third house, known as the Rose House (1953), initially designed and built for Harry Seidler's brother but then sold to Julian Rose; more recently it has been reacquired by the family. These three buildings, particularly the Rose Seidler House, launched the architect's long and highly successful career in Australia. Today, Harry Seidler is often described as the godfather of Australian Modernism, and he was certainly the most visible and influential of the European émigré architects who arrived there in the years just before and after World War II, bringing the ideas and ideals of the International Style along with them.

Glass Houses
The New Belvederes

8   Ludwig Mies van der Rohe – Farnsworth House,
Plano, Illinois, United States, 1951

Ludwig Mies van der Rohe
Farnsworth House
Plano, Illinois,
United States, 1951

Lina Bo Bardi
Casa de Vidro
São Paulo, Brazil, 1951

Philip Johnson
Glass House
New Canaan, Connecticut,
United States, 1949

C reating and crafting a new home is an intimate and demanding process. The relationship between architect and client can be intense and sometimes deeply personal, because it inevitably involves a journey of understanding. To produce the house that a client really wants, the architect must delve deep into his client's wishes and desires, along with the way that they live – or want to live – their day-to-day lives. Just as a house should embody a response to site and surroundings, it should also be a response to the needs, dreams and aspirations of those paying the bills.

The peculiar relationship between architect and client has been likened to that between doctor and patient, priest and penitent or psychotherapist and subject. It is a bond that develops over time, given that the process of designing and building a home is seldom rapid, and involves, inevitably, many highs and lows. Perhaps it should not be a surprise that every now and again this bond becomes something more than a professional, working relationship. Perhaps we should not be shocked when infatuation, admiration and perhaps even passion complicate the creative endeavour.

Farnsworth House, the ultimate universal space

The curious connection between Ludwig Mies van der Rohe and Dr Edith Farnsworth has been the subject of much conjecture and has even been turned into both a stage play and a film. It is hard to know the full truth about their relationship, but it's clear that there was an infatuation and an affair interwoven with the design and build of one of the most significant and widely referenced modern houses of the 20th century. The Farnsworth House (1951) in Plano, Illinois (see page 138), took the idea of universal space and transparency to a new extreme within a glass pavilion that held what was essentially a single open-plan room.

Dr Edith Farnsworth was a kidney specialist who worked in Chicago and was a single woman with a powerful intellect and a strong, independent spirit. Mies van der Rohe was a respected architect with an international reputation. A German émigré and former head of the Bauhaus, with a portfolio of pioneering European projects, including the Villa Tugendhat of 1930 (see page 78), Mies moved to Chicago in 1938 and took up the directorship of what was soon to become the Illinois Institute of Technology. He had married Ada Bruhn in his 20s and they had three daughters together, but the couple had separated in 1921. During the late Twenties and the Thirties, his companion was Lilly Reich, an interior designer who co-designed many of Mies's most famous pieces of furniture, including the Barcelona collection. The companion of his American years (1938–69) was the artist Lora Marx, whom he first met in 1940.

Farnsworth was introduced to Mies van der Rohe at a party in Chicago in 1945, just after the end of World War II. This was a time, naturally, of great optimism and hope, with thoughts focused upon renaissance, revival and a new world order. Farnsworth wanted to build a weekend home and had just bought a parcel of land by the Fox River at Plano, around 80km (50 miles) west of Chicago. Deeply impressed by Mies, she invited him to design the house, trusting him not only to craft a home that would suit her needs, but also to create a building of architectural significance. It is clear that she had a good deal of confidence in her architect and allowed him the creative freedom to produce something extraordinary. Without knowing it, Farnsworth had initiated one of the most profoundly influential buildings of the Modernist movement. She had started a revolution that was to change the whole way that we live in our homes and order our personal spaces.

Whether you love it or hate it, the Farnsworth House is an extraordinary achievement for its time. The building is a single-storey glass pavilion that seems to hover above the meadow upon which it gently sits. Eight vertical steel beams support the slender framework of the house, which is painted a crisp white. A large verandah at one end of the building is neatly contained within the precise geometrical outline of the composition. The simple beauty of this crafted belvedere conceals only the complexity of the thought processes and thinking time that lay behind it, with Mies reworking the design many times over, stripping it back to its purest form.

The idea of elevating the building came from the need to minimize any flood damage from the river that runs alongside, but also helps to enhance and invigorate the entire composition and the ethereal character of the Farnsworth House. The floor-to-ceiling glass windows create a powerful impression of transparency, allowing the eye to look right through the building and connecting the interiors with the meadow alongside and the trees beyond it. Mies told the critic Christian Norberg-Schulz, 'If you view nature through the glass walls of the Farnsworth House, it gains a more profound significance than if viewed from outside. It becomes part of the larger whole.'[1]

The house pursues many ideas explored by Mies in his ground-breaking Barcelona Pavilion of 1929 (see also page 67). This temporary pavilion was commissioned by the German government for the International Exposition held in the Spanish city but was later rebuilt as a permanent feature at the foot of the stone steps that climb up to Barcelona's Montjuïc Castle. The Barcelona Pavilion offered sublime delight and was well ahead of its time. Glass walls dissolved the boundaries between indoor and outdoor space, which included water pools set within pristine courtyards. The minimalist purity of the space was offset by the use of richly patterned onyx and marble walls and other intricately patterned natural finishes. The furniture – including Mies's famous steel and leather Barcelona chair – was designed in sympathy with the fluid, uninterrupted interiors. Yet this was an exhibition pavilion rather than a home. With the Farnsworth House, Mies seized the opportunity to explore his ideas on a truly domestic scale, with the willing support of his client.

The ideas contained within the house are just as radical and far-reaching as its outward appearance. The transparency of the building was made possible by the lack of any solid walls or partitions in the house and the use of a 'free plan'. The idea of a free plan had already been explored by a number of pioneering Modernist architects, including Le Corbusier, who included it in his manifesto for modern architecture, 'Five Points of Architecture' (see page 71). Yet Mies progressed the concept of an open-plan area, or 'universal space', and took it to a completely new level of purity and accomplishment, designing a fluid and flexible interior space uninterrupted by columns or internal supporting walls.

Such universal spaces were made possible by the advanced engineering and new materials of the early 20th century. With traditionally built stone, brick and timber buildings, the opportunities to create a universal space were limited, and only larger buildings with soaring rooflines, such as cathedrals, temples and barns, generally offered wide-open volumes. Period stone, brick and timber houses were usually compartmentalized into a series of individual rooms, often arranged around a fireplace, and supported by beams and internal load-bearing walls. But the arrival of steel-framed construction allowed the load of a building to be taken by the skeleton alone, freeing up the space within. Strong, slender beams and slimmed-down frameworks also permitted the spaces between to be filled with glass, creating a non-structural 'curtain wall' to the exterior, which introduced transparency and plenty of sunlight. They enabled a new generation of glass houses and see-through palaces that would have delighted one of their earliest advocates, Joseph Paxton, designer of London's Crystal Palace of 1851, which housed the Great Exhibition.

Mies van der Rohe applied the curtain wall and universal space principles to soaring skyscrapers, like the 1951 Lake Shore Drive Apartment towers in Chicago (see page 193). But he also embraced the same thinking, on a more modest scale, at the Farnsworth House. The living space within the building was not split up or sectioned off, but left free-flowing, fluid and open. A desk faces the verandah at one end, forming a miniature study, which runs through into a seating area, while a teak-faced cupboard to the rear helps lightly delineate the sleeping zone at the back. Mies also designed a 'service core': a compact unit, like a piece of furniture, which contained a fireplace and two small bathrooms on one side and a galley-style kitchenette on the other. The unit did not quite touch the ceiling, allowing the whole house to be read by the eye as one single, unified space. Living areas were defined by the placement of furniture rather than solid partitions, while different zones could be created by something as simple as the positioning of a rug and some chairs on the travertine floor.

Today we have grown used to the idea of open-plan living, but back in 1951 the idea was still experimental, especially when applied to an entire home. Open-plan sitting and dining rooms eventually became a staple of mid-century modern houses, but a room that was a fully universal space was a radical rarity. It was the kind of thinking that was to revolutionize the whole way that we think about living space in our homes, marking a key moment in the shift away from compartmentalized living within a series of interlinked boxes towards more flexible and airy spaces that combine a whole series of functions within one open floor plan.

Few of us now want to live, like the Victorians, in a series of different and isolated compartments, each tailored to one specific purpose, such as dining, working and relaxing. By and large we prefer a more informal approach, where many functions and uses are contained within one more generously scaled space. And we no longer see our kitchens as service spaces to be tucked away and inhabited by domestic staff. Instead, they have become an integral part of modern-day living and brought into the heart of the home. Nor are we content with a small sash window that frames a micro-managed view of the outside world. We crave light and a strong relationship between inside and outside space; even in the city we ask for a vista and a vivid sense of connection with the world beyond our four walls.

The Farnsworth House provided the archetypal glass box and continues to inspire the design of countless contemporary homes. In addition, it has led to thousands of linear glass extensions grafted onto period homes to create new family living, dining and kitchen spaces arranged on an open-plan principle and infused with a spirit of informality as well as practicality. Likewise, it's hard to think of open-plan loft living or contemporary barn conversions without the model of the Farnsworth House. It provided a key marker upon the path to this modern way of living.

However, Edith Farnsworth decided that she was not happy to be the guinea pig. She wanted a house of distinction, but she also wanted a house that she could live in. The mosquitoes from the Fox River plagued her. In winter, condensation ran down the single-glazed panes of glass and pooled on the travertine floors. She felt that she was on display within a glass case that offered little or no privacy, while Mies the maestro tried to stop her whenever she attempted to sneak in some of her own furniture.

Their relationship broke down and the 'romance' unravelled – the two of them ended up in court arguing over cost overruns and unpaid bills. Mies ultimately won the case and many would suggest that he also won the aesthetic and architectural argument, given the importance and ongoing influence of the house he had built for Edith Farnsworth. Yet she was the one left to live with the house day to day, while Mies went on to bigger projects and fresh ideas. She called it her 'Mies-conception' and complained, 'I can't even put a clothes hanger in my house without considering how it affects everything from the outside.'[2]

Edith Farnsworth gives us the great case study in architect–client relations, suggesting the importance of establishing a clear brief and close understanding of the final goals and ambitions for a home that is made to order. The house itself was transparent, but the personal relationship between Mies and Farnsworth was muddy, complex and opaque. We feel for her and are sorry for her disappointment. Yet we hope that she found some comfort as an inadvertent revolutionary and as Mies's partner in a process that changed the way we live in the modern world.

There are a few points that are deeply telling about her long-term relationship with her own house. Rather than selling up or knocking it down, she continued to live here for the best part of 20 years. When she built a garage for her car, she placed it at a respectful distance from Mies's building. And when she eventually sold up, the final straw was said to be the widening of the nearby highway, which compromised the setting and left her with the sound of traffic echoing in her ears. She argued that the house was essentially unlivable, yet she stayed on for nearly two decades, hopefully finding some kind of happiness along the way. Edith Farnsworth changed the world of architecture and transformed the modern home, even if she just wanted a nice house on a meadow for the weekends.

Today, her home still has the power to inspire. A visitors' centre has been built a good walk away from the house and well out of sight, requiring a gentle journey through the woods and along the river, which gradually builds a sense of anticipation. When the outline of the 'floating room' finally reveals itself, it's almost like visiting an altar to modernity where the idea of 'home' has been distilled down to its very essence.

The greenery of the meadow and of the surrounding trees means that the white geometry of the building sings out, but your gaze still passes through the glass walls to the landscape beyond. The river bank feels surprisingly close and the water worryingly high as it tumbles past. The guide talks of the troubling floods that have damaged the house a number of times over the years, with water lapping at the windows, and branches and debris swirling past. It's hard not to imagine the river fish pausing as they pass and looking in for a moment, in a strange reversal of the aquarium effect that Edith Farnsworth was so worried about.

Mies's famous aphorism 'less is more' was taken to fresh heights at the Farnsworth House. Edith Farnsworth herself suggested that 'less is not more – it is simply less'. But her opinion has not stopped minimalist architects and designers taking Mies's lessons to new levels of pared-down perfection. The Farnsworth House and the Barcelona Pavilion are buildings where everything is on display, which means that the interiors have to be perfectly crafted, the glazing clean and pristine, while the furniture assumes the poetic importance of sculpture in an art gallery. This is the philosophy behind 'less is more'. It is not meant as an excuse for laziness, but as a thoughtful way of achieving clean lines and accentuating the importance of carefully curated materials, furnishings and design solutions.

Glass House, a pavilion for viewing nature

'Less is more' may not have suited Edith Farnsworth but it was a notion that was soon embraced by others and is still very much in currency today. Chief among Mies's disciples was the American architect Philip Johnson, who built a close cousin to the Farnsworth House that has proved almost as influential, infused with its own individual narrative. Though preceding the Farnsworth House, the Glass House (completed in 1949) was largely shaped by Mies's ideas and philosophy, as Johnson knew him well, and this great architectural magpie was familiar with the plans for the Farnsworth House before it was even built.

As a curator at the Museum of Modern Art (MoMA) in New York, Johnson coined the term 'International Style' with the 1932 exhibition *Modern Architecture: International Exhibition*, which he co-curated with Henry-Russell Hitchcock, and the book they co-authored, *The International Style: Architecture Since 1922* (see page 123). Both the exhibition and the book featured Mies van der Rohe's work prominently. Johnson organized Mies's first visit to the United States and commissioned him to design the interiors of his own New York apartment. In later years they collaborated on the design of the Seagram Building in Manhattan.

Philip Johnson was always a curator as much as an architect. It was only in his mid-30s that he actually resigned his role as director of MoMA's architecture department and began training as an architect at Harvard Graduate School of Design, under Mies's former Bauhaus colleague Marcel Breuer, graduating in 1943. Even in later years, his attitude to architecture remained curatorial (he described himself as 'a chameleon, so changeable'), experimenting with a number of different architectural styles and forms

Philip Johnson – Glass House, New Canaan, Connecticut, United States, 1949

over the course of a long career. Some of these experiments met with more success than others.

At his 19-hectare (47-acre) estate on the edge of the Connecticut town of New Canaan, shared with his partner, art curator and collector David Whitney, Johnson created what he called a visual 'diary' of his changing interests over a span of 50 years. The first and most important building in his diary was the Glass House.

One of the chief advantages that Johnson's house has over Edith Farnsworth's home is the setting. There is no highway here to spoil the atmosphere, nor any danger of flooding or clouds of mosquitoes. The house sits on the brow of a green hill, with towering trees close by, and is set well away from the nearest road. It looks down into a gentle valley where a small lake forms a focal point. Here, surrounded by the green acres, there is peace and quiet, with the house forming a true belvedere tied intimately to the natural surroundings. Johnson described his new home as 'a pavilion for viewing nature'.

The house itself adopts much of the Miesian language: the steel frame, the glass walls, the flat roof and the universal plan. Instead of floating a little above the ground, like the Farnsworth House, the building sits on a modest brick plinth that also forms the floor of the interiors. The only solid floor-to-ceiling element is a brick drum, which projects upwards and through the roof of the building like a vast chimney. The drum contains a small bathroom on one side and a fireplace on the other.

With the exception of the brick drum, the space is essentially uninterrupted. Like Mies, Philip Johnson employs the concept of zoning, using furniture, cupboards and rugs to help delineate certain areas within the universal space. A suite of Mies's furniture forms a seating area laid out upon a soft white rug, sitting upon the herringbone brickwork that makes up the floor. As with the Farnsworth House, the sleeping zone is demarcated only by a storage cupboard that does not reach the ceiling, while a study area is defined by a desk and chair. Another timber unit forms a kitchenette/bar. There are also a few select artworks, including a painting by Nicolas Poussin on a stand and a sculpture by Elie Nadelman. Yet the real work of art here is, of course, the surrounding landscape, which the architect called 'very expensive wallpaper'.

One original departure from Mies came in the form of the Glass House's lesser-known twin, the Brick House, completed at the same time and linked to the Glass House by a grassy court. But while the Glass House is open and transparent, the Brick House was largely closed and much more enigmatic, illuminated by skylights and porthole windows. The Brick House was devoted to service spaces and a guest room, freeing up its twin from the burden of placing such amenities on show or trying to disguise them. In other words, Johnson created an entire service building rather than a service core.

Over the years that followed, Johnson created a campus of separate buildings and other structures spread out upon the estate, but without compromising the Glass House in any way. Some of these additions were abstract in nature or formed pieces of landscape art. They included a Ghost House formed by a latticed metal framework draped in green creepers, as well as a scaled-down neo-classically inspired Pavilion in the Pond. Other key buildings included the Painting Gallery – where the paintings were arranged on spinning pivots, like a vertical Rolodex – and a Sculpture Gallery, as well as a Study. Together these buildings formed a house of many parts, arranged within the landscape, yet none came close to the importance and drama of the Glass House itself.

As a wealthy man of independent means, Johnson could do exactly as he liked on his own estate. His great advantage with the Glass House, compared with Mies's experience with Edith Farnsworth, was not only the setting but also the fact that there was no client but himself, which meant no compromises to be made or arguments to be aired. Johnson worked with almost total freedom at his New Canaan retreat and left the house, after his death, to the National Trust for Historic Preservation. It was certainly his greatest achievement.

Casa de Vidro, a tree house in Eden

At around the same time that Johnson and Mies van der Rohe were working on their North American glass houses, a South American glass house also sprang up. Architect Lina Bo Bardi's very own belvedere, in Morumbi, on the green outskirts of São Paulo in Brazil, was completed in 1951.

Bo Bardi had been born in Rome and had worked with Gio Ponti in Milan before founding her own architectural practice. But her offices were destroyed during World War II and, afterwards, she and her husband – the writer and curator Pietro Maria Bardi – decided to emigrate to Brazil, travelling together by ocean liner, with all their possessions packed into trunks. Within a year, they had famously collaborated on the creation of the Museum of Art São Paulo (or MASP), which her husband founded and Bo Bardi designed – creating a colourful, floating box that became a striking urban landmark in the centre of the city.

Casa de Vidro ('glass house') was a more personal project where the aim was, as Bo Bardi put it, 'to come extremely close to nature using all available means'.[3] The site itself was a nature preserve, with possums, armadillos and nighthawks. After all the destruction that the Bardis had witnessed in Europe, this was a kind of Eden, and the house created a picture frame around this extraordinary garden.

Bo Bardi raised her Casa de Vidro among the trees and pierced its heart with a living tree growing up and through an elevated, floating courtyard.

Lina Bo Bardi — Casa de Vidro, São Paulo, Brazil, 1951

The impact is extraordinary, suggesting a transparent tree house, or observatory, surrounded by the wild, subtropical greenery.

Bardi raised her home, situated on a sloping site, into the air and created a processional series of ladder-like stairways that reach into the house via the undercroft. The main living spaces look across the tree canopy while also revolving around the elevated courtyard. The interiors are layered with colourful mosaic floors, furniture of Bardi's own design and small treasures brought from Italy. All of the service spaces and bedrooms are pushed to the rear, where the house meets the slope of the hill. It is an architectural wonderland where nature itself, as Bardi intended, plays the starring role.

Today, Morumbi is a wealthy and leafy suburb of São Paulo. Although it has been swallowed up by the epic sprawl of the metropolis, Casa de Vidro retains its resonance. The building combines one of Bardi's great preoccupations – elevation – with transparency to powerful effect and accentuates the drama accordingly. This glass house may not be as well known as Mies's and Johnson's, but it has an originality and presence all of its own. It is a floating house full of light, perched among the trees, and offers a completely fresh perspective upon its surroundings. There are two big ideas here rather than one, with each of them explored to the full.

The Farnsworth House, the Glass House and Casa de Vidro are now all open to the public. They are places of pilgrimage for the devotees of 'less is more' and admirers of the International Style, Modernism and modern architecture in general. The three houses have become key reference points in the canon of 20th-century design. With their open plans, flat roofs, crisp geometry, clean lines and pared-back interiors, they continue to define for many the idea of 'modernity' itself, as exemplars of architectural transparency.

Mid-Century Modernism
Scandinavian by Design

9   Jakob Halldor Gunnløgsson – Gunnløgsson House,
Øresund Strait, Denmark, 1958

Arne Jacobsen
Round House
Zealand, Denmark, 1957

Hanne and Poul Kjaerholm
Kjaerholm House
Rungsted, Hørsholm,
Denmark, 1962

Jakob Halldor Gunnløgsson
Gunnløgsson House
Øresund Strait, Denmark, 1958

Jørn Utzon
Utzon House
Hellebaek, Helsingør,
Denmark, 1952/1959

Alvar Aalto
Maison Louis Carré
Bazoches-sur-Guyonne,
France, 1959

During the mid-century period, architects and designers began to relax into modernity. Over time, the manifestos and grand promises of the pre-war, pioneer Modernists gave way to a more optimistic, expressive and even playful approach that was both innovative and engaging. Mid-century masters and makers built upon the lessons and principles established by the early Modernists, yet they added another important layer of character and warmth, which helped to define one of the most engaging and seductive styles of the 20th century. Given the originality and artistry of post-war furniture, ceramics, textiles and a new generation of domestic consumer appliances and gadgets, as well as the fresh dynamism of Fifties and Sixties architecture, the mid-century home was the place where all of these things came together within an aesthetic that still continues to resonate and fascinate in the early 21st century.

Mid-century design was a broad church and, like Modernism itself, there were many different groups and sub-groups within the congregation. In the United States, design, architecture and manufacturing surged during the Fifties on the back of a consumer boom that helped to fuel the growth of creativity, as seen in the Desert Modernism of the West Coast (see page 102), the exemplars of the American branch of International Style (see page 122) and the experimental spirit of landmark houses such as Mies van der Rohe's Farnsworth House and Philip Johnson's Glass House (see pages 140 and 146). In many European countries, including Britain, Germany, France and Italy, the focus was on reconstruction and revival, which gave architects both challenges and opportunities. During the Fifties and Sixties, European architects and designers applied themselves to this task with great energy and ambition, looking for new ways of building and fresh tectonic solutions to meet the urgent demand for modern homes. Further afield, in South America, Australia, Asia and other parts of the world, there were influential regional Modernists (see page 204), such as Oscar Niemeyer and Geoffrey Bawa, who built their reputations during the mid-century period. Yet, for many, the most accomplished proponents of mid-century style will always be Scandinavian.

When we conjure up an image of the mid-century modern residential aesthetic, the chances are that it will have a Nordic flavour that comes not just from the architecture but also from the interiors, furniture, textiles, textures, colours and patterns. Scandinavian architects and designers, especially, managed to splice the ideas and ideals of early Modernism with a love of craftsmanship and a passion for natural materials, especially wood. There was a definite openness to modern, industrially made materials like steel and concrete, but also to more traditional materials such as stone, timber and brick.

Emerging from the war years, Scandinavian architects and makers found themselves well placed to develop and promote their work both at home and abroad. Rather like in Italy, most designers and producers worked within a system of small ateliers and workshops built upon the skills of talented and trained artisans, and they soon stirred back into life during the late Forties and Fifties. The Nordic countries began grouping together to market their design output internationally, exhibiting at trade fairs and expos while Scandinavian architects such as Arne Jacobsen, Alvar Aalto and Jørn Utzon began to pick up important commissions abroad.

Certain sectors of Scandinavian design were particularly strong, including glassware, ceramics and furniture, where Hans Wegner, Poul Kjaerholm, Bruno Mathsson, Grete Jalk and many others are still revered. A number of these mid-century modern masters were multidisciplinary, applying themselves to many different threads and strands of design including architecture, interiors, furniture and lighting. This gave their residential work, especially, a striking sense of cohesion and charm.

One of the greatest of these multitalented designers was Arne Jacobsen. After training initially as a stonemason, Jacobsen went on to study architecture at the Royal Danish Academy of Fine Arts in Copenhagen, and became familiar with the work of Le Corbusier, Mies van der Rohe and Walter Gropius (see pages 69, 78 and 125) during the Twenties. Much of his early work was residential and in Denmark. But even during the Thirties, Jacobsen was taking a holistic approach to his projects, such as his Bellevue Sea Bath of 1932 at the coastal resort of Klampenborg, where the architect designed everything from the watchtowers for the lifeguards to the entry tickets. After World War II, Jacobsen continued seeking this kind of synergy between the various design elements of a project. Most famously, there was the SAS Royal Hotel in Copenhagen (1960), where Jacobsen involved himself in every aspect of the architecture and interiors of the building, including his much loved Egg and Swan chairs, which were first designed for the hotel. Similarly, his work on St Catherine's College, Oxford (1964), was all-encompassing and included his Oxford desk, chair and lighting designs; Jacobsen even specified what kind of fish should be chosen for the ornamental ponds.

Living in the round at the Round House

There was a domestic dimension, of course, to both the SAS Royal Hotel and St Catherine's. But Jacobsen also designed many apartment buildings and private houses, with one of the most expressive and enticing of these being his 1957 Round House upon a peninsula known as Sjaellands Odde situated on the Zealand coast, northwest of Copenhagen. Here, Jacobsen was asked to design a new family house by the sea for the manager of a fish-smoking plant, Leo Henriksen, and he went full circle.

The idea of living in the round sat perfectly within the growing mid-century preoccupation with geometrical forms. Increasingly, during the late Fifties and Sixties, architects began to grow frustrated with the linear precision of the rectangular forms and glass boxes of the International Style and began to consider alternative plans and ideas. This gave birth to a disparate collection of round houses and other circular buildings in various parts of the world, including Australia, North Africa and America, where one thinks of Richard Foster's Round House (see page 224).

Arne Jacobsen had been interested in circular structures for a long time. Back in 1929, working alongside the Danish architect and designer Flemming Lassen, he won a competition to design 'The House of the Future', which was also round and was conceived with space enough for a helipad up on the roof. The house was built for an exhibition in Copenhagen and also featured wind-down windows, a boathouse and a garage with a Dodge Coupe. Not surprisingly, the project earned itself a lot of attention.

The Sjaellands Odde Round House has less in the way of gadgets but more in the way of a sophisticated mid-century style, featuring – naturally – interiors, furniture and lighting designed by Jacobsen himself. The architect positioned the single-storey, steel-framed house in a slight dip in the landscape, with some protection from the onshore winds offered by a bank to one side. One of the key challenges of the circular form lay in how to order the floor plan and circulation routes through the building, while offering a balance

Arne Jacobsen – Round House, Zealand, Denmark, 1957

between open-plan living spaces and private havens for the family. Jacobsen decided on a radial plan, with the entrance leading into a central circular hallway that connects the various segments of the home. There's a spacious living area to one side, arranged around a fireplace and leading out to a terrace, while also connecting with a dining area alongside, which can be separated off as needed by a sliding curtain, while the kitchen is separate. Most of the family bedrooms sit within the other semicircular half of the Round House, apart from the master suite, which sits within a semicircular segment grafted on to one side of the building, offering some parental privacy.

Kjaerholm House: organic textures plus a sea view

The beauty of the Danish coast was also a source of temptation for other architects and designers, who decided to build for themselves by the sea. They included Hanne and Poul Kjaerholm, who built a waterside house for themselves and their children at Rungsted near Hørsholm, within commuting distance of Copenhagen. Kjaerholm House (1962) was very much a collaboration between architect Hanne Kjaerholm and her husband, Poul, a celebrated furniture designer. They had acquired a modestly sized plot of land but with a wonderful open view out across the Øresund Strait, which they wanted to maximize to the full. While Jacobsen's Round House sought to protect itself from the wind and weather on an exposed coastline, here at Rungsted the intention was to form a close relationship with the water and draw the sea view into the home itself.

The Kjaerholms had to work with a limited budget, as well as a limited site, yet managed to achieve so much. Having explored and dismissed the idea of a two-storey building, Hanne Kjaerholm developed plans for a single-level home of timber and brick. The innovative floor plan was designed to make the most of the sea vista, while also balancing the desire for open living with the need for privacy. The house largely turns its back on the narrow driveway and entrance, while the layout that Hanne devised features two parallel hallways, or lines of circulation, with a compact kitchen, bathrooms and services between them; the parental bedroom sits at one end of the building and the children's room at the other. These spaces take up around half of the house, but the other half is devoted to an open living room with a line of floor-to-ceiling windows framing the view of the sea. The glass slides back, connecting this already generous space with a long verandah sheltered by the overhanging eaves of the roof, which is supported by a line of whitewashed brick piers, while a waterside terrace and garden offer a modest hinterland between the house and the beach.

Inside, the Kjaerholms created a feeling of warmth. The 'great room' has two or three focal points, if we include the view itself, the brick fireplace and perhaps also the library wall of books at one end. The timber beams are exposed, while wall panels also feature extensively, and on the floor the Kjaerholms used tiles made from natural fibres, adding another layer of organic texture. Poul Kjaerholm's furniture takes pride of place, of course, including his PK9 dining chairs and table at one end of the open living space, a desk and chairs at the other, armchairs around the fireplace towards the centre and a PK24 chaise longue by the window. For much of his furniture, Poul Kjaerholm used super-strong steel frames but then typically complemented these with leather or cane seats, balancing the industrial and the organic. There was a lightness to these pieces and a sense of modernity that came from the metalwork and engineering – seen in Poul Kjaerholm's

Hanne and Poul Kjaerholm – Kjaerholm House, Rungsted,
Hørsholm, Denmark, 1962

cantilevered chairs, for example – yet the natural textures were very much in keeping with the Scandinavian focus upon craft and the handmade.

Gunnløgsson House and its echoes of Japan

Kjaerholm's furniture also appears prominently in another Danish coastal house of roughly the same period and not far away, designed by a good friend of his, the architect Jakob Halldor Gunnløgsson. Built for himself and his wife, Lillemor, the 1958 Gunnløgsson House (see page 152) has many elements in common with the Kjaerholm House. Again, it is single storey and faces the Øresund Strait, offering a glorious sea vista. Key points of difference are the subtle but pervading Japanese influence and the alternative approach to flexible spatial planning, reminiscent of the space-saving ideas seen on ships or in compact apartments.

Shortly after Gunnløgsson's marriage to Lillemor, who was the daughter of a sea captain, the couple went on a honeymoon tour of Japan and Asia, and the visit stirred his interest in traditional Japanese architecture and design. In fact, this influenced a number of Modernist architects in the West, especially those who favoured a more organic approach to design, including – most famously – Frank Lloyd Wright (see page 84). Upon the couple's return from honeymoon, Gunnløgsson (who was a successful practising architect as well as a lecturer and then a professor at the School of Architecture within the Royal Danish Academy of Fine Arts in Copenhagen) set to work on designing the couple's new, single-level house at Rungsted.

The processional entry sequence, in particular, holds echoes of Japan. A sheltered porch, set within the linear outline of the house, leads to the front door and the internal hallway. This has the feel of a Japanese *genkan*, an entryway where you might remove your coat and shoes, and put on your slippers. A parallel line of recessed timber cupboards, painted black, feature sliding doors that open to reveal vivid red shelving. The polished finish on much of the wooden wall panelling in the building itself has the feel of lacquer, while Gunnløgsson also used sliding panels to partition certain parts of the house, reminiscent of Japanese *shoji* screens.

Spatially, the arrangement of the Gunnløgssons' residence was certainly innovative. The house featured brick walls at either end, a timber frame and a wall of floor-to-ceiling glass connecting with a verandah and the sea view, rather like the Kjaerholm House. But given that the Gunnløgsson House was designed just for the two of them, the architect adopted a fluid floor plan, not unlike the universal spaces explored by Mies van der Rohe at the Farnsworth House and by Philip Johnson at the Glass House (see pages 140 and 146). The majority of the house is essentially open-plan, with the entry hallway opening out into a study and then leading through into the seating area, arranged around a monolithic fireplace, with a fitted sofa against one wall and the views of the sea itself, while the dining area floats alongside.

Both the galley kitchen and the one double bedroom can be either read as part of this universal space or partitioned using the sliding screens. There is an ingenuity to this highly adaptable arrangement, in which Gunnløgsson has made the most of every iota of available space, using integrated storage, shelving units and other space-saving measures, such as the fold-down trellis table on the verandah. There is a cabin-like character to the bedroom especially, which includes a modern take on a ship captain's chest that serves as a dressing table. The bank of fitted cupboards to one side holds a secret door to the bathroom alongside, which is the only fully separate and private room in the house, illuminated by a skylight.

Such ideas have fed into the design of countless urban apartments and micro flats, where every bit of space is valuable and amenities and storage solutions need to be compact. In the Gunnløgssons' home, the design approach helps to preserve the sense of openness, allowing this modestly scaled building to appear much larger than it really is, while constantly steering attention to the bank of picture windows and the sea. The entire house is unified by the use of a small but beautifully crafted selection of materials, including the timber panelling and grey Kolmården marble floors. Much of the loose furniture here is by Kjaerholm, of course, including examples of his famous PK25 lounge chair with its light, matt chromed steel base and strung seat and back made with flag halyard, a strong rope commonly used on board ship to hoist flags and sails; the same nautical material was used by Danish designer Hans Wegner in his 1950 Flag Halyard chair. With his own home and other residential commissions, as well as larger projects such as Tårnby City Hall (1959), Gunnløgsson became well known across Denmark. But other Scandinavian architects began to spread their wings further afield, establishing international reputations.

Jørn Utzon – Utzon House, Hellebaek, Helsingør, Denmark, 1952/1959

Jørn Utzon and Utzon House

Among the best known of these Scandinavian architects was another Dane, Jørn Utzon, who won the competition in 1957 to design the Sydney Opera House, setting in motion a controversial and often convoluted 15-year process to create one of the most iconic 20th-century buildings in the world. But, before this win, Utzon's focus was largely on residential work in Scandinavia and other freelance design commissions.

There was the 1955 lakeside Middelboe House that Utzon designed at Holte, near Copenhagen, for Sven Middelboe, the design manager of a lighting company. Here, Utzon raised almost the entire house on a steel framework and precast concrete pillars to give the family the best possible view across Lake Furesø, leaving just the entrance and utility spaces at ground level next to a sheltered area for parking a car, boat or bikes.

Between 1950 and 1959, Utzon worked on the various phases of Utzon House, his own family home at Hellebaek, around 40km (25 miles) north of Copenhagen. It has been described as a landmark of warm Danish Modernism. Jørn and Lis Utzon bought the land just after a 1949 trip to the Americas, when they met Frank Lloyd Wright but also visited Mayan pyramids in Mexico. They camped out at Hellebaek during the summer of 1950, trying to work out the best position and orientation for a house that would be truly contextual.

Utzon designed a small, low-slung pavilion where the north-facing wall was made of brick and largely closed, while the south-facing façade featured a wall of glass. This fed out to a terrace looking across the grounds to a small stream. Inside, rather like Gunnløgsson, the architect sought to make the most of the available space with a largely open-plan 'great room' and a compact galley-style kitchen, along with two small bedrooms for the children at one end of the pavilion and a third bedroom for themselves at the opposite end. The combination of brick, timber joinery and expanses of glass gave the house an organic character, drawing some inspiration from Wright's Usonian houses (see page 91), which were modestly sized but offered a strong indoor–outdoor relationship.

This first phase of the house was completed in around 1952, but by the time of the Opera House victory in 1957 the Utzons had a third child, and the architect began thinking about extending the family house in a way that both enhanced and changed its character. The material language was the same, using Flemish bonded brick once again, and the idea of a pavilion in the landscape remained. Essentially, Utzon added a second building running parallel to the first and, again, the northern wall was largely closed while the southern one featured expanses of floor-to-ceiling glass. The space between the two pavilions was filled by a courtyard, with a glass link to one side of it connecting the two structures, and a covered carport and entry sequence to the other side. Sitting at the centre of the enlarged plan, the courtyard provided not only an important outdoor room, with a level of enclosure and shelter, but also a new focal point for the house as a whole. Like the terraces that bordered the building, the floor of the courtyard was brick, which helped unify the entire composition while tying the house back to the earth.

After the floor plan of the original pavilion was rearranged, it became a studio and library, where Utzon developed his plans for the Sydney Opera House. The new addition offered space enough not only for a more generous sequence of family bedrooms, but also room for a new living and dining area plus an open kitchen, all looking out upon the courtyard alongside.

With this phase completed in around 1959, the Utzons' family home was now much larger and more ambitious, but it still preserved the valuable sense of connection with nature and the landscape, partly achieved through the introduction of the pivotal courtyard. In this way, it achieved a similar purpose to the plan of architect Josep Lluís Sert's 1958 courtyard house in Cambridge, Massachusetts (see page 129), yet the setting was more rural in feel than urban. Here in Hallebaek, privacy was not such an issue, yet the idea of a semi-sheltered outdoor room still had great resonance, creating an open heartland to the house that was full of light, fresh air and promise.

It was an idea that Utzon pursued with the design of 60 houses at nearby Helsingør. Known as the Kingo Houses, these were completed in 1958, the year before his extended family home was finished. They, too, are constructed of brick and feature an L-shaped floor plan plus a walled courtyard; a similar idea was used at another Utzon housing development, known as the Fredensborg houses, finished in 1963, the year that the Utzons headed off to Australia. The courtyard formation at both projects meant that residents each had their own private outdoor room, with its promise of sunlight and connectivity with nature.

Even after the Utzons left Australia in 1966 and settled in Mallorca, the idea of a series of interlinked pavilions punctuated with terraces and court-yards resurfaced at Can Lis, their house by the sea at Portopetro, Mallorca, which Utzon designed in 1972, using stone this time rather than brick.

Alvar Aalto and Maison Louis Carré

During the Fifties and Sixties, the great Finnish Modernist architect Alvar Aalto was also tempted abroad. He was involved in apartment buildings in Germany and projects in Italy, Iceland and America, including one of his most astonishing houses, situated to the west of Versailles in the Yvelines department of France. In 1939 Aalto had created one of the great, pioneering early Modernist houses, in the form of Villa Mairea in rural Noormarkku in western Finland, a house that echoed the woodland setting and sought a fresh kind of synergy with nature itself (see page 97). He spent some time in the United States during World War II and just afterwards, teaching at MIT and working on American projects, but then largely settled back into life and work in Scandinavia following the death of his wife, Aino, in 1949.

Alvar Aalto – Maison Louis Carré, Bazoches-sur-Guyonne, France, 1959

By the mid-Fifties Aalto had married his second wife, fellow architect Elissa Mäkiniemi, and the couple began to travel. There was the Hansaviertel Apartment Building project in Berlin (completed in 1957), and in the previous year they had met the French art dealer and gallery owner Louis Carré in Venice, where Aalto had designed the Finnish Pavilion for the 1956 Biennale. The two men, who had many acquaintances in common, became great friends. Having considered and rejected the idea of commissioning Le Corbusier, Carré asked Alvar Aalto to design a new home for himself and his wife, Olga, on a hillside near Bazoches-sur-Guyonne.

Situated around 48km (30 miles) from Paris, the house, which was completed in 1959, was intended to offer the Carrés a rural escape, with the benefit of a prominent position looking out across the landscape from the top of the hill. More than this, however, Maison Louis Carré was a house of art. It hosted many important pieces from Carré's own collection, including works by Picasso, Fernand Léger, Paul Klee, Pierre Bonnard and Alberto

Giacometti. But it was also a place for entertaining artists and clients within a home that needed to be welcoming but also well suited to gatherings and happenings. Carré explained his and Aalto's attitude to the materials that would be used to achieve this:

> I wanted a house with materials that had lived. This was an unconscious reaction to steel architecture. Consequently, I needed stone, brick – because brick has become nobler through its use – and wood. There again, Aalto was perfect for me. He was extremely sensitive to materials. I think that is related to his poetic talent: he is a poet.[1]

Aalto designed the house with a layer of Chartres limestone topped with brick, while creating a distinctive monopitch roofline (slanting in just one direction) that almost mirrors the falling slope of the hill itself. The Carrés largely lived on the ground floor, although there was a small upper storey towards the top of the pitch, which held servants' quarters.

Stepping into the house, one was met by an extraordinary hallway with a high, vaulted ceiling clad in strips of Finnish red pine. Louis Carré called this great wave of timber Aalto's 'masterpiece':

> Aalto outdid himself…It is a kind of cupola. From the beginnings of architecture, a cupola has always been the most difficult thing to achieve. But this vault is not a copy of something else; it is an endless wave. It is the sign, the value of the house.[2]

The hallway is a reminder of the importance of an entrance not only in offering the hand of welcome, but – as Carré suggests – in setting the tone and character of a house from the start. Here, there is the drama that comes of height, volume and light, with a clerestory window over the main doorway introducing sunlight to the space. But there is also the warmth that comes from the joinery, used in combination with terracotta floor tiles, while the space was further enhanced by the apt positioning of sculpture and art.

More than this, the hallway represents the key junction in the house. Steps lead down to the main reception room, which is an inviting space in itself, with its fireplace and a line of windows looking down the hill. But the hall also leads into a dining room to one side, while a latticed timber gate sits behind a line of custom storage cupboards. This is the dividing line between the 'public' side of the house and the private side, which includes both service spaces, such as the kitchen and the master suite, and a guest bedroom. The clarity of this line creates a house better suited to entertaining, even if there is a greater degree of formality in the arrangement than might be the case in many modern houses. Sometimes these events were, in themselves, significant and open, with the Carrés creating a kind of amphitheatre with a ziggurat of stepped seating laid out upon the landscape towards the back of the house, suited to musical and theatrical productions.

As with Villa Mairea, there is a striking sense of cohesion to the house that comes from Aalto's involvement in each and every detail of the architecture and interiors. This encompassed everything from custom door handles in brass and leather, to the furniture and also the lighting. The latter included custom designs such as the multidirectional ceiling lamps in the dining room that could direct light onto both the table below and the paintings upon the walls. Designs from Aalto's own furniture collection for Artek were mixed with multiple bespoke designs for desks, tables, armchairs and more.

This was 'soft' Scandinavian mid-century modernity at its best, even if the setting was the French countryside. It was emblematic of the way that Nordic style spread its influence internationally, with a global reach that saw elements of the aesthetic making its presence felt in places such as England, the United States and Australia, as well as many other parts of the world. Even now, the mid-century modern aesthetic exemplified by Scandinavian residential, interior and furniture design remains a much loved favourite.

Blue-Sky Thinking
Modernist Mavericks
& Prefab Pioneers

10   Eric Lyons – Span Houses, Cator Estate,
Blackheath, London England, 1958

Richard Buckminster Fuller
Dymaxion House
various locations,
United States, 1945

Eric Lyons
Span Houses
various locations, England,
1950s–1960s

Matti Suuronen
Futuro House
various locations,
Finland, 1968

Joseph Eichler
Eichler Homes
California, United States,
1940s–1960s

Jean Prouvé
Prouvé House
Nancy, France, 1954

Eduardo Longo
Casa Bola
São Paulo, Brazil, 1979

Modular and mass-produced houses and housing were a great source of fascination for many Modernist architectural pioneers. The idea of manufacturing modern homes in factories and then assembling them on location sat well with the early Modernist ideal of making the world a better place through innovative design. What's more, it was the key ambition voiced by Walter Gropius and the Bauhaus masters (see pages 78 and 124) of making good design more affordable, more available and, therefore, more democratic. Constructing a house in a factory, either in full or in part, provided a prefabricated kit of parts that could be assembled more quickly and more cheaply on site than with traditional ways of building. The 20th-century production line techniques developed by Henry Ford and the car industry in Detroit could be used to make a true 'machine for living in' that could potentially transform the lives of thousands or perhaps even millions of people. No wonder, then, that the goal of designing and building a prefab house with mass appeal became something of a Holy Grail for architects and designers.

There were early experiments with prefabrication and modular building systems during the first half of the 20th century. But World War II lent the whole enterprise a fresh relevance, given the epic need for reconstruction and emergency housing, particularly in parts of Europe that had suffered carpet bombing and the destruction of residential quarters in many major cities. New housing was needed and it was needed fast. Architectural designers and engineers like Richard Buckminster Fuller and Jean Prouvé thought they had the method, if not the means, to meet this demand.

Beyond the need for post-war homes in the United Kingdom and Europe, there was also a growing feeling of marketplace potential for affordable but truly modern homes during the Fifties and Sixties. Design-led developers began thinking not only about prefabrication, but about creating mid-century modern pattern books that allowed buyers to choose a standardized design with the option to modify and tailor the specification of the house according to budget and need. This was the thinking behind Span housing projects in the United Kingdom and the Eichler Homes developments on the American West Coast, both of which had a huge impact on the evolution of modern living, as more and more homeowners found themselves at home in a mid-century architect-designed building. It's also true that, while many of these prefab and modular housing programmes were truly pioneering, there was the suspicion that they were ahead of the curve, as consumers were struggling to buy into the idea of factory-built or modular pattern-book houses with a modern aesthetic. The majority of these grand projects struggled to succeed financially, suffering major setbacks with every wave of economic turbulence, while many crashed along the way. It's only now, in the early 21st century, that prefabrication and modular building systems are finally beginning to enter the mainstream.

Buckminster Fuller's Dymaxion House and other ideas

One of the most influential prefab visionaries and dream catchers was the American architectural designer, engineer, inventor and theorist Richard Buckminster Fuller. He was driven by the idea not of 'less is more' but of 'more for less', arguing that we need to approach design in a sustainable way, considering our use of resources, materials and energy in a sensitive manner for the good of 'spaceship Earth'. In this way, and many others, Fuller was certainly ahead of his times and became a mentor for generations of younger architects and designers who have taken inspiration from his preoccupation with environmentalism and prefabricated buildings.

Fuller studied at Harvard University but was expelled twice before joining the US Navy, serving as a communications officer and a rescue boat commander during World War I. After leaving the forces, Fuller began applying himself to construction and engineering. By 1929 he had developed the first ideas for the Dymaxion House, which took its name from a combination of the words 'dynamic', 'maximum' and 'ion'.

Fuller drew upon his love of sailing and boat design for the Dymaxion House, which was a compact hexagonal building with roof, hull and floor plates radiating outwards from a central supporting pillar. Like a yacht, the building was divided into a series of compartments and cabins, holding the kitchen, bathroom, services and bedrooms. For Fuller, the unfortunate timing of the Wall Street Crash and the Great Depression meant that securing funding for his concept house was almost impossible.

During World War II, Fuller promoted the idea of Dymaxion Deployment Units for military use and, towards the end of the war, realized there would be a golden opportunity to manufacture mass-produced housing for the

Richard Buckminster Fuller – Dymaxion House, various locations, United States, 1945

reconstruction effort in Europe and elsewhere. The first full-scale prototype of the Dymaxion Dwelling Machine was finished by 1945, resembling a kind of hybrid of a boat and automobile, with its streamlined body made of aluminium panels supported by a lightweight steel skeleton. Weighing around 2,700kg (6,000lb), the entire kit house could be shipped to site in a large tube and rapidly assembled in around two days, at a cost of roughly $6,500, which was similar to the price of a good car. The intention was to mass-produce the silver-domed Dymaxions at the Beech Aircraft factory in Wichita, Kansas.

At last Fuller managed to attract investors and a long list of potential clients, with thousands of enquiries coming in, while *Fortune* magazine also gave the Dymaxion its blessing. But just at the crucial moment, with the Dymaxion almost ready to go into production, Fuller and his engineers fell out over tweaks to the final design, causing his backers to lose patience and start walking away from Fuller Houses Inc. One of the investors, William Graham, bought the two remaining prototypes and put them together to extend his own Wichita home; Graham's 'Wichita House' is now in the Henry Ford Museum in Detroit.

There were other disappointments for Buckminster Fuller. During the Thirties, he had developed a Dymaxion Car, which looked rather like a Flash Gordon spaceship on three wheels, with a streamlined fuselage and a tail fin, but when the design was exhibited at the 1933 Chicago World's Fair, another car drove into Fuller's prototype and killed the driver. Neither Fuller nor his car was to blame, but it led to the interest in the Dymaxion Car fizzling out.

Eventually Buckminster Fuller hit the big time during the Fifties with his patented invention of the geodesic dome. This enabled him to advance some of the ideas contained within the Dymaxion House, while simplifying both the concept and the engineering. The domes were light, strong and easily adaptable in terms of scale and context, working as a single unit or in conjoined multiples. It was the US military that first picked up on the potential of Fuller's geodesic structures, using them as field pavilions and emergency shelters; substantial domes could be easily lifted by military helicopters and transported. Later, they featured in projects as diverse as the Amundsen–Scott South Pole Station and the American Pavilion at the 1967 Montreal Expo. Over 300,000 domes have been built around the world, including some for residential use, suggesting that there is certainly a demand for prefabricated buildings that might work in a wide range of scenarios and situations.

Futuro House, the spaceship pod

Curiously, there are many parallels to be drawn between the troubled story of the Dymaxion House and the development of another photogenic prefab, the Futuro House, designed by Finnish architect Matti Suuronen. After studying architecture at Helsinki University of Technology, Suuronen launched his own architectural practice and became interested in the structural possibilities of plastics, especially fibreglass.

During the mid-Sixties a friend asked Suuronen if he could design a ski cabin suited to extreme conditions, which would also be simple enough to build on mountainsides. Suuronen came up with an archetypal UFO: a saucer-shaped building, or bubble house, made from insulated fibreglass-reinforced polyester plastic, and complete with fold-down, airliner-style entry hatch and stairway. The entire house was light enough to be transported by lorry or helicopter as a complete structure, or it could be delivered as 16 separate segments, which could be bolted together in a day.

All that was needed on site were four base plates, or piers, to support the steel leg struts of the flying saucer, plus a connection to services.

Suuronen started working with the Finnish company Polykem, a plastics specialist. Together they began perfecting a design, complete with porthole windows, that could be mass-produced in factories. The first cabin was delivered to Finnish TV personality Matti Kuusla in 1968, who put his Futuro House next to a lake in rural Southern Savonia, northeast of Helsinki. From the start, the marketing strategy adopted by Polykem and its publicity consultants was clever. Kuusla, for instance, was offered a discounted deal on his bright yellow saucer in exchange for some press coverage, even if this was not always flattering.

The second house was shown at a 1968 trade fair in London, held on board a ferry on the Thames, and with interest well and truly sparked Polykem went into production. A year later, Futuro was launched in the United States with a marketing partner in Philadelphia, entrepreneur Leonard Fruchter, who saw an opportunity to market this house as a holiday and weekend home. Again, the marketing drive was well timed, with a *New York Times* headline reading 'Saucer-Shaped House Arrives on Earth' published on 20 July 1969, which happened to be the day that 'Eagle', the Apollo 11 lunar module, touched down upon the surface of the moon.

The Swedish Air Force bought three Futuros, which it airlifted for use as lookout posts, and others appeared in Russia, South Africa and elsewhere in the world. Suuronen and Polykem developed a second prefab, a fibreglass bungalow known as Venturo, in 1971. But the whole business model collapsed with the global oil crisis two years later, which not only sent the cost of producing plastics spiralling upwards but also saw potential customers falling away as the resulting economic recession took hold.

Rather like Fuller's Dymaxion House, initial interest and excitement in the Futuro fell away and production was stopped. It's thought that perhaps 60 or so Futuros still survive, many of them either museum pieces or collectors' items. But they do have a kind of cult status within the design community as an emblem of Space Age optimism and also as an innovative model for prefabrication. The kind of approach pioneered by Suuronen and Polykem has been adopted, in part, by 21st-century hotel chains, for example, who produce bathroom pods, kitchenettes and other elements in factories ready for delivery onto site, speeding up the whole construction programme with these modular units.

Prouvé's pioneering prefabs and Prouvé House

Another of the great pioneers of prefab houses was the French architectural designer and engineer Jean Prouvé. He described himself as a *constructeur* and always adopted an engineering-led approach to design, combining technical innovation with practicality. Prouvé spent a great deal of time fine-tuning prototypes in his workshops at Nancy and nearby Maxéville, developing his own projects and also collaborating with other designers and architects, including Charlotte Perriand, Pierre Jeanneret and Le Corbusier.

For some, Prouvé is best known as a furniture designer and maker. Like Walter Gropius, Marcel Breuer and the Bauhaus masters, Prouvé was interested in the combination of modern industrial and factory-produced materials, especially steel and plywood, with production-line techniques that could replicate and reproduce standardized designs at an affordable price. Many of his most famous designs, including his Standard chair (1934) or his Guéridon table (1949), consisted of a small number of component parts. Given that many of the production runs were relatively small, Prouvé's original designs are now highly collectable, although there have also been 21st-century reissues at a more manageable price.

But Jean Prouvé's other great passion was for prefabricated houses and buildings. The challenge of creating adaptable, transportable and affordable structures suited to a whole range of uses was a preoccupation, or perhaps an obsession, that carried through Prouvé's sometimes turbulent career all the way from the Thirties to the Sixties.

As happened with Buckminster Fuller, early interest in Prouvé's ideas for prefabricated structures came from the military. In 1939 he received an order from the French army for 275 patented demountable barrack units composed of a simple steel frame infilled with wooden wall panels. Production of these units was interrupted by the rapid German invasion. But some of the ideas behind the portable barracks then fed into the design of Prouvé's Maisons à Portiques of 1945, developed with Charlotte Perriand and Pierre Jeanneret. These 37sq m (400sq ft) demountable houses were manufactured as emergency housing for those who had lost their homes

Jean Prouvé – Prouvé House, Nancy, France, 1954

during World War II, with around 400 units produced for the French Minister of Reconstruction. Here, again, the component parts had to be easily transported and assembled, usually by two people. A floor plate was set upon eight small pillars or brick stacks to lift the house off the ground, and then a central steel spine held up by splayed leg supports formed a strong and secure fulcrum for the roof beams; again the walls were ready-made with wooden panels and integrated windows.

These simple but ingenious prefabs were born of necessity, but they provided Prouvé with the impetus he needed to take his thinking even further. By the end of the Forties, he had developed much more sophisticated concepts for prefabricated 'Standard Houses'. The designer's conversations with the Ministry of Reconstruction eventually led to the construction of ten test houses at Meudon, near Paris, developed with Prouvé's brother Henri. These buildings were not only larger than the previous designs, but they incorporated a fresh structural system that used steel and aluminium components rather than timber.

The houses at Meudon were single storey but the floor plates were partially raised up on stone piers, creating an undercroft used as a carport, while the rear was supported by earth banks formed by the gently undulating topography. Again, there was a standardized modular kit of component parts arranged around a steel spine, but with supports in the shape of supersized staples or croquet hoops. This time, the walls were made of aluminium panels using layers of glass wool for insulation, while the compact floor plan positioned the bedrooms to one side of a central hallway and an open living and dining area to the other, as well as a semi-connected kitchen with a serving hatch. In addition to the Meudon houses, Prouvé completed another 15 Standard Houses at other locations.

At around the same time, Jean and Henri Prouvé developed the Maison Tropicale concept, with a design adapted to the climatic conditions of Africa and the need to pack the entire building onto a transport plane. A key element of this new prefab system was its integrated natural cooling techniques, with a verandah arranged around a more enclosed central space, perforated wall panels and a ventilation stack for directing hot air out of the building via an opening in the roof. In the end, the rising costs of the buildings meant that just three of these were delivered and constructed on site, with one in Niger and two in the Congo.

Jean Prouvé continued developing modular building systems, helping to shape this nascent modern genre. But in 1952, just two years after the designer was awarded the Légion d'Honneur, he lost control of his own workshop and factory in Maxéville after his business partners pushed him out of the enterprise that he had created. This was, of course, a deeply troubling time for Prouvé, who effectively had to rebuild his career and his finances.

Despite these troubles, there was a silver lining in the form of his own family home in Nancy, a city in the northeast of France, which the designer built in just three months in 1954, largely using a collection of leftover prefab parts. It was to be a constant presence in his life for many years as he went back and forth between it and Paris.

The setting was a steep hillside overlooking Nancy. The site was only affordable, said Prouvé, 'because no one wanted to live on such sloped property'.[1] The designer used his 'leftovers' to create a single-storey pavilion pushed into a plateau on the site, with Prouvé and his family helping the builders at weekends to keep the costs down. For the façade, there were port-hole panels from the Maison Tropicale and wall units from the Standard Houses. Prouvé positioned a long circulation corridor to the rear, where the house met the hill, complete with a run of integrated shelves and storage. This connected the study and kitchen at one end with the bedrooms at the other. The more open, central living space pushed out from the main body of the house and featured expanses of glass framing the views of the city below.

Prouvé thought the house might last ten years but it is still very much intact. Born of adversity, Prouvé's home helped to prove the effectiveness of the modular systems that he had pioneered over the preceding years. For many, Jean Prouvé remains the godfather of prefabrication. Looking at the most successful prefabricated houses of the 21st century, such as the IT HOUSE designed by Taalman Architecture, one can still see Prouvé's hand in them, but his work has also helped to inspire designers looking to provide emergency shelters for disaster relief and refugee crises.

Span Houses: modern prefabs in small developments

As well as experiments with prefabricated houses, the mid-century period also saw the evolution of a number of modern housing developments that used some modular elements along with pattern books of approved house designs, which could be replicated many times over. In the United Kingdom the best known were the Span developments pioneered by archi-tects Eric Lyons and Geoffrey Townsend (see page 168). During the Fifties and Sixties, Span built over two thousand houses, mostly within the outer boroughs of London or the Home Counties, while the name itself was inspired by the idea of 'spanning the gap' between typical Metroland estates and one-off architect-designed homes.

Eric Lyons started off working with Walter Gropius (see page 125) and Maxwell Fry in 1936–7 when Gropius was in London, just before he emigrated to America. Lyons first met Geoffrey Townsend when they were both taking classes in architecture at the Regent Street Polytechnic and they remained friends, working together at a practice in Richmond. After the end of World War II, Lyons and Townsend, along with many other architects, began focusing on reconstruction in and around London. They began with a development of flats in Twickenham with four blocks of maisonettes set within landscaped grounds and courtyards. Within just a few years, Span was born.

Lyons and Townsend joined forces with Leslie Bilsby, the owner of a successful construction company, which had worked with a number of early Modernist architects including Patrick Gwynne and Wells Coates (see pages 75 and 187). Bilsby and Townsend became joint managing directors of Span, which they founded in 1954, while Lyons was the chief architect; one of Lyons's assistants, Ivor Cunningham, was a talented landscape designer and also played an important role.

Over the following years, Lyons developed a series of prototypical houses and exemplars for a collection of Span developments in southeast London's Blackheath district, and in Richmond, Weybridge, West Byfleet and Ashstead in Surrey. Some were flats but most consisted of houses, either in terraces or clusters. Rather than having separate, private gardens, most Span developments featured large communal gardens and open spaces, while cars were kept at a distance. Rooflines were usually mono-pitch (sloping in just one direction) and there were generous windows that introduced plenty of light and framed the garden views. Eric Lyons also used warm, familiar materials such as brick and timber cladding. Inside, Lyons opted for open-plan living spaces. The 'T8', for instance, was a two-storey house with a double-aspect living and dining area on the ground floor and three bedrooms above. Underfloor heating was fitted as standard.

The creation of a set of standardized designs offered economies of scale, but also opportunities to use some prefabricated modular components to keep costs down. The use of communal gardens helped to increase the density of the developments, while fostering a communal spirit, as did the residents' associations that were set up to help manage and look after these new communities, based on the principle of shared responsibility. Span developments are still popular today, with some – such as Parkleys close to Ham Common, near Richmond, and Cedar Chase in Taplow, Buckinghamshire – now included within designated conservation areas.

The legacy of Eichler Homes

On the West Coast of America, the developer Joseph Eichler was the most successful at scaling up mid-century living within dedicated neighbourhoods and 'tracts' of modern houses. Rather like Lyons and Townsend in the UK, Eichler's ambition was to translate mid-century modern design principles from individual custom houses to large-scale developments offering new homes that would be more available and affordable. With the invention of a dozen new neighbourhoods in California, the developer managed to build around eleven thousand 'Eichler Homes' characterized by open-plan living, a vivid inside–outside relationship and sleek, contemporary lines.

It was, in part, the experience of living in a house designed by Frank Lloyd Wright (see page 84) that catalysed Eichler's own interest in modern design and fresh patterns of living. He began tapping into the consumer boom of the late Forties and early Fifties, when the economy was thriving and optimistic home buyers gradually opened their minds to innovation and the ambition of 'making it new'. From early on, Joseph Eichler saw the advantage of drawing upon the skills and talents of free-thinking Modernist architects, including A Quincy Jones, Frederick Emmons and Raphael Soriano, who contributed to the Case Study House Program, which helped define the Desert Modern style (see pages 102 and 112).

Eichler respected the American ideal of a single family home with its own private garden and garage, along with tract layouts that prioritized the automobile. But Eichler's houses tended to turn their backs to the street, with the possible exception of a prominent entry porch, while orientating the main living spaces to the rear gardens. Here, the houses unfolded, with floor-to-ceiling glass linking open-plan living areas to the adjoining terraces and outdoor rooms. These were all ideas well established by ground-breaking homes such as Richard Neutra's Kaufmann House in Palm Springs (see page 107) and the Case Study House Program, but here the thinking was applied to developments of tens or hundreds of individual family homes.

Usually single-storey, the houses were timber-framed, post-and-beam structures with flat or shallow-pitched roofs. Inside, there was underfloor heating, the provision of generously scaled living spaces with fireplaces, and the use of more natural materials such as timber and brick, as well as expanses of glass. Outside, there were outdoor rooms and sometimes swimming pools. Contemporary admirers of Eichler's houses talk of the sense of openness, the quality of the light, the feeling of warmth and the flexibility offered by the way that the internal living space extended into the garden.

Joseph Eichler –
Eichler Homes,
California,
United States,
1940s–1960s

Rather like Span Homes, Eichler tracts were also conceived with an awareness of 'community'. Joseph Eichler believed in diverse neighbourhoods and adopted a policy of non-discrimination, while also adding parks and community centres to larger estates. The majority of the Eichler tracts are situated around San Francisco, but there are also developments in Southern California and Palm Springs. One of the largest tracts was in San Mateo County, where 'The Highlands' grew to a community of 700 Eichler Homes, including an experimental steel-framed version. The company was a great success during the Fifties and early Sixties, until eventually Eichler began to overextend himself, and the business went bankrupt in 1967. It was a sad end to a great idea and ideal, yet there is a strong physical legacy within the stock of Eichler Homes, along with the design ideas and social principles that Joseph Eichler explored in his work.

Casa Bola and the dream of pod life

One of the most radical and fascinating experiments in prefabricated, modular housing systems came from Brazilian architect Eduardo Longo during the Seventies. Longo's idea was to build a superstructure with slots for a whole series of living pods. This framework would hold all of the services and circulation routes in one neat, ordered grid, allowing the pods to be stacked within a high-rise collective. Each sphere would be a self-contained, multilayered home, while the organization of the superstructure meant that each one would have its own privacy and a flow of light and air around it. Longo explained how his idea developed:

> I became interested in spherical buildings when I was searching for an ideal volume that could become an industrially produced, modular apartment. Weight was a very important issue and no volume is lighter than a sphere.[2]

To test the idea, Longo built a prototype known as Casa Bola, or 'Spherical House', on the flat roof of his home and studio in São Paulo, using a circular steel frame that was then coated in layers of moulded concrete. Rather like Futuro and Dymaxion, the interiors of Casa Bola have the compact feel of a boat or yacht, with the hull morphing into many integrated elements such as beds, kitchen counters, steps, shelves and desks. The potential of every last bit of space is maximized to the full over four and a half levels, with the bedrooms towards the bottom of the sphere; the main entrance, the kitchen and dining area towards the centre; and the principal living spaces right at the top, where there are larger windows and plenty of sunlight.

Longo painted the house exteriors a vivid sky blue but inside everything is white, creating a sense of quiet and cohesion. There is also a playful sense of humour to the project, with a spiralling yellow escape slide down to the garden. The architect moved into Casa Bola with his wife and two children, while a client commissioned a second spherical home, which hovers above a hillside, perched on a single supporting stem. This equally extraordinary house was painted red and features a vast cyclops' eye window to the front. Longo's concept of mass housing networks using his spherical apartments has not yet come to fruition, but the architect has not lost faith in his concept.

Eduardo Longo – Casa Bola, São Paulo, Brazil, 1979

Sky-High Living
Towering Ambitions

11   Chamberlin, Powell & Bon – Barbican Estate,
London, England, 1976

Wells Coates
Isokon
London, England, 1934

Le Corbusier
Unité d'Habitation
Marseille, France, 1952

Berthold Lubetkin
Highpoint I and II
London, England, 1935/1938

Chamberlin, Powell & Bon
Barbican Estate
London, England, 1976

Ludwig Mies van der Rohe
Lake Shore Drive Apartments
Chicago, Illinois,
United States, 1951

The shape of our cities has changed dramatically since the beginning of the 20th century. Most major urban centres have expanded outwards over time, as their populations have grown with the gradual drift from the countryside to the city. This relentless expansion has swallowed suburbs and greenfield land, as cities become megacities or collide with one another and fuse to become part of an epic sprawl. Yet, at the same time, many cities have also grown upwards, towards the sky, within a process that has also been transformative.

This skyward push might have begun in America and the West during the early 20th century, yet it has gradually become a global phenomenon, evidenced by the countless towers of São Paulo, Hong Kong, Mumbai, Seoul and other metropolises around the world. Skyscrapers have always been controversial, particularly among conservationists who argue in favour of preserving key sightlines in cities such as London, Milan and New York, but also among those concerned about our right to natural light and privacy. Inevitably, 'supertalls' and 'superskinnies' have an impact upon their neighbours and the quality of life down at street level.

Yet Modernist architects, in particular, have long argued that skyscrapers and residential high-rises are an essential component of modern cities. 'Supertall' towers can certainly accommodate the homes of hundreds of individuals and families in one place, reducing the need for sprawl. At the same time, they are usually located close to public transport hubs and within easy access of other centrally situated amenities, reducing the need for private car ownership, cutting down on transport miles and therefore reducing energy consumption and pollution. If a high-rise building is also energy efficient or even self-sufficient, then the environmental implications become even more important.

These are complex arguments. But just as fascinating is the way that the evolution of 20th-century apartment buildings have helped to influence residential design more generally. Within high-rises, space and light have always been at a premium, leading to design solutions that maximize both. This has helped to encourage the push towards open-plan living, with spaces that combine many functions in one fluid space. Similarly, integrated balconies and winter gardens help to extend the perception of open space and provide some connection with the natural world, even on a very small footprint.

One of the first truly modern compact kitchens, known as the 'Frankfurt kitchen', was originally designed in 1926 by the Austrian architect Margarete Schütte-Lihotzky for use in a series of innovative apartment buildings built in the German city during the Twenties. Thousands of these ingenious, space-saving designs were produced for both apartments and houses, while Schütte-Lihotzky's ergonomic, thoughtful and functional design influenced the look and feel of the kitchens that many of us have today. Similarly, contemporary shower rooms and micro *en suite* bathrooms are partly a result of the growing pressure on space within our cities, especially within the context of high-rise living. The same is true of integrated storage, furniture and other built-in elements of the home. In these ways and others, high-rise living has played a part in shaping the homes we live in, whether apartments or houses.

A sense of community at the Isokon Building

One of the most original early Modernist apartment buildings in London was the Isokon building, also known as the Lawn Road Flats, designed by the architect Wells Coates. Sitting among the Georgian terraces of leafy Belsize Park, adjacent to Hampstead, the Isokon apartment building felt way ahead of its time when it first opened its doors back in 1934. Today the sleek apartment building still feels fresh, with its crisp, sculpted outline and floating balconies cantilevered from the façade of the building. It was the achievement of a lifetime both for design-world entrepreneur Jack Pritchard and for Wells Coates. For a fleeting moment in the late Thirties, this was the social and creative hub of north London, hosting a succession of writers, artists and architects while Pritchard and his wife, Molly, took up residence in the penthouse apartment. One of its most famous residents, the novelist Agatha Christie, compared the building to a great ocean liner, floating among the trees.

The son of Canadian missionaries, Wells Coates was born in Japan and travelled widely with his parents before studying at the University of British Columbia at Vancouver. He served with the Canadian army and flying corps during World War I, before continuing his studies and then moving to London, where he obtained a PhD in engineering. He worked briefly as a newspaper journalist but then began a career in design, founding his own

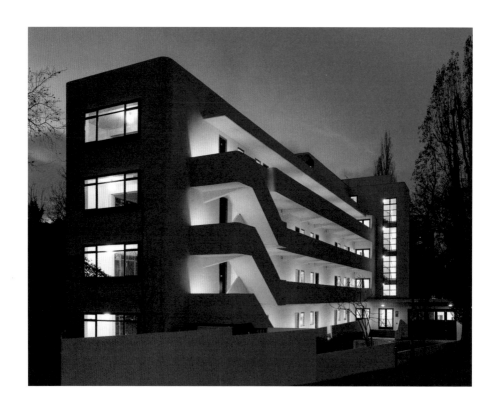

Wells Coates – Isokon, London, England, 1934

practice in the late Twenties. A flamboyant and sometimes eccentric figure, Coates turned his talents to many different areas of design, from architecture to interiors and product design.

Coates was a great believer in a new order of architecture and design and was a co-founder of the Modern Architectural Research Group, or MARS, the English arm of the Congrès Internationaux d'Architecture Moderne, or CIAM (see page 122). He visited the Bauhaus in 1931 with Jack Pritchard and two years later was a delegate at the famous CIAM conference, attended by Le Corbusier, Walter Gropius and others, which was held on a liner as it sailed across the Mediterranean.

Jack and Molly Pritchard first became aware of Wells Coates's work through plywood. Jack Pritchard was the UK dealer for Venesta, a Baltic plywood manufacturer, and noted Coates's use of plywood within some of his shop interiors for Cresta Silks. The Pritchards acquired a site on Lawn Road, a short walk from the Belsize Park underground station, in 1929. Initially, they considered building a terrace of interlinked houses and started working with Coates on that basis. But Coates encouraged the Pritchards to think about building a block of serviced flats on the site instead, and a company, Isokon, was formed to develop the building. Molly Pritchard sketched out a memorandum in 1932, detailing the elements that each apartment would include, and a prototype flat was shown at the Exhibition of British Industrial Art in Relation to the Home, held at Dorland Hall, London, in the summer of 1933. The Isokon building itself was finally completed a year later.

The four-storey building, made of reinforced concrete – the first time this had been used in British domestic architecture – initially held 22 single flats, or 'minimum' apartments, as well as three studio apartments and five larger flats, including a penthouse that was perched on top of the four storeys. There was also parking for ten cars and staff quarters, with a full 'domestic service' available. The apartments themselves were modest in size and featured built-in furniture to Coates's design, with the extensive use of plywood throughout. The kitchens and bathrooms were small and relatively basic, but complemented by a larger, communal kitchen on the ground floor. Two staff flats and the communal kitchen were later converted into the Isobar, a members' restaurant and club with interiors by Marcel Breuer, who became an early resident here, along with fellow Bauhaus émigrés Walter Gropius and László Moholy-Nagy. The social life of the apartment building was lively and intellectual, with the Pritchards hosting parties up in the small penthouse and on their large adjoining roof terrace, and with the Isobar drawing in artists and creatives from across Hampstead and north London, including Barbara Hepworth, Ben Nicholson and Henry Moore.

The blueprints of the building were conceived by Coates and the Pritchards in a spirit of optimism, lifted by the desire to create a new type of building: a social, serviced and democratic ship of state with a strong sense of community. Wells Coates went on to design two other apartment buildings, in Brighton and London, and later served with the Royal Air Force during World War II, developing designs for fighter planes. In 1951 Coates designed the Telekinema for the Festival of Britain; a venue for showing films and large-screen television broadcasts, it was one of the festival's most popular attractions and became the home of the National Film Theatre from 1952 to 1957. Yet money worries and a sense of disappointment and unfulfilled dreams blighted Coates's later years. He taught at the Harvard Graduate School of Design for two years and then moved back to Canada.

The Isokon name, however, lives on. The apartment building has been lovingly restored by Avanti Architects, and the penthouse is now owned by an admirer of Coates's work. Jack Pritchard also developed a line of Isokon furniture in the late Thirties, making use of the talents of the Bauhaus émigrés who had become friends and fellow residents. The pieces were largely made of plywood, drawing on Pritchard's own experience of the material, and the collection included a number of designs by Gropius and Breuer. The Isokon Furniture Company was forced to close in 1939, when materials became scarce and Gropius and Breuer moved to America. However, in the early Sixties it was restarted, and in the early Eighties the brand was successfully resurrected as 'Isokon Plus', with the furniture made under licence and many of the most famous designs reissued.

Lubetkin and Highpoint I and II

Another Modernist émigré who arrived in London during the Thirties was Berthold Lubetkin. The founder of the progressive architectural unit Tecton, Lubetkin became a highly influential figure in a very short space of time, sealing his reputation with a series of landmark projects over the pre-war years. Chief among them were the two Highpoint apartment buildings in Highgate, where he also created a home for himself perched atop Highpoint II, blessed with one of the best views in London.

Lubetkin was born in Tbilisi, Georgia, the son of a businessman specializing in imported ticketing machinery. As a child Lubetkin joined his father on a number of business trips to various parts of Europe, lending him an outward-looking perspective upon the world. He studied in St Petersburg and Moscow, where he was living when the Russian Revolution ignited. In 1922 he travelled to Berlin, initially working as a translator, and continued his studies in Berlin, Austria and Poland, where he completed a diploma in architecture. From Poland, Lubetkin moved on to Paris in 1925, working for a time with the early Modernist pioneer Auguste Perret, who developed early systems for building with concrete. Lubetkin extended his architectural studies at the École des Beaux-Arts and at the École Supérieure de Béton

Berthold Lubetkin – Highpoint II, London, England, 1938

Armé, where he added to his growing knowledge of concrete construction (*béton armé* is reinforced concrete) and got to know the work of Le Corbusier.

An invitation to design a house for a potential client drew Lubetkin over to London in 1931. Although the project never went ahead, he was soon immersed in the world of English architecture and design, forming a practice called Tecton in 1932 with a group of younger English architects, some of them with strong social connections that helped generate leads and contacts for commissions. A young Denys Lasdun, who went on to design the Royal National Theatre (1976), joined the practice a few years later.

A number of early Lubetkin/Tecton commissions were for zoo buildings, including the gorillas' Round House (1933) at London Zoo and also the sculptural Penguin Pool (1934), developed with the Danish engineer Ove Arup. The fluid, imaginative geometry of the Penguin Pool, in particular, with its oval outline and intertwined ramps, set Lubetkin apart from many of his Modernist contemporaries, who seemed to view the architectural world as a series of straight lines. Lubetkin's work, again and again, sought to subvert the simple cube and create a more dynamic and expressive composition. Other zoo commissions followed, including buildings at Dudley Zoo in the West Midlands and Whipsnade Zoo in Bedfordshire. At Whipsnade, Lubetkin also designed a modest, modern 'dacha' for himself, known as Bungalow A, or Hillfield (1936).

During the early Thirties, Lubetkin met the businessman Sigmund Gestetner, who owned a company making office equipment. They found a site in Highgate, north London, where they set about creating a new kind of apartment building that could house Gestetner's workers in affordable apartments. Highpoint I, completed in 1935, holds 60 apartments in an H-shaped building floating on a series of concrete piloti in the Corbusian style. The plan of the building allowed Lubetkin to maximize views and privacy for the flats, which were surrounded by landscaped gardens, complete with a swimming pool and tennis courts. The ground floor was largely given over to a broad, open hallway leading to a communal gathering space, originally designed as a tea room overlooking the gardens.

Detailing and specifications were carefully considered throughout, and the reinforced concrete apartment building, with structural engineering by Arup again, was an instant success, although it did attract a more affluent, middle-class ownership than originally anticipated. In 1937, the building was featured at the exhibition *Modern Architecture in England* at the Museum of Modern Art in New York.

When the owners of the neighbouring house sold up, Lubetkin persuaded Gestetner to buy the land to build a companion building, Highpoint II. After a protracted planning process, Lubetkin won permission for a complementary building with just 12 luxurious apartments, including a penthouse for himself and his family. It was completed in 1938.

The penthouse of Highpoint II was a highly personal space, sitting on top of an extraordinary building, featuring apartments rich in light and volume, but also designed with practicality and easy living in mind. The heart of the penthouse was a large open-plan space, with a parabolic roof, featuring skylight slots at the ends of the barrel-vaulted ceiling and extensive ribbon windows to either side of the apartment. The ceiling was painted a sky blue and the tiled floor was a dark, earthy tone. The two-bedroomed flat featured colour, texture and pattern, including idiosyncratic wallpapers and pine cladding around the entrance area and fireplace. Lubetkin designed a number of pieces of furniture especially for the space, including characterful armchairs in Norwegian yew and cowhide.

Highpoint II, which served as Lubetkin's home until 1955, was widely praised. Visitors included Le Corbusier, who described it as 'an achievement of the first rank, and a milestone which will be useful to everybody'.[1]

There were other Lubetkin projects of the Thirties, in particular the Finsbury Health Centre (1938) and an innovative Modernist house known as Six Pillars in Dulwich (1935), both in London. But Lubetkin's work on large-scale social housing projects was interrupted by the war, and during the Fifties he became disillusioned by his constant battles with planners and local authorities. He went into self-imposed exile in Gloucestershire, with his work only positively reassessed and rediscovered towards the end of his life.

Lake Shore Drive Apartments, a big step forward

In the United States, one of the greatest exemplars of modern high-rise living was Ludwig Mies van der Rohe's twin-tower project in Chicago known as the Lake Shore Drive Apartments, completed in 1951. Chicago has always been a focal point for the evolution of the skyscraper, from early

Ludwig Mies van der Rohe – Lake Shore Drive Apartments,
Chicago, Illinois, United States, 1951

steel-framed high-rises by Louis Sullivan through to architect Fazlur Khan's 1973 Sears Tower (now known as the Willis Tower), which was the tallest building in the world for nearly 25 years. There was also Bertrand Goldberg's distinctive pair of circular apartment buildings known as Marina City, completed in the late Sixties. But Mies's Lake Shore Drive apartment buildings stand out as landmark prototypes, which have helped to inspire multiple modern imitators all around the world.

The address 860–880 Lake Shore Drive represents the most ambitious collaboration between the former Bauhaus director and the property developer Herbert Greenwald, who became the architect's greatest supporter and patron during his American years. The two friends had already worked together on the design and build of the Promontory Apartments, also in Chicago, which was completed in 1949. But the Lake Shore Drive project was a step forward in almost every respect.

Mies designed the pair of 26-storey towers on the edge of Lake Michigan using a steel skeleton and floor-to-ceiling windows. Each has a disciplined, rectangular outline and features a frame of black metal on the façade, which helps to reinforce the strict sense of geometry. Also known as the 'Glass House Apartments', the two buildings share many of the same 'skin and bones' architectural principles of Mies's Farnsworth House (see page 140), which was completed the same year and also used a skeletal steel frame and curtain walls of glass. On Lake Shore Drive, many of these glass walls framed open views out across the lake itself, which resembles an inland sea. Residents have spoken about their intense relationship with Lake Michigan, comparing the experience to being on a ship, as the weather, the light and the elements constantly change according to the time of day and the time of year.

But there are also strong parallels between the original floor plans set out by Mies for these apartments and the internal layouts of the Farnsworth House. His priority was to preserve the sense of openness while avoiding any unnecessary interruption of the curtain walls. So, within each apartment, the kitchen and bathroom(s) are pushed to the rear, towards the central circulation core, while the living and dining areas are combined within one open-plan space that benefits from the views. Inside the one-bedroom apartments the partitioning between the living space and the sleeping area was also lightly done, as at Edith Farnsworth's house, lending the interiors a fluid universality. This was the intention, at least, before Greenwald's backers began insisting on a more conventional, cellular approach, leading to a greater sense of separation for the bedrooms.

Even so, the Lake Shore Drive Apartments offered a radically different alternative to life in a suburban home, within a modern village in minia-ture. There were originally 90 three-bedroom apartments in no. 860 and 158 one-bedroom apartments in no. 880. The hotel-style entrance lobby on the ground floor, with its own glass enclosure, became a staple of late 20th-century apartment buildings, along with galley kitchenettes and space-saving bathrooms. They offered a kind of template for sky-high living, which Greenwald and Mies reinforced in 1955 with a second pairing of apartment buildings nearby, at 900–910 Lake Shore Drive, known as the Esplanade Apartments. Meanwhile, in the commercial sector, Mies's 1958 Seagram Building in New York offered a clear template for the modern, curtain-walled office building and the corporate high-rise.

Unité d'Habitation and the city of towers

In Marseille, another hugely influential apartment building, completed just a year later than Mies van der Rohe's Lake Shore Drive Apartments, provided an alternative model for the high life and captured the attention and imagination of countless European architects and urban planners. The 1952 Unité d'Habitation by Le Corbusier was the culmination of decades of thought about the shape and organization of modern cities and the need for mass-produced housing to meet the growing demand for new homes within the cityscape. Le Corbusier had started thinking about mass-housing concepts as far back as 1915, when he sketched out plans for a 'Town Built on Piles': a whole neighbourhood created within one super-building. He set out his ideas more fully in his book of essays, *Vers une Architecture*, published in 1923 (and in English as *Towards a New Architecture*, in 1931). In it he discusses the need not only for the mass production of well-designed homes but also for '*les Villes-Tours*' ('Cities of Towers'), a phrase Le Corbusier borrowed from his mentor, Auguste Perret:

> In these towers which will shelter the worker, till now stifled in densely packed quarters and congested streets, all the necessary services, following the admirable practice in America, will be assembled, bringing efficiency and economy of time and effort, and as a natural result the peace of mind which is so necessary. These towers, rising up at great distances from one another, will give by reason of their height, the same accommodation that has up till now been spread out over the superficial area; they will leave open enormous spaces in which would run, well away from them, the noisy arterial roads, full of traffic which becomes increasingly rapid. At the foot of the towers would stretch the parks: trees covering the whole town. The setting out of the towers would form imposing avenues; there indeed is an architecture worthy of our time.[2]

Le Corbusier, always a grand dreamer, took inspiration not only from American skyscrapers, concrete construction, ocean liners and principles of mass production but also from the need for communal space and gardens, parks and fresh air, playgrounds and playing fields. His utopian

Le Corbusier – Unité d'Habitation, Marseille, France, 1952

Cities of Towers concept imagined clusters of towers 60 storeys high, set among parkland, while his 1922 concept of *Immeubles-villas* (translated as 'Freehold Maisonettes') which was also included in his book, envisaged a block of 120 maisonettes (two-storey apartments) set around a large central atrium, each one with its own 'hanging gardens' and balconies integrated within the outline of the superstructure. These ideas embrace Le Corbusier's idea of the home as 'a machine for living in' (see page 69), yet they also seek to create a precious private realm for each resident, which includes open family space and access to gardens or roof terraces.

The epic destruction of the war years offered Le Corbusier an opportunity to begin applying some of these ideas on a large scale. The Unité d'Habitation was a commission from the French Ministry of Reconstruction. The building took five years to complete, with delays caused by budget constraints, controversy over the social implications of the design and the sheer scale of the project, with its 337 apartments contained in a single 12-storey block.

Using reinforced concrete, Le Corbusier raised the entire community off the ground upon a series of vast piloti. Le Corbusier himself is said to have described the structural organization of the building as 'like wine bottles in a rack', with apartments 'pushed' into the superstructure. There were central circulation routes, or streets, along with an ingenious method of slotting apartments around these corridors using a combination of maisonettes that spanned the width of the building and offered large windows and balconies to either side. The result was a house in miniature, arranged over two levels, with spatial and volumetric variety and some sense of a garden city because of the private balconies and the outdoor rooms that they provided. Le Corbusier also worked with designers Charlotte Perriand and Jean Prouvé (see page 175) on a portfolio of furniture and integrated elements for the apartments, including built-in cupboards and bookcases.

Le Corbusier never underestimated the importance of private space at the Unité d'Habitation. Yet there were also important communal amenities, especially up on the roof, where there was a nursery school, a gym and roof terraces. A famous period photograph shows children playing in a circle alongside one of the vast concrete ventilation funnels on top of this concrete community.

Ironically, the Unité d'Habitation was and is one of the most divisive buildings in Europe. For some, it is the most rounded and thoughtful of Le Corbusier's micro-towns and an inspirational model for urban social housing. For others, it was the match that sparked a thousand mistaken imitations and social housing experiments that blighted cities across Europe, the Americas and beyond. The truth probably lies somewhere in between these diametrically opposed positions.

Barbican Estate, an urban community

It's certainly true that Le Corbusier's theories and his buildings helped to inspire the creation of countless high-rises around the world during the Sixties and Seventies. Some of these were successes, but others were poorly conceived, hastily built and badly maintained, leading to a kind of urban heart failure that resulted in segregated urban ghettoes. The dysfunctional and dystopian aspects of such buildings are captured in J G Ballard's 1975 novel *High-Rise*, in which a godlike Modernist architect nests in a penthouse apartment while his self-designed tower disintegrates beneath him.

But there are many post-war and mid-century high-rises that remain beloved, even if the material is concrete and the style is clearly Brutalist (see page 232). One of the most characterful of these developments is the Barbican Estate on the edge of the City of London, built between 1965 and 1976 by architects Chamberlin, Powell and Bon (see page 184). Of the many large-scale developments completed across the UK during the post-war period, the Barbican Estate is – arguably – one of the closest to the Corbusian ideal of a City of Towers. There are three residential towers, each 42 storeys high, but also terraced blocks, the Barbican Centre arts complex, a school, a public library, a museum and other elements, all interspersed with courtyards, garden squares, elevated walkways, water features and other open spaces.

The complex sits upon a site of around 14 hectares (35 acres) that was badly damaged by bombing raids during World War II. The need for reconstruction offered an almost unprecedented opportunity not just for urban infill but to create an entirely new community in the heart of London, with space enough to establish a social and cultural mix while also meeting the need for new homes.

Within the residential part of the Barbican Estate there was a whole range of apartments of various sizes and scales, suited to a wide spectrum of different needs. They included everything from penthouses to small sub-podium flats (below the podium level on which the building stands, and facing the sunken gardens or lake), initially made available for rent. Many apartments had their own private balconies or terraces while all had large windows and plenty of light, helped by the intelligent master planning of the Barbican Estate and the way that the various blocks looked over open spaces of one kind or another. Internally, there was a great deal of ingenuity throughout the design of the apartments themselves, with spacious, open-plan living spaces, and galley kitchens tucked away to one side. Bathroom pods were compact and usually self-contained, windowless elements. The specifications and quality of the kitchens and bathrooms were always high, with many apartments today still holding on to their original layouts, kitchen units and integrated storage cupboards.

Residents have talked about the special sense of community at the Barbican, as well as the peace that comes from an entire estate without cars and traffic noise. Here, human beings rather than cars or machines are at the centre of everything. There is a true diversity to the community itself, with some apartments still rented while many others have been bought by their residents under 'right to buy' programmes, and right from the start the complex has been well maintained and looked after. Evidence of the enduring appeal of the Barbican came with the recent opening of a fourth residential high-rise, Blake Tower, which was converted from a YMCA hostel into new apartments by architects and designers Conran & Partners. Demand for these fresh Barbican flats was high.

High-rise living remains a divisive subject in certain parts of the world. Like any home, a well-designed skyline apartment offers the potential for pleasure and delight, while a poorly conceived high-rise flat can be little more than a prison. But as the pressure to provide new urban homes grows, along with the desire among buyers to live centrally in the great cities of the world, then inevitably the push is upwards. For many architects and planners, there is a feeling that we have reached a moment of choice that has far-reaching implications for us all. Either cities continue to grow and spread outwards, as we build on fields and farms, or we go up. Architect Renzo Piano, who has designed a number of skyscrapers and high-rises, sums up the issue:

> We woke up at the beginning of the new century and finally discovered that the earth is fragile and must be defended. The first thing to defend is land. There is a nostalgic, almost romantic idea that it is more ecological to make a small building – forget it, this is the worst way to consume land. This is the reason that cities grow. It is more socially correct to intensify the city and free up space on the ground. The earth is fragile, the city is fragile and vulnerable, so we have to be careful.[3]

Barragán & Co.
Regional Modernists

12 Luis Barragán – San Cristóbal, Los Clubes, Mexico City, Mexico, 1968

Luis Barragán
San Cristóbal
Los Clubes, Mexico City,
Mexico, 1968

Oscar Niemeyer
Casa das Canoas
Rio de Janeiro, Brazil, 1953

Jean-François Zevaco
Villa Sami Suissa
Casablanca, Morocco, 1947

Geoffrey Bawa
Lunuganga
Bentota, Sri Lanka, 1969

Charles Correa
House at Koramangala
Bangalore, India, 1988

The post-war period saw a dramatic acceleration in the process of globalization. Images and ideas travelled the world as never before within a revolution in communications, but so did people, carried by a new generation of airliners. They included corporate businessmen, entrepreneurs and salesmen looking to spread their wings internationally, but there were also architects and designers, who increasingly began working overseas. This sat well within the concept of an 'International Style' (see page 122), encompassing a set of common principles grounded in Modernist thinking. For global firms especially, including tech companies and hotel groups, exporting a common architectural approach to their buildings and projects fitted neatly with the ambition of inventing a clear and cohesive corporate identity that transcended borders.

Yet even as globalization gained traction, there was also an increasing respect for regionalism. This was true of architecture in particular, where 'regional Modernism' offered a counterbalance for the rise of the International Style, with far-reaching implications for residential design and the modern home. When it came to house and home, internationalism suggested the dominance of a familiar set of modern principles, such as skeletal structural frameworks in steel or reinforced concrete, curtain walls, banks of glass, a strong inside–outside relationship and, within the home, a push towards open-plan living spaces. While regional Modernists often embraced such elements, they also stressed the importance of context and the need for homes tailored to the climate, conditions and culture of a specific part of the world, which might include references to vernacular traditions, as well as the use of local materials and building techniques. In other words, while globalization stressed the importance of conformity and familiarity, regionalism spoke of the value of difference and originality.

Even within a single continent or country, such differences could be dramatic. In the United States, for instance, among mid-century houses we can see a difference between Californian Modernism, a modern New England aesthetic and 'Florida modern', where architects such as Ralph Twitchell and Paul Rudolph developed a fresh design philosophy suited to the subtropical climate of the state during the Fifties and Sixties. Further afield, in South America, Africa, Asia or India, there was a wide spectrum of regional variation spread out under the big, broad umbrella of mid-century

Modernism. Architects and designers in all parts of the world brought something interesting and important to the table as they looked to create an architectural style that embraced modernity but was also a response to the setting and surroundings of a particular part of the world.

In his own definition of 'Critical Regionalism', architectural critic Kenneth Frampton talks of the influence of 'site specific factors' and 'reinterpreted vernacular elements', but also of the importance of multiple sensory factors:

> Critical Regionalism emphasizes the tactile as much as the visual. It is aware that the environment can be experienced in terms other than sight alone. It is sensitive to such complementary perceptions as varying levels of illumination, ambient sensations of heat, cold, humidity and air movement, varying aromas and sounds given off by different materials in different volumes, and even the varying sensations induced by floor finishes, which cause the body to experience involuntary changes in posture, gait, etc. It is opposed to the tendency in an age dominated by media to the replacement of experience by information.[1]

This focus on tactility and the importance of touch, sound and smell, as well as sight, points to the vivid experiential quality of so much regional Modernist architecture, with its rich variety of materials, textures and surfaces. More than this, there is a much greater openness to colour, pattern and a range of finishes than might be the case within the limitations of the International Style. At the same time, regional Modernist architects such as Luis Barragán and Oscar Niemeyer stressed the emotional and poetic aspects of the art of architecture, as well as the intellectual and the technical aspects. They clearly recognized that the personal and individual act of creating a home involves both the head and the heart.

Barragán, emotional architecture and San Cristóbal

The Mexican mid-century master Luis Barragán trained as an engineer, yet his temperament was one of an artist and a romantic. He was well aware of Modernist manifestos and travelled widely in Europe during the Twenties, where he attended lectures by Le Corbusier. Yet his work was deeply rooted in the context of Mexico itself with its haciendas, churches, pueblos and village squares. While many Modernists argued for an architecture of openness and connectivity, Barragán spoke of the importance of privacy and solitude. This could only be achieved through the poetry of the wall itself, offering a protective enclosure around one's own architectural space. For Barragán, walls were a thing of beauty and a canvas to be layered with texture and colour. Rather than being a barrier to the landscape, he felt they should be seen as part of the landscape, as in a walled garden or outdoor room. Landscape design and architecture were intimately linked in Barragán's mind, with his residential work especially embracing gardens, courtyard spaces, fountains and pools. They all became part of his poetic design philosophy. In his Pritzker Prize acceptance speech in 1980, Barragán said:

> It is alarming that publications devoted to architecture have banished from their pages the words Beauty, Inspiration, Magic, Spellbound, Enchantment, as well as the concepts of Serenity, Silence, Intimacy and Amazement. All these have nestled in my soul, and though I am fully aware that I have not done them justice in my work, they never cease to be my guiding lights…Serenity is the great and true antidote against anguish and fear, and today, more than ever, it is the architect's duty to make of it a permanent guest in the home, no matter how sumptuous or how humble.[2]

As well as serenity and solitude, Barragán also emphasized the spiritual dimension of space and the ways that it might enable an individual not only to escape but to recharge and 'take stock'. As an architectural designer, Barragán created sacred spaces such as a chapel in Tlalpan, a haven completed in 1960 for a Catholic convent within a neighbourhood of Mexico City. Yet many of his houses also highlighted this feeling of spiritual serenity, including the ranch house of San Cristóbal at Los Clubes, completed in 1968 (see page 202).

Barragán has described his work as 'autobiographical', given the way it draws inspiration from his memories and experiences of his country. Beyond his own home in Mexico City, one of Barragán's most personal projects was certainly San Cristóbal, which drew upon his recollections of growing up on his father's ranch on the one hand and his passion for horses and riding on the other:

> I spent my youth on horseback, looking at houses that sang over the earth, passing by popular festivals; I remember the play of shadows that always fell over the walls as the late sun was weakening, and no matter how much the shadows changed the angles were either attenuated or the lines were cut off. From here also comes my fixation with aqueducts. At Mexican ranchos you always see streams of water; you would never have a house or an architectural ensemble without a pond, or a stream, or a fragment of an aqueduct. Nothing could distract me from thinking of horses.[3]

San Cristóbal was designed to be just as much a home for horses as it was for their owner, Barragán's client Folke Egerström. The ranch sits within a walled compound, where a staff apartment, garage, swimming pool area and service spaces form a hinterland between the street and the main family residence. Here, the house consists of one wing largely devoted to the main living spaces, including a large living room, and another to the bedrooms. But the house itself is one linear, or cubic, element within a much larger composition in which the horse is king. There are stables and a hay barn, but also a paddock, an exercise ground and a central courtyard complete with a horse pool fed by a fountain. The walls that help to enclose these different spaces have been painted in a vibrant range of colours, including pink, purple and terracotta. High trees sit around the boundary, adding greenery, while the fountain provides a constant musical accompaniment.

The result is a thoughtful, abstract version of a hacienda with great planes of colour drawing the eye, while the fountain, the water pool and the horses themselves delight the senses. There is a sense of peaceful seclusion, certainly, but here at the ranch there is also a theatrical quality, with this open stage set for the balletic movement of the equine actors. Just as importantly, architecture and landscape blur into one, but not through the use of glass walls. Instead, there is a constant interplay between inside and outside space, between tectonic intervention and natural elements. At

San Cristóbal, as elsewhere, Barragán suggested that gardens should not be ornamental but should be spaces to be used and enjoyed to the full, within an ethos that he described as 'emotional architecture'.

Casa das Canoas, a laboratory of ideas

There are certain parallels that can be drawn between the work of Luis Barragán and that of another Latin American maestro, Oscar Niemeyer. They shared a suspicion of the dogmatic rigour of the International Style and argued in favour of an approach that mirrored the character of their own countries, while taking a contextual approach to site and setting. There was a mutual love of garden design, with a significant interplay between architecture and landscaping, as well as an emotional and sometimes playful outlook that put both architects at odds with the more academic critical theorists among the international design community.

Yet while Barragán adopted a broadly cubist approach to architectural form, with a love for the tectonic presence and implied mass of high walls, Niemeyer's passion was for curves. This had not always been the case, as suggested by a number of Niemeyer's early houses from the Forties, which had a strong Corbusian quality, with a regular use of piloti (structural pillars), ribbon windows and integrated roof terraces. But gradually, Niemeyer began to push back against linear forms and rectangular buildings as he embraced a distinctive style that was more dynamic, with the use of fluid forms and sinuous curves. 'I am not attracted to straight angles or to the straight line – hard and inflexible – created by man,' he said. 'I am attracted to free-flowing, sensual curves.'[4]

Niemeyer praised the 'plastic freedom' offered by concrete, which he moulded and sculpted at will: 'First were the thick stone walls, the arches, then the domes and vaults,' said Niemeyer. 'Now it is concrete-reinforced that gives our imagination flight, with its soaring spaces and uncommon cantilevers.'[5]

Unlike many European Brutalists (see page 234), who used concrete in uncompromising linear shapes and forms, Niemeyer wanted to create sculptural buildings that offered true 'architectural spectacle'. Like his contemporary in Mexico, Félix Candela, Niemeyer experimented with over-arching concrete roof shells that sheltered all of the internal space beneath, as seen in his Church of Saint Francis of Assisi in Pampulha

(1943). By the early Fifties, he was celebrating 'plastic freedom' on a vast scale, as seen in his famous curving Copan Building in São Paulo – with 1,160 apartments arranged over 38 storeys, it twists and turns in the cityscape. Designed in 1951, it was not completed until 1966.

At around the same time that Niemeyer was working on the Copan Building, he also designed and built one of his most rounded and accomplished houses, embracing this fresh sense of plastic freedom. This was Oscar Niemeyer's own family home in Rio de Janeiro, completed in 1953, which – like many examples of architects' own, self-designed houses – was a laboratory of ideas.

Niemeyer chose a hillside site at Canoas, on the green edge of Rio, where the city meets the greenery of a number of nature reserves and parks. Given the verdant, tropical surroundings, this setting has a semi-rural feel rather than an urban atmosphere. The architect collaborated on the gardens with his great friend the celebrated landscape designer Roberto Burle Marx, adopting a semi-naturalistic approach that sees the trees and planting edging towards the house and even inside it, taking root within internal planters.

Niemeyer pushed the house into the hillside itself. The upper level is a light and largely transparent pavilion, with a curvaceous concrete canopy sheltering the main living spaces, as well as part of the adjoining terrace. Rather like John Lautner's Elrod House in Palm Springs (see page 117), the rock of the hill pushes through the band of windows and into the building itself, further enhancing the sense of connection to the natural world.

Internally, the house is arranged over two levels. The pavilion is largely open-plan, with seating and dining areas plus a small galley kitchen tucked away behind a wooden screen. The rock marks the point where the stairs lead down to a semi-subterranean floor, set into the slope of the hill, which holds the family bedrooms and bathrooms. These are the night-time spaces within an almost cave-like haven, while the pavilion above is full of light. Creating this hidden basement devoted to the sleeping spaces makes practical sense, but also helps to reduce the overall impact of the house upon the landscape. Niemeyer suggested that he wanted his buildings 'to be as light as possible, to touch the ground gently, to swoop and soar, and to surprise'.[6] Casa das Canoas achieves all of these things.

Oscar Niemeyer – Casa das Canoas, Rio de Janeiro, Brazil, 1953

In 1956 the new president of Brazil, Juscelino Kubitschek, visited Oscar Niemeyer at his home. He asked the architect to help him build a new capital, Brasília, which was to become Niemeyer's greatest achievement. Here, the architect used concrete like an artist, creating dynamic structures such as the Metropolitan Cathedral (1970), with a roof like a crown of thorns, and the inverted dome that forms the Chamber of Deputies in the National Congress Building (1960). Niemeyer's Brasília helped to define the modern identity of a nation, infused with a sense of sculptural artistry.

'Maghreb modern' and Villa Sami Suissa

The Moroccan architect Jean-François Zevaco has sometimes been described as North Africa's answer to Oscar Niemeyer. Zevaco was one of the principal post-war exponents of what we might call 'Maghreb modern', which took ideas and principles developed by the early European Modernists and adapted them to the climate and conditions of North Africa. Born in Casablanca, Zevaco studied at the École des Beaux-Arts in Paris, before returning to Morocco to establish an architectural practice in his home city.

The port city of Casablanca has long been an economic hub, both for Morocco itself and the wider region. During World War II, Allied forces took control of the city from Vichy France and it became a focal point for American forces during the final years of the war. Later, Casablanca played an important part in the push towards independence, which came in 1956. Given its proximity to Europe and its position as Morocco's largest city, it also became a focal point for modern architecture, including architect Léonard Morandi's Liberty Building of 1951, which was the tallest residential building in Morocco upon its completion, as well as one of the highest towers in Africa.

Casablanca was home to a number of influential Modernist architects. Elie Azagury was another native of Casablanca who studied in Paris and went on to design a collection of houses in the Moroccan city during the Fifties and Sixties, including his own home, splicing a Brutalist approach with vernacular influences drawn from the Maghreb. Wolfgang Ewerth was born and trained in Germany, but set up a practice in Casablanca in 1954, designing a series of striking mid-century villas, including the 1954 'Villa for Dr B'. This round house, also known as the Villa Camembert, combined the post-war passion for vivid geometrical forms with Moroccan interiors, and included a grand salon decorated with traditional zellij tilework.

Jean-François Zevaco's Villa Sami Suissa of 1947 was an early but highly sophisticated exemplar of the Maghreb modern style. Zevaco had grown impatient with the rectangular compositions adopted by many of the Modernist masters and had begun to experiment with expressive shapes and forms. For example, his 1951 Clubhouse at Casablanca Tit-Mellil Airport was a partially elevated building featuring an observation deck, which pushed outwards at one end like the rounded prow of a ship.

Situated close to the sea in the Anfa district of Casablanca, Villa Sami Suissa was designed for a property developer, Sami Suissa. It was arranged on two principal levels, plus a basement holding service spaces and staff quarters. The living spaces on the ground floor spilled out onto a large private garden, complete with terraces and a swimming pool. The bedrooms on the upper level were protected by a sinuous roof canopy, which extended beyond the core of the house itself and helped to shade a wraparound balcony, offering an elevated deck overlooking the gardens. Also known as the Butterfly House,

Jean-François Zevaco – Villa Sami Suissa, Casablanca, Morocco, 1947

it had a butterfly (V-shaped) roof reminiscent of a number of Niemeyer's designs (including the 1943 Casa Kubitschek, or Kubitschek Residence, which he built for Brazilian politician Juscelino Kubitschek, the future president). Villa Sami Suissa is now a restaurant, known as Villa Zevaco.

After a major earthquake hit the Moroccan city of Agadir in 1960, Jean-François Zevaco played a key part in the reconstruction programme with his innovative Courtyard Houses (1965), which won an Aga Khan Award for Architecture. The cluster of 17 modern houses in the centre of Agadir was partly inspired by traditional Moroccan riads (with a garden in the centre) and dars (with a central courtyard). Like them, the houses featured private courtyards and patios protected by boundary walls, offering light and, just as importantly, fresh air, which percolated through the houses.

Tropical Modernism and Lunuganga, Geoffrey Bawa's masterpiece

Another accomplished pioneer of the 20th-century courtyard house was the Sri Lankan-based architect Geoffrey Bawa. Rather like Luis Barragán, Bawa saw gardens and outdoor rooms as an integral part of the home rather than as separate elements. Developing his own unique version of 'Tropical Modernism', the architect created buildings that flowed from inside to outside and back again. His work was tailored to the climate, with its heat and monsoons, while Bawa's patios and outdoor rooms helped to ventilate the interiors of his buildings. These integrated courtyards and terraces included water features and planting, freshening the spaces around them but also ensuring that nature was always respected and revered.

The son of Anglo-Asian parents, Geoffrey Bawa was born in 1919 in what was then called Ceylon. He originally studied law at Cambridge University and practised as a lawyer for a time in Colombo before realizing that he had taken the wrong turning. After spending some time travelling, he enrolled at the Architectural Association in London, graduating in 1957 and returning to Sri Lanka to open his own architectural office. Over time, Bawa became one of the most respected architects in Asia, fusing Modernism with vernacular references and demonstrating an ingrained respect for local materials and craftsmanship. There were major projects including hotels, university campus buildings and the Sri Lankan Parliament Building in Colombo, which Bawa completed in 1982. Yet the architect is probably best known for his houses, including his own, in both town and country.

Bawa's house in 33rd Lane, Colombo, was designed and built over the space of a decade during the Fifties and Sixties. It was an organic process, with Bawa gradually acquiring four existing bungalows and either replacing or remodelling them to create one substantial residence. Towards the street, there was a new town house with two main levels plus a roof terrace. But the house flowed backwards onto its site, within a complex sequence that included guest quarters, a master suite and then the main living spaces beyond. Almost every significant room connected in one way or another with an outside space or lightwell. There was very little in the way of decoration but, as well as incorporating planting, Bawa added character through the use of architectural salvage, such as supporting columns recovered from period Sri Lankan houses that had been demolished.

There was a similar design process at Bawa's country home, even if the context was very different. Lunuganga, meaning 'salt river', which is now run as a hotel, is widely regarded as the architect's masterpiece. In 1948 Bawa bought an overgrown rubber plantation of around 10 hectares (25 acres), resting on two lush hills bordered by Dedduwa Lake and the Bentota River. With the ocean nearby, it is a place of extraordinary fertility and natural beauty.

At first Bawa did little with the estate, which is at Bentota, around 60km (40 miles) south of Colombo, concentrating instead on his architectural studies. Work only began in the Fifties and then accelerated during the Sixties, as Bawa rebuilt and enlarged an existing bungalow on the site and began adding a series of complementary structures, including a studio, a pavilion, a guesthouse and other ancillary spaces. Completed in 1969, Lunuganga became a house of many parts, and again the gardens were a vital part of the mix, although they unfolded on a far grander scale than could ever be the case in Colombo.

Architecture and landscape constantly intersect and overlap at Lunuganga, with particular consideration given to key sightlines and vistas, including views over the lake and towards the temple of Katakuliya in the distance. There are terraces and walkways, a water garden and a 'field of jars'. As with the house in Colombo, almost every architectural space has a

Geoffrey Bawa – Lunuganga, Bentota, Sri Lanka, 1969

strong relationship with a corresponding garden room, from framed views of the tropical greenery through to a collection of verandahs, terraces and secluded spots for enjoying the surroundings. More recently, when one of Bawa's Colombo projects – the Ena de Silva House – was threatened with demolition, the Bawa Trust managed to save it and move the entire building to Lunuganga. Given the architect's great love of salvage and recycling, one can only assume that Bawa himself would wholeheartedly approve.

For Geoffrey Bawa and many other regional, Tropical Modernist architects, definitions of house and home were not limited to internal, enclosed space. A garden court, terrace, verandah or patio was not just an extension of the home but a vital part of it, essential for enjoying everyday life in a place that might be hot and humid, wet or dry, depending on the season or time of year. This meant a choice of outdoor rooms that were either open to the elements or sheltered by a roof or canopy, allowing for the possibility of spending time in the fresh air even during the rainy season or monsoon weather. These garden rooms help cool air to circulate through the entire building and, as such, have an important functional purpose, yet they also enhance the overall feeling of space and openness, while – as Barragán might have put it – offering serenity, beauty and enchantment.

Open-sky spaces in Correa's home at Koramangala

Similarly, the design approach adopted by the Indian master architect Charles Correa placed great importance upon garden spaces and 'rooms open to the sky', including in his own family home and studio in the neighbourhood of Koramangala, in Bangalore. Correa was well versed in the lessons of Western-centric Modernism, having studied in both Mumbai and at the University of Michigan, followed by attaining a master's degree at the Massachusetts Institute of Technology. Yet his work was always firmly rooted in the context of India. Correa explained the reason for the Indian approach:

> In India, the sky has profoundly affected our relationship to built form and to open space. For in a warm climate, the best place to be in the late evenings and in the early mornings is outdoors, under the open sky. Hence, to us in Asia, the symbol of education has never been the Little Red Schoolhouse of North America, but the guru sitting under the tree. True Enlightenment cannot be achieved within the closed box of a room – one must be outdoors, under the open sky.[7]

Correa sought to integrate open-sky spaces in all of his projects, both residential and non-residential, and in his work as an urban planner. Naturally, the provision of courtyards and garden rooms was an essential component of his Koramangala home, completed in 1988. The design of the house changed a number of times, even after building work began, but the central courtyard was the one truly consistent element, with all of the main living spaces and the architectural studio arranged around it and connected with it; at the centre of the courtyard, the architect placed a large Champa plant (*Plumeria*). Around the house there were gardens and verandahs, as well as the 'kund' – a water pool that was often regarded as a sacred space. Again we might circle back to Barragán, who also regarded water pools and fountains as an important and delightful element within a garden room and one that added a valuable meditative and spiritually uplifting dimension.

Charles Correa – House at Koramangala, Bangalore, India, 1988

Houses of the Future
The Dynamic Age

13   Antti Lovag – Palais Bulles, Théoule-sur-Mer,
Nice, France, 1989

Charles Deaton
Sculptured House
Genesee Mountain
Colorado, United States, 1965

Richard Foster
The Round House
Wilton, Connecticut
United States, 1968

Staffan Berglund
Villa Spies
Torö, Finland, 1969

Antti Lovag
Palais Bulles
Théoule-sur-Mer,
Nice, France, 1989

Within the world of architecture, as in so many other walks of life, the Sixties was a time of liberation. The linear precision of early Modernism and the International Style began to give way to a late mid-century aesthetic that was more expressive, playful and decidedly dynamic. There was, during this time, a concerted attack upon the power of the straight line and the rectangle, as architects and designers began to think outside the box. The American architect Charles Deaton reflected this approach during the mid-Sixties when he asked:

> People aren't square, so why should they live in squares? I believe people look better and feel better among curves – they make people feel less confined. In other words, curved buildings provide a natural setting for curved people. I can reason with a cube, but I cannot cherish one.[1]

Architects and designers like Deaton began to question the rational, functionalist logic of linear forms and adopt an approach that was more sculptural. Within the art world, similarly, cubism gave way to abstraction and Op Art, as artists and illustrators explored the full spectrum of geometry. Increasingly, architects began experimenting with houses and buildings that were circular or triangular or hexagonal, while there were also butterfly (V-shaped) roofs, over-arching canopies and soaring shell structures.

At the same time, there were dramatic advances in engineering and new materials that enabled such experiments. Architects and structural engineers pioneered fresh techniques for creating thin concrete vaulted roofs and superstrong shells, as well as perfecting ways of spraying concrete over lightweight steel frameworks to create more sculptural, rounded tectonic forms. There was a growing sense of the 'plasticity' of cement, referring to its malleability and versatility, which took concrete way beyond the familiar notion of the 'wall' while twisting and turning in the most unexpected and surprising ways.

This plasticity was, of course, echoed and influenced by a new generation of modern products made of moulded plastic. They included iconic pieces such as the Panton chair – conceived in 1960 and marketed in 1967 as the result of a collaboration between Danish designer Verner Panton and the

Swiss-German manufacturer Vitra – which was the first injection-moulded plastic chair to be made in a single piece, using glass-reinforced polyester. There were Charles and Ray Eames's 1950 Shell chairs in plastic or fibre-glass, as well as Robin Day's famous Polypropylene stacking chair of 1963. Within the world of lighting, George Nelson created his famous Bubble lamps by spraying thin layers of plastic onto a wire frame. Achille and Pier Giacomo Castiglioni used a similar idea to create their own lightweight Cocoon and Taraxacum lampshades during the early Sixties.

Innovative collections of plastic furniture by designers such as Joe Colombo, Vico Magistretti, Marco Zanuso and many others made their way into the home, usually characterized by their bright colours and sinuous shapes. These were not disposable pieces, but they were fresh, fun and affordable. Unlike today, when the focus is very much upon the environmentally damaging use of disposable plastics and packaging, back in the Sixties plastics were collectively seen as a kind of wonder material, with designers and architects looking at ways in which they could maximize their potential.

When the Brazilian master architect Oscar Niemeyer (see page 208) spoke of 'total plastic freedom', he was referring to the plasticity of concrete. During the Sixties, in his work on the new Brazilian capital, Brasília, Niemeyer made the most of this new-found freedom and remained devoted to the curve. Similarly, the Mexican architect Félix Candela pioneered lightweight concrete vaults and shells during the Fifties and Sixties, with his work often sitting in the borderland between architecture and super-sculp-ture. In 1962 Candela collaborated with the ex-Formula One racing driver and architect Héctor Alonso Rebaque on the construction of Rebaque's home at El Pedregal, Mexico City, where a soaring, parabolic roof canopy – or saddle roof – shelters a dramatic, double-height living space.

In the United States, architects such as John Lautner and Eero Saarinen (see pages 117 and 126) stepped away from the constraints of linear forms, exemplified by – among other projects – Saarinen's North Christian Church of 1963 in Colombus, Indiana and his TWA Flight Center of 1962 at John F Kennedy International Airport in New York.

In Europe, the French architect Claude Parent railed against the box while arguing in favour of what he called the *fonction oblique* and a design philosophy that promoted free forms. Parent believed that fluid architectural compositions liberated not only the imagination, but also internal space, which was suddenly free of the conventions imposed by the right angle and compartmentalized rooms. He explored this to the full with his 1965 Maison Bordeaux Le Pecq near Bois-le-Roi in northern France, where he designed an extraordinary home for the artist Andrée Bordeaux-Le Pecq, featuring a pagoda-style roofline formed by a triptych of copper-coated concrete birds' wings.

There was certainly an experimental, avant-garde quality to these futuristic homes, as well as an element of abstraction. Even for the Sixties, such buildings were well beyond the ordinary and they pushed at the limits of the possible. Yet they were also evidence of an architectural energy that is still very important today, suggesting that houses and other buildings do not need to conform to a linear stereotype. Seen from the perspective of the Sixties, these were the houses of the future; and now, in the early 21st century, such shape-shifting dynamism is being more widely explored once again, as we recognize that the box is not always best.

Star quality in Sculptured House

Charles Deaton's Sculptured House in Colorado came to define the future after taking a starring role in Woody Allen's 1973 sci-fi comedy *Sleeper*, which was set in 2173. The house certainly has star quality, drawn from its dramatic clamshell aesthetic and its prominent position perched upon a Colorado mountain, floating above a blanket of pine trees. Compared with the more traditional houses in the valley below, the Sculptured House certainly feels as though it belongs to another century.

During the Sixties and Seventies, Deaton was best known for his stadium designs and banks. The Sculptured House (1965) is the architect's only known residential design and was very much a dream house, intended for himself and his family. An amateur pilot, Deaton scouted for a suitable location from the air and eventually found an idyllic 6-hectare (15-acre) setting on Genesee Mountain, where the views stretch all the way to the Rockies in the west and the Denver plain to the east.

Deaton explored his first ideas for the house in the form of a maquette, or preliminary plaster sculpture, which became the basis for sketches and drawings of his 'sculptured' mountain home. Construction began around

Charles Deaton – Sculptured House, Genesee Mountain,
Colorado, United States, 1965

1963, with the creation of a concrete pediment anchored to the bedrock below; this pediment also holds the entrance, hallway and staircase. To create the clamshell that hosts the main portion of the house, Deaton constructed a steel-mesh framework, which was coated in concrete. It was finished with an outer, protective layer of synthetic rubber, known as Hypalon, which was mixed with white pigment and ground walnut shells, echoing the plaster finish of the original maquette. This clamshell was designed to hold all of the principal living spaces, facing a long sequence of windows where the shell opens to the view, as well as connecting with an elevated terrace.

But, having begun the house, Deaton found it difficult to finish it. With the combination of the mountain site and the unconventional construction system, the cost of the project began to climb and the architect would come over at weekends, often with his family, to try to make progress. The architect's daughter Charlee Deaton describes the slow progress:

> We lived on the same mountain that the house was being built on, so I grew up with it and witnessed it being developed. It was slowly evolving through my childhood and it was stop–start. It is a stunning location – we used to say that we could see clear out to Kansas.[2]

Eventually Charles Deaton had to let the house go, and it fell to his daughter and her husband, architect Nick Antonopolous, who used to work in his father-in-law's practice, to finish the building for a new owner. The interiors of the main house were finally completed and the couple also designed an 'extension' to the house, which was pushed into the hillside without upsetting the integrity of the original building. Charlee Deaton comments:

> I think my father would have been very pleased with the finished house. We were really appreciative of the opportunity to finish it in the way that it was meant to be, as it is such a strong piece of sculptural design.[3]

The revolving Round House

Another of the great American houses of the future was Richard Foster's Round House in Wilton, Connecticut, which he finished in 1968. Again, this was the architect's own family home, lending Foster the freedom to

Richard Foster – The Round House, Wilton, Connecticut, United States, 1968

experiment. It was a golden opportunity that Foster certainly embraced to the full, creating a building that was both dynamic and kinetic.

During the mid-century period, the idea of living in the round was explored by a number of influential architects, including Arne Jacobsen, who designed his own version of a round house in Denmark, completed in 1957 (see page 156). But Foster's house was not only round – it also rotated upon a central axis, offering an ever-changing perspective upon the New England landscape. Such a concept might sound simple, yet it required an extraordinary level of ingenuity.

Foster studied at the Pratt Institute School of Architecture and graduated in 1950, when he joined Philip Johnson's architectural practice

Staffan Berglund – Villa Spies, Torö, Finland, 1969

(see page 146). He contributed to a number of key Johnson projects during the Sixties, including the New York State Pavilion for the 1964 New York World's Fair, and carried on working with Johnson even after founding his own practice, Richard Foster Associates.

The idea of a rotating house that follows the sun had been tried before, back in the Thirties, when Italian engineer Angelo Invernizzi designed and built the Villa Girasole – or 'Sunflower House' – near Verona. Two motors turned the entire two-storey house on circular tracks, sitting upon a round base station set into a hillside, while at the point where the house pivots Invernizzi added a tower resembling a lighthouse. This was a complex and extraordinary venture, but Foster's design offers a much purer, sculptural form, with the round body of his shingle-coated building perched upon a single slender stem.

Foster found a site on the edge of Wilton, Connecticut, where a drive-way tucked between neighbouring houses led down to a point at which the land began to dip away to the nearby woods, while also looking towards the waters of the local reservoir. This almost bucolic hillside spot, opening up towards the landscape, offered the perfect setting for Foster's own sunflower house. 'The site is a natural amphitheater,' the architect said back in 1968. 'When the idea came to me, the only problem was finding the right parts. As far as I know, this hasn't been done before in any country.'[4]

The stem holds the entrance hall and a spiral staircase, around which the building slowly revolves by a full 360 degrees at the flick of a switch, with a choice of forward and reverse. The 22m- (72ft-) diameter house takes 48 minutes to turn fully, using a ball-bearing mechanism inspired by rotating radar antennae and gun turrets. Given that all the services for the house pass through this core, one of the greatest challenges is how to keep everything connected while the house is in motion, requiring a ring-based electrical circuit that is always in contact with the turning circle and a circular tray for collecting waste water, which is then neatly drained away via a single pipe in the stem. Storage tanks and other services are hidden away in a concealed attic.

Up on the principal level of the house, all of the living spaces and family bedrooms radiate outwards from the central, circular hallway arranged around the stem and the staircase. These spaces flow towards the band of floor-to-ceiling glass that wraps around the house, as well as a circular balcony beyond the glass. This creates a futuristic belvedere, with a continual sense of connection to the landscape enhanced by the choice of movement and a shifting vista, ranging from meadow to woodland to the long view of the lake.

Richard Foster hoped that the idea of kinetic living might catch on, and in this sense the Round House was a kind of prototype. Even if such ideas have remained in the slow lane, there has been a growing interest in the idea of contemporary kinetic houses and buildings, particularly those that follow the sun while drawing in solar energy. Conversely, kinetic systems can also be used to lessen the impact of the sun, reduce overheating and cut down on the need for air conditioning.

But the Round House, which has recently been restored by new owners, did make Foster an architectural celebrity during the late Sixties. As well as newspaper and magazine coverage around the world, the house even appeared in advertisements for bourbon, which offered a tempting vision of the future, best enjoyed with a drink in hand.

Villa Spies, a futuristic lookout station

If the Round House came to define Richard Foster's career, then the same was true of another single house, Villa Spies, designed in the late Sixties by the Swedish architect Staffan Berglund and completed in 1969. He had responded to an architectural competition, launched by the Danish travel and airline entrepreneur Simon Spies, to design 'Bubbles of Pleasure'. Spies's original idea was to create a series of prefabricated holiday homes, which would be dotted throughout the Nordic landscape. He launched an open call for ideas, and the winning entry was Berglund's. The pleasure bubbles never went into production but the flamboyant and somewhat eccentric Spies asked Berglund to translate his ideas into a country escape for himself and his guests, out on the Stockholm archipelago.

Simon Spies set his heart upon a clifftop site on the small isle of Torö, one of the many thousands of islands and islets that make up the archipelago. Like his contemporary Richard Foster, Berglund opted for a circular form. Sitting upon the rocks, it looked out over the sea like a futuristic lookout station, complemented by an adjoining terrace and a bowl-shaped swimming pool (known as the 'bird bath') teetering on the edge of the cliff.

Berglund used a plastic roof, with a central bubble skylight made of translucent fibreglass, to shelter the principal level of the house. This is a largely open-plan living area, facing a bank of floor-to-ceiling windows offering a panoramic view across the archipelago. At the centre of this space was another kinetic element, which offered a neat party trick: at the touch of a button a disc rose magically from the floor to reveal a secret dining pod, complete with integrated table and seating. Period photographs show the magnificently bearded Spies sitting on an Aarnio Bubble chair perched upon the 'roof' of the pod as it rises upwards in grand, theatrical style.

There was a galley kitchen to the rear and sliding doors to the master suite; guest bedrooms were tucked away in the basement. The choice of furniture fitted the Sixties aesthetic, with Italian furniture by Joe Colombo and the Castiglioni brothers. There were also concealed speakers throughout for piped music, motorized sun shades for the windows and slide projectors. This was the ultimate party house and Spies made the most of it. 'He was a wonderful man, with a deep interest in psychology,' said Berglund. 'And he loved nothing better than surprising his guests.'[5]

The combination of the flying-saucer aesthetic and such a dramatic coastal location aroused plenty of curiosity, which is just what Spies wanted. A great marketing man and publicity hound, Spies savoured the image of a Pop Art playboy, and his villa was the ultimate version of a statement home. More than this, it was emblematic of a shift from soft Scandinavian Modernism to the iconoclastic Nordic dynamism of Sixties designers such as Verner Panton, Yrjö Kukkapuro and especially Eero Aarnio, whose fibreglass Pastil chairs from 1967 featured in Spies's home. These were designers who explored the possibilities of plastic to the full while experimenting with ergonomic forms, body-centric shapes and playful Pop Art colours, all feeding into chairs and sofas that looked completely different from anything that had ever come before.

Palais Bulles and other bubble buildings

While Simon Spies wanted to create a collection of houses that were 'bubbles of pleasure', one of Eero Aarnio's most famous designs was known as the Bubble chair (1968), which was made of transparent Perspex in a demi-egg shape and suspended from the ceiling, offering a floating designer-bubble of joy. The idea of the bubble also crossed over into the Space Age concept of capsules, landing pods and UFOs. At the same time, the bubble represented the polar opposite of the linear precision favoured by architects of the International Style, an aesthetic that was still very current during the Sixties and Seventies. Such bubbles were, therefore, countercultural and deliciously avant-garde.

The architectural bubble was taken to a new extreme by the French fashion designer Pierre Cardin and his experimental Hungarian architect, Antti Lovag. Born in Italy, Cardin worked with Elsa Schiaparelli in Paris before founding his own fashion house in 1950. Credited with the invention of both mini and maxi skirts, Cardin was also one of the first designers to build a global brand through perfumes, cosmetics and licensing while stepping across into other disciplines, including car design.

Cardin also took inspiration from the early days of space exploration and the moon missions, even creating a spacesuit design for NASA at one point. His own house near Cannes, in the South of France, has a Space Age surrealism to it, formed from a vast collection of intersecting pods. Palais Bulles, or the Bubble Palace, takes the notion of dynamic architecture to another level entirely.

'I've always been fascinated by circles, spheres and satellites,' Cardin has said. 'When I heard about a project to construct a house entirely out of round surfaces, I knew it would correspond perfectly with my universe.'[6]

The idea of bubble buildings was explored by a handful of architects during the Sixties. They included Pascal Häusermann, Charles Haertling, Jacques Couëlle, Haim Heifetz and Antti Lovag, who worked with Jean Prouvé (see page 175) before starting his own practice in the South of France. Lovag, Couëlle and their close contemporaries were interested in organic architecture and took inspiration from natural forms, yet their buildings were mostly conceived with sculpted concrete, often lending them a decidedly futuristic appearance. Lovag's houses usually consisted of an interconnected set of capsules, or cells, resembling a bee's nest or a cluster of seashells, colonizing the topography of a site. Like Charles Deaton, Lovag argued that curves were made for comfort:

> I began to think about improvised buildings, cobbled together on site and adapted to a particular person's desires or idea of a house. I began experimenting with frameworks that could be bent and changed and with techniques of concrete surfacing. That way, forms could move again.[7]

Rather like Deaton and his Sculptured House, Lovag created lightweight metal meshes and then coated them in concrete. But instead of constructing a single sculptural piece, the architect crafted an entire collection of capsules for Pierre Cardin, punctuated by apertures and sky domes, forming a vast bubble house with multiple blinking eyes. The project was begun in 1975, on a hillside site between Cannes and Saint-Raphaël, looking over the Côte d'Azur. Lovag's original client was an industrialist who died before the house had progressed very far. When Cardin heard about the project, he was soon seduced by the idea and began working with Lovag on the evolution of his maritime palace.

Cardin acquired the house in 1992, extending it on a grand scale (with a swimming pool and outdoor theatre) and designing the interiors. Much of the furniture at Palais Bulles was designed by Cardin himself within an otherworldly aesthetic, which banishes the right angle. Rather like the Sculptured House, which sat comfortably within the 22nd century, there is a cinematic, sci-fi quality to the bubble palace (see page 218). Sometimes it feels like part of a dreamscape, but such buildings offer an alternative architectural reality that remains a valuable source of inspiration for today's advocates of an adventurous attitude to shape and form.

A Brutal World
Concrete Solutions

14   Paulo Mendes da Rocha – Millán House, São Paulo, Brazil, 1970

Alison and Peter Smithson
Upper Lawn
Tisbury, Wiltshire,
England, 1962

Paulo Mendes da Rocha
Millán House
São Paulo, Brazil, 1970

Agustín Hernández
Casa Hernández
Mexico City, Mexico, 1970

Mario Botta
House at Riva San Vitale
Ticino, Switzerland, 1973

Tadao Ando
Koshino House
Kobe, Japan, 1984

During the Sixties and Seventies, Brutalism established itself as the purest and most uncompromising form of modern architecture. Raw, radical and unadulterated, Brutalism was usually expressed in the form of exposed concrete, lending the style a love-it-or-leave-it aesthetic. It was a movement principally associated with high-rises, tower blocks and major cultural buildings, yet it also impacted upon the shape, form and materiality of the modern house.

The term Brutalism first surfaced during the early Fifties when the British architects Alison and Peter Smithson used the phrase 'New Brutalism' to describe a house that they hoped to build in Soho, with an architectural structure that would be exposed and explicit. The Smithsons argued in favour of a design philosophy that allowed the methodology and materiality of a building to be clearly read, with no interference from decorative ornament and little in the way of superficial finishes that might hide the thinking and intent behind it.

The influential architectural critic Reyner Banham soon picked up on New Brutalism and connected it to the *béton brut*, or raw concrete, favoured by Le Corbusier and others. He also linked it to the *art brut*, or raw art, aesthetic pioneered by French artist Jean Dubuffet during the late Forties and early Fifties, which argued for the raw, unfiltered expression of ideas through sculpture and painting. In a famous 1955 essay in the *Architectural Review*, Banham sought to define New Brutalism as a fresh movement, focusing on the work of the Smithsons but placing it in a broader cultural context. In the essay, Banham summarized the qualities of Brutalism as: '1, Formal legibility of plan; 2, clear exhibition of structure, and 3, valuation of materials for their inherent qualities "as found".'[1]

The material in question was, of course, concrete. For many Modernists and for the followers of Brutalism in particular, concrete was the great modern material. Malleable, adaptable and seemingly invincible, concrete made its presence felt in high-rises and superstructures (see page 198) yet was also 'plastic' enough to be shaped and moulded into sculptural forms (see page 208). It helped buildings to be taller, stronger and more dynamic, as well as lifting them into the air on piloti, or pillars, while reinforced concrete skeleton frames enabled curtain (non-load-bearing) walls filled with glass. This was modernity in motion, so why hide its beauty and intent?

Brutalists believed in the 'character' of concrete, as well as its tectonic prowess. Surfaces were left unadorned or lent further texture through bush or pick hammer treatments and incisions that carved into the surface to expose the aggregates within. There was something almost geological to such a process, as well as the strata that cast concrete tended to create upon a building. Concrete set in wooden formwork, or shuttering (moulds made from planks), borrowed the pattern of the grained timber, lending it almost organic personality. It was one of the few materials that managed to engage almost the entire congregation within the Modernist church, from organic architects such as Frank Lloyd Wright to Le Corbusier to Alvar Aalto to Alison and Peter Smithson. But the Brutalists took their passion for *béton brut* to a new extreme.

Upper Lawn, the modern cabin

Flamboyant, outspoken and sometimes a little eccentric, Alison and Peter Smithson met at the School of Architecture in Newcastle (which was then part of Durham University) and, for a short time, were one of the most influential power couples in British architecture and design. They first made their reputation with the design of a secondary school in Hunstanton, in north Norfolk, which was completed in 1954, and they sealed it ten years later with the Economist Building in St James's, London.

The Smithsons' most controversial and divisive project was Robin Hood Gardens (1972) in the London borough of Tower Hamlets. The council housing estate was composed of two long concrete buildings holding just over two hundred flats, overlooking a large communal green space with a small man-made hill and trees. There was a considered mixture of single-level apartments and maisonettes (two-storey apartments), ranging from two to six bedrooms, with echoes of the mix of spaces seen at Le Corbusier's Unité d'Habitation in Marseille (see page 196). The Smithsons also developed the idea of the spacious promenades seen within the Unité d'Habitation, creating their famous 'streets in the sky' situated on every third floor.

The decks of Robin Hood Gardens were intended to be elevated street-scapes that would foster a sense of community, providing spaces to meet, talk and play with other residents. In reality, the design was poorly executed and the build quality low, creating a series of problems that only got worse over time. With their dead zones and blind spots, the communal streets became a magnet for all kinds of antisocial behaviour, including vandalism, while residents also complained of an ongoing lack of privacy. Despite a concerted campaign by Smithson supporters to protect the estate and its architecture, Tower Hamlets eventually decided to tear down Robin Hood Gardens and rebuild, damaging the Smithsons' legacy in the process.

One of the Smithsons' more successful projects was their own country cottage in Wiltshire, which certainly feels a world away from Tower Hamlets. During the late Fifties, the London-based Smithsons bought a small farmstead near Tisbury, complete with a derelict cottage and walled courtyard, surrounded by open fields. Here, they designed a new two-storey cottage (completed in 1962) around the remnants of the old one, including the stone boundary wall separating the site from the farm track alongside, and an old chimney. The architects used a lightweight timber structure, with banks of glass framing the views, together with bands of zinc cladding. There are poured concrete floors on the ground floor, plus an exposed concrete pillar at one corner where the glass windows fold back and retract.

As one might expect, surfaces are raw and unapologetic. Upper Lawn is a kind of modern cabin, in rectilinear form, with a simple wooden ladder linking the two levels. The lower storey features a simple kitchenette and services, while the upper level is an open-plan living area with the best of the views. At first, the Smithsons used to camp out here using roll-up bedding, although a recent update has seen some more 'comforts' added, including a wood-burning stove. On the upper level, the vista of the open fields and distant woodland is the dominant element, framed by the large windows.

There are some crossovers here with the Brutalist aesthetic, particularly in the use of honestly expressed materiality, the legibility of the plan and the clear expression of the structural framework. But just as important was the Smithsons' notion of 'found space'. They first explored this idea within the two 19th-century period houses that served as their London homes, where they slotted themselves and any new services into the existing shells of the buildings while carefully preserving and protecting their original character, which was left as untouched as possible. Similarly, with Upper Lawn, the ghost of the old cottage is still there in the stone walls, the chimney stack and even the old tiled floor in the courtyard, which was once

Alison and Peter Smithson – Upper Lawn, Tisbury, Wiltshire, England, 1962

part of the internal portion of the original farm labourers' house. This approach translates into what we might now call 'adaptive reuse': the recycling of the existing elements of a building rather than erasure of the past.

Mendes da Rocha's Brutalism and Millán House

For all the rural delights of Alison and Peter Smithson's Upper Lawn, it is true that Brutalism established itself as a primarily urban phenomenon during the Sixties and Seventies. Housing projects, museums, campus universities, hospitals, churches and chapels all adopted the Brutalist style, which spread its wings internationally. *Béton brut* was embraced in many different parts of the world, including the Soviet states, India and Japan, where the monumentality of raw concrete superstructures echoed the growing ambition of architects and urban planners.

One of the great epicentres of Brutalism was Latin America, which developed its own powerful take on the aesthetic during the post-war period. Hot spots included Mexico, where Félix Candela (see page 221) established himself as one of the great pioneers of sculpted concrete forms, and also Brazil, where the Paulista school of architecture was intimately associated with the evolving Brutalist aesthetic. This loose collective of like-minded architects, centred upon São Paulo, tended to favour heroic, geometric blocks and linear forms, rather than the dynamic curves associated with Candela and Oscar Niemeyer (see page 208).

The most famous exponent of Paulista Brutalism was Paulo Mendes da Rocha. Having studied at São Paulo's Mackenzie Presbyterian University College of Architecture, Mendes da Rocha opened his own practice in the city in 1955. There were major cultural projects such as the Brazilian Museum of Sculpture (1988) and sacred spaces such as the Chapel of Saint Peter (1987), both in São Paulo. But most striking of all was the way Mendes da Rocha successfully translated monumental Brutalism into a residential style, seen within a series of extraordinary houses designed and built during the Sixties.

Describing his buildings as 'instruments of life', Mendes da Rocha also suggested that 'architecture is a human endeavor inspired by the nature all around us. We must transform nature; fuse science, art, and technology into a sublime statement of human dignity.'[2] In a vast metropolis such as São Paulo, the notion of creating 'instruments of life' that offer dignity, privacy and protection becomes a serious challenge. The architecture of the city has increasingly tended towards a fortress mentality, where houses are hidden away behind high walls and protective boundaries, and there is certainly a strong sense of the fortress in Mendes da Rocha's houses, where nature itself is present but set within secret gardens and secure courtyards. His highly engineered, concrete structures resemble geological forms, like rocks and boulders in the cityscape. In this respect, it's interesting to note the architect's love for the 'unknown architects' who built Stonehenge and the pyramids.

Mendes da Rocha's São Paulo sequence of residential urban fortresses included his own home, completed in 1967. Set upon a small hill and surrounded by a walled garden, the *concretão* (concrete) house is single storey but raised up on reinforced pillars, creating an undercroft hosting a carport and entry sequence. The linear planes and surfaces of the house are bare and exposed, revealing the marks of the timber board shuttering used to support the walls as they rose on site. As per Reyner Banham's definition of Brutalism, the materials are honestly expressed and the entire form and structure are explicitly revealed.

In 1969, Mendes da Rocha completed a house for civil engineer Mario Masetti. Here, again, the architect used the idea of elevation, which reinforces the idea of fortress-like protection, as well as offering a fresh perspective on the cityscape. Vast beams and columns raise the house above terraces and a patio with a swimming pool, while a semi-spiral staircase twists upwards to meet the main entrance to the building. Bands of windows and skylights feel like incisions within this floating cave, while even elements such as the fireplace and shower enclosure are made of raw concrete.

A year later, in 1970, Mendes da Rocha completed another house in São Paulo, for the art dealer Fernando Millán. From the street, Millán House (see page 232) hardly looks like a home at all, with few obvious signals of domesticity. The linear concrete form and closed walls create an enigma, reinforced by the glimpse of an external concrete staircase heading towards the flat roof. Stepping inside the walled compound, the idea of a fortress home remains, with the two-storey building only revealing itself by degrees. There's an entrance courtyard, with verdant planting tucked to one side, and also a semi-sheltered swimming pool on an upper terrace, where the external stairway leads up to a roof garden.

Inside, the entire house is arranged around a central, double-height living room, illuminated by skylights. This part of the *béton brut* building offers an internal focal point, connecting with other parts of the house and overlooked by mezzanine walkways and circulation routes. A spiral staircase to one side of this space links the two floors and offers a sculptural element that slightly softens the raw, linear monumentality of the building. With its unadulterated concrete floors and walls, combined with the top-lighting from the skylights, Millán's living room has the atmosphere of an art gallery. Here, as in Mendes da Rocha's other houses, the building is largely inward-looking, with carefully edited openings and apertures to the outside realm and to the gardens, which are also edited and controlled. Now owned by another gallerist, this is truly a house of extremes.

Casa Hernández, geometry in raw concrete

Mexican architect Agustín Hernández also offers a lesson focused upon extreme living. One of the region's great original thinkers, Hernández combined a love of raw concrete with a passion for epic, gravity-defying structures that splice futurism with references to Mayan cities and their pyramids. Hernández explains his unique approach:

> To be a creator, you have to be original. I tried to be different. I tried to look for a real Mexican architecture, to look for a way to revisit the pre-Hispanic roots of our history. It was about looking for identity and a synthesis of all the different cultures around Mexico and I also love science and science fiction.[3]

As with Mendes da Rocha's work, there is a monumentality that echoes the superstructures of the distant past yet also shows a striking sense of modernity, partly derived from the bold use of bare concrete. But instead of exploring linear forms and fortresses, Hernández is best known for his 'floating machine houses': extraordinary residential sculptures raised above the cityscape of Mexico City upon structural mono-pillars.

Agustín Hernández studied architecture at the National Autonomous University of Mexico, and early commissions included the 1968 Folkloric Ballet School for his sister, the choreographer Amalia Hernández, for whom

Augustin Hernández – Casa Hernández or 'Praxis', Mexico City, Mexico, 1970

the architect also designed a house, completed one year later. There were already suggestions of Hernández's unique philosophy within the design of Casa Amalia, which featured a dramatic, pyramid-shaped living room punctuated with furniture designed by the architect.

Hernández's 'floating machine houses' included the Casa en el Aire ('House in the Air', 1991) in Mexico City, designed for his cousin. With its abstract geometry and sheer monumentality, the building was also enigmatic, resembling a technical facility, scientific laboratory or observatory, sitting on the edge of a steep hillside.

Most famous of all was Hernández's own house and studio, Casa Hernández (also known as Praxis), completed in 1970, which has the look of an angular concrete spaceship hovering above the rugged, sloping topography of Mexico City's Bosques de las Lomas district. A slender concrete tower roots the building into the slope of the hill, while allowing for a degree of movement at times of seismic stress; it has survived a number of earthquakes and tremors unscathed. The angular concrete body of the house, holding two principal levels, is held aloft by the tower above an entry level that connects with the nearby street as it runs along the top of the hill. The complex, angular geometry of the house offers a fusion of squares and triangles expressed in raw concrete. Inside, semi-industrial elements such as the spiral steel staircase, with its individually sprung steps, echo the sense of the architect's home and studio as a kind of machine, yet at the same time the form of the composition is decidedly sculptural, as Hernández confirms:

> My houses do look like sculpture. If you are making architecture, not just construction, then you do have to create a higher level of aesthetics and make it into an art. That's the difference between construction and architecture.[4]

Mario Botta's sculptural House at Riva San Vitale

The concept of a tower house, like Casa Hernández, creates an opportunity to provide a substantial amount of living space upon a small footprint. This has real benefits when a site is difficult to build on and where there's a desire to lessen the physical and environmental impact of a building in a sensitive setting. That was very much the case with another tower house,

Mario Botta – House at Riva San Vitale, Ticino, Switzerland, 1973

the House at Riva San Vitale, in Ticino, Switzerland, designed by the Swiss architect Mario Botta. Here, the setting is a hillside overlooking the waters of Lake Lugano and the mountains beyond, offering the challenge of capturing and celebrating this epic panorama while minimizing the impression of the house upon the landscape.

Mario Botta sits within a proud Swiss Brutalist architectural tradition. Having served an apprenticeship in Lugano, he studied in Milan and Venice, where he worked with Le Corbusier, who was also born in Switzerland. In Venice, Botta worked with Louis Kahn (see page 254), whose ambitious projects of the Sixties and Seventies were monumental in both scale and ambition. Botta established his own practice in 1970, and the House at Riva San Vitale, completed in 1973, played a key part in establishing his reputation in Switzerland and beyond.

The house was commissioned by a family who had known Botta for many years and had previously asked him, when he was still a student, to refurbish an apartment for them. The clients inherited the site overlooking the lake and, from the start, wanted to avoid the traditional pattern of house and garden while creating something fresh and original.

This part of Ticino is populated by many old bird-hunting towers, known as *roccoli*, so the idea of a rural tower was not completely new – yet the form of the house, made with concrete blocks, certainly was. Botta used the bare blocks to create a relatively simple geometric form with a square footprint and four levels. Yet within this outline, he offered a whole range of spaces that were anything but simplistic, with complex shifts in volume as well as the provision of integrated terraces, all sitting within a single monolithic box.

The house is accessed from the brow of the hill, where a distinctive steel-framed bridge, with red paint picking out its metal lattice, stretches out over the slope of the hill to connect with the tower at its uppermost level. Here, there is the main entrance to the house and a studio space but also a terrace looking out towards the open vista. A central staircase leads down to the master suite on the floor below, with the children's bedrooms on a separate level further down, ensuring a degree of privacy for both generations. The bottom level holds the family's social spaces with interconnected kitchen, dining and living areas, as well as another large terrace with openings in the boundary wall to the landscape. A large bank of glass between the terrace and the internal living spaces allows in plenty of light, but also connects with the views.

Again, the approach seems almost sculptural, as though Botta were carving into a solid block of concrete to create the openings and spaces within it. There's a powerful contrast between the feeling of mass offered by the shell of the building and the surprising sense of openness of the spaces within this Brutalist envelope, while the landscape itself offers a constant natural foil to the man-made character of the tower.

The house sits within a particularly Swiss predilection for sculpted Modernist buildings in the Brutalist style, including houses by architects such as Peter Märkli and Wespi de Meuron Romeo Architects. Following the success of the House at Riva San Vitale, Mario Botta himself cemented an international reputation with a portfolio that included a significant number of sacred spaces, such as Évry Cathedral in France (1995), the Chapel of Saint Mary in Ticino (1996) and the Cymbalista Synagogue and Heritage Center in Tel Aviv (1998). The combination of intrinsic materiality and a cohesive minimalist approach to the surfaces of both interior and exterior space lent itself to the sense of meditative restfulness required in such spiritual spaces.

Tadao Ando and the Koshino House

The same is true of the architectural outlook of the great Japanese architect Tadao Ando, who is highly regarded for the pure geometry of the Church on the Water in Hokkaido (1988) and the Church of the Light in Osaka (1989).

Rather like Mario Botta, Tadao Ando began his career designing residential projects, which played a key part in the early evolution of his practice.[5] Having established his atelier in Osaka in 1969, one of Ando's first completed projects was the Tomishima House (1973), which he later bought to use as his architectural office. A few years later, in 1976, he built the concrete Row House in Osaka, which offered a blank wall of concrete to the street but was built around an internal courtyard.

Then, in 1984, came the Koshino House, within a semi-rural setting near the city of Ashiya, in the prefecture of Hyogo, west of Osaka. This hillside 'landscraper', tucked into the sloping topography, also uses concrete to the full, while exploring Ando's ideas of 'site-craft' (his term for the careful blending together of building and site).

For Ando, and many other Brutalists, concrete is a poetic material as well as a tectonic one. It has a character of its own and offers countless possibilities in terms of colour, texture and form, as Ando says:

> Every concrete mix and pour has a different character. It is not like steel or glass, which has a more consistent nature. Concrete can vary greatly. Le Corbusier used concrete as if it were clay. He used its plastic quality almost as if he were sculpting. Louis Kahn used concrete as if were hard steel. The same material – two very different effects.[6]

Ando himself has used concrete walls in a very individual way. For him, concrete creates the opportunity to change and challenge perceptions of space, light and the natural world. Through a process of enclosure, in combination with a minimalist approach to materials and finishes, Ando accentuates the importance of highly edited and finely filtered glimpses of sunlight and nature, as he explains:

> Such things as light and wind only have meaning when they are introduced inside a house in a form cut off from the outside world. The isolated fragment of light and air suggests the entire natural world. The forms I have created have altered and acquired meaning through elements of nature (light and air), which give indications of the passing of time and the changing of the seasons, and through connections with human life.[7]

Through introspection and reduction, Ando focuses on small, quiet moments and sensory experiences that sometimes border on the spiritual or the emotional – offering, as he put it, 'environments that will give people a refreshing new perception of things'.[8] At the Koshino House, which the architect created for a fashion designer, the parallel rectangular blocks that form the house are pushed into the hillside with one holding the main living spaces and another a run of bedrooms. The semi-subterranean situation of the house, and a studio built in 1984, means that every connection with the outside world is carefully controlled: 'The goal was a house in which the power of nature that penetrates it, is made conspicuous by a thorough purification of the architectural elements.'[9]

Such editing, both in form and materials, concentrates the mind. It also offers a polar opposite to the ideal of Californian Modernism (see page 102), where the focus is on maximum connectivity with nature and the dissolution of boundaries between inside and outside space. Like a church or a chapel, narrow shafts of light filter into the house and illuminate the raw textural surfaces of the concrete walls and interiors, which are more than minimalist.

Clearly, there is an overlap between Ando's version of Brutalism and the minimalist aesthetic, as seen at the Koshino House. But the house, along with other Tadao Ando 'landscrapers' such as the Naoshima Contemporary Art Museum (1992), also suggests a way of building in the landscape that mitigates the impact of architectural forms through semi-submersion. It's an idea that has been gaining greater traction over recent years, as architects look for ways to balance architectural interventions with the need to protect and preserve precious landscapes.

Over recent years there has also been a marked resurgence of interest in Brutalism as an aesthetic movement. The style seems to have finally come in from the cold, celebrated in a number of recent books devoted to the subject, while some Brutalist buildings have been updated and repurposed. They include Richard Seifert's landmark Brutalist office building in London, Centre Point, which was a highly controversial addition to the skyline when it was first completed in 1966. Recently converted into residential apartments by Conran and Partners, the distinctive, concrete-clad high-rise is emblematic of the way in which such buildings are being rediscovered and, in some cases, adapted for residential use. In this respect such historical Brutalist buildings have, in themselves, become 'found spaces', as the Smithsons might have put it.

Less is a Bore
Po-Mo & Beyond

15   Robert Venturi – Vanna Venturi House, Philadelphia, Pennsylvania, United States, 1964

Robert Venturi and
Denise Scott Brown
Venturi–Scott Brown House
Philadelphia, Pennsylvania,
United States, 1972

Robert Venturi
Vanna Venturi House
Philadelphia, Pennsylvania,
United States, 1964

Louis Kahn
Esherick House
Philadelphia, Pennsylvania,
United States, 1961

Charles Gwathmey
**Gwathmey Residence
and Studio**
Amagansett, Long Island,
New York, United States, 1965

Ricardo Bofill
La Fábrica
Barcelona, Spain, 1975

Turning their backs upon Mies van der Rohe's famous mantra 'less is more', the disciples of Post-Modernism argued that 'less is a bore'. Coined by the godfather and godmother of Po-Mo, Robert Venturi and Denise Scott Brown, the phrase pointed to the spirit of inclusion that characterizes the movement. Why, they asked, would you limit yourself to Modernism when there was a whole world of architecture and design, both past and present, which might inspire and delight you? Why take such a narrow pathway, when there were so many freeways, railroads and open routes leading in all directions?

Post-Modernism is often presented as a rejection of Modernism. Certainly there was a frustration with the limitations of Modernism, encapsulated in the idea of 'less is more', the fusion of form and function and the sense that ornament is a crime (see page 66). But, as the influential architect and critic Charles Jencks pointed out, Post-Modernism was not just a process of reaction but a process of inclusion, which embraced all kinds of architecture and design, including Modernism, while threading these influences together within something that was new, original and often playful.

The eclectic interior of the Venturi–Scott Brown House

This idea is perhaps best expressed by Robert Venturi and Denise Scott Brown's dining room. Here, in their own home on the edge of Philadelphia, the couple painted the names of their heroes within the band of wall space between the picture rail and the ceiling. These names include many of the masters of Modernist architecture, such as Frank Lloyd Wright, Le Corbusier and Alvar Aalto, who was a particular favourite. But we also have neo-classicists such as John Soane and John Vanbrugh, along with the Baroque architect Francesco Borromini, the Arts & Crafts pioneer Edwin Lutyens, plus Ludwig van Beethoven and Michelangelo, while a smaller band of lettering below offers a second tier of cultural giants, spanning the arts and the centuries.

Robert Venturi and Denise Scott Brown's home carries this idea of open-minded eclecticism even further, offering a powerful case study of 'practising what you preach'. The house itself, in the Art Nouveau style, dates from 1909 and retains many of its original architectural features and interior detailing. The couple painted and stencilled the walls, while layering the house with a mix of furniture, ceramics and art. There are armchairs and sofas from the old Traymore Hotel in Atlantic City, which was torn down in the Seventies at around the same time that Venturi and Scott Brown were first furnishing their home. There are collections of chairs, books, paintings and prints and many other treasures, including neon lights and signage. One of the first things that you see as you walk into the entrance hallway is a McDonald's sign with a pointing arrow, reading 'Welcome'; there's also a Burger King sign just down the hallway, suggesting that other brands might also be available. The library holds a collection of model signage from Las Vegas, framed in Perspex (Plexiglas) containers, offering memory boxes of Venturi and Scott Brown's time researching and writing their pivotal Po-Mo book, *Learning from Las Vegas*, which suggested that 'we learn from the architecture and urbanism of gaming as much as we do from gothic cathedrals'.[1] The house is an amalgamation of thousands of objects and ideas.

'I love the eclectic quality of combining all of these things,' Robert Venturi said. 'We did experiment with certain things in this house, like the patterns on the walls, but that's more about us. We had fun doing all these things.'[2]

'Fun' is an important word. When it comes to our own homes, they are not only high-minded expressions of our own cleverness but places where we should be able to have some fun. This was, the Po-Mos argued, where Modernism went wrong. Where was the room for fun in a steel-framed glass box? Where would you put all the treasures from your travels through time and geography? Surely a house should leave space for self-expression and for play, mixing the low with the high, the instinctive with the intellectual, the passion with the prose. Venturi explained the couple's approach:

> You must learn from the past and your environment. Denise and I are never bored when we travel, even when we take the train between New York and Philadelphia. We look out the window and see beautiful old churches from earlier prosperous blue-collar neighborhoods, great generic industrial loft buildings, very beautiful billboards that enliven the landscape. We learn from gas stations as well as Borromini and Chartres.[3]

Post-Modernists embraced the idea of eclecticism with open arms, throwing out the Modernist rulebook, but only after reading it closely. And, if we are honest, most of our homes are eclectic. Even architectural and aesthetic purists tend to sneak in some treasures from their trips and a few tokens from their adventures. Some of us might collect art, books, vases, ceramics or sculptures. There may be family pieces that we have inherited, which might have travelled down through the centuries. Such pieces are personal, closely treasured and often eclectic. If Po-Mo taught us anything, it was not to worry about it.

Robert Venturi and the Vanna Venturi House

Robert Venturi studied architecture at Princeton University and went on to work with Eero Saarinen (see page 126), with whom he did not feel particularly 'at home'. After Venturi's father became ill, he returned to Pennsylvania and spent 18 months helping to look after the family's fruit-produce business. He worried that he might be trapped, but managed to set himself free and started working with his mentor, Louis Kahn, in Philadelphia. During the late Fifties, Venturi taught at the University of Pennsylvania, where he first met Denise Scott Brown, and after their marriage in 1967 Scott Brown became a partner in an architectural practice that Venturi had founded seven years earlier.

Among Robert Venturi's most influential architectural projects was one of his first: a house in Chestnut Hill, Philadelphia, completed in 1964, for his mother, Vanna Venturi. The Vanna Venturi House (see page 248) managed to fulfil a series of ambitions. Above all, it had to please his mother who, by this point, was a widow living on her own. It needed to offer a suitable setting for her lifestyle, as well as fitting in with the pleasant and leafy suburban surroundings, within a picturesque neighbourhood towards the northern edge of Philadelphia. But, more than this, the commission offered Venturi a golden opportunity to explore his own ideas about architecture within a project that became one of the most important early houses in the Po-Mo canon. Venturi wrote of the house:

> My mother's house was designed for her as an elderly widow, with her bedroom on the ground floor, with no garage because she didn't drive, and for a maidservant and the possibility of a nurse – and

also as appropriate for her beautiful furniture, which I had grown up with. Otherwise she did not make demands on the architect, her son, concerning its program or its aesthetic – she was beautifully trusting.[4]

The resulting house is modestly scaled but layered with a multitude of ideas and points of reference that spilled from Venturi's imagination. The Vanna Venturi residence features many of the familiar touches of the traditional American home, such as the pitched roof, the porch, the stacked chimney and hearth. But all of these things are subtly re-evaluated and subverted within what amounts to a complex process of questioning accepted wisdom, while travelling through the history of architecture within one small house, as Venturi describes:

> It connects with ideas of mine of the time involving complexity and contradiction, of accommodation to its particular Chestnut Hill suburban context, to aesthetic layering I learned from the Villa Savoye, its pedimented roof configuration derived from the Low House of Bristol, Rhode Island, its split pediment derived from the upper pediment of Blenheim Palace, the duality composition derived from the Casa Girasole in Rome and involving explicit applied elements of ornament. But it is a modern house; my mother enjoyed living in it and also entertaining the many young architects who visited it.[5]

As with so much Post-Modern architecture and design, part of the 'fun' lies in the various layers of meaning, which offer a collection of stories within stories. But, at the same time, one does not have to recognize all of the references in order to enjoy the house. An essential part of its playfulness lies in the subversion of expectation and the creation of surprises within the *promenade architecturale* (processional journey or pathway) that carries you towards and through the house. At first glance, the façade looks symmetrical, yet the more you look, the more the surprises gradually reveal themselves: the slightly off-centre chimneypot, the irregular window pattern, the unusual entry sequence where the front door is also off-centre and angled. The games continue inside this house of fun that offered a Post-Modern manifesto in miniature.

Louis Kahn and Esherick House

One of the key differences between Robert Venturi's early work and the portfolio of his mentor, Louis Kahn, surrounded the question of monumentality. Kahn was always a difficult architect to categorize, which some might argue makes him decidedly Post-Modern, yet others identify him as a free-spirited Modernist and still others call him a Brutalist. It's a free choice, but it's certainly fascinating to compare and contrast the Vanna Venturi House with Kahn's Esherick House, which is – quite literally – five minutes' walk away.

Kahn was something of an architectural outsider, yet at the same time his work has been hugely influential, particularly for younger generations of architects. His family had moved from Estonia to the United States and settled in Philadelphia, which was a constant presence in his life even when Kahn was working internationally in the last decades of his career. The family struggled financially, but Kahn showed an early talent for the arts and won a scholarship to the University of Pennsylvania. During the Twenties and Thirties, he worked for a number of architectural practices before founding his own office in 1935. During the late Twenties, he took a formative grand tour around Europe, including trips to Italy and Greece, and also a visit to Egypt, and he was seduced by the scale and grandeur of ancient and classical architecture.

It was this journey, in part, that led Kahn to question the orthodoxy of the International Style and begin searching for a design philosophy of his own that sought to reinterpret the ambitious monumentality of the past. He wrote:

> No architect can rebuild a cathedral of another epoch, embodying the desires, the aspirations, the love and hate of the people whose heritage it became. Therefore the images we have before us of monumental structures of the past cannot live again with the same intensity and meaning. Their faithful duplication is unreconcilable. But we dare not discard the lessons these buildings teach, for they have the common characteristics of greatness upon which the buildings of our future must, in one sense or another, rely.[6]

Louis Kahn – Esherick House, Philadelphia, Pennsylvania, United States, 1961

As Kahn's career slowly progressed, not helped by his uncompromising character and unwavering passion for his architectural principles, his buildings increasingly sought to find this kind of 'greatness'. They included the Salk Institute for Biological Studies in La Jolla, California (1965), the Indian Institute of Management in Ahmedabad, India (1974) and a 20-year project to design the new National Assembly Building of Bangladesh at Dhaka, which was only completed a decade after his death. These were vast projects, which explored not only questions of light and scale but also materiality and form, with Kahn exploring complex geometries while often adding surprises and moments of asymmetrical irreverence that were provocative and playful.

Kahn eventually achieved monumentality and a kind of architectural immortality. But it was at great personal cost, with constant money worries and a deeply complex personal life that encompassed three partners and three separate families. His body was found in March, 1974, in a restroom at Penn Station in New York, where he had paused en route to Philadelphia after returning from a working trip to India. It took three days for police to identify one of the greatest 20th-century architects in the world, and it later transpired that, at the time of his death from a heart attack, he was deeply in debt and close to bankruptcy.

Like many of his contemporaries, much of Kahn's early work was focused on houses and housing. Louis Kahn's client in Chestnut Hill was an independent woman, living on her own, who owned and ran a bookstore in the neighbourhood. Like Vanna Venturi nearby, she wanted a house that was fully tailored to her needs and to the setting. Margaret Esherick bought herself a parcel of land, which was the last to be built upon in this quiet cul-de-sac, looking out onto a large rear garden bordered by woodland.

Completed in 1961, the Esherick House manages to explore, on a relatively limited suburban footprint, some of the architectural ideas that Kahn took to fresh extremes in the years that followed. Constructed with cement blocks, which were smoothly rendered, the two-storey house is relatively closed to the street but opens up towards the rear garden. Rather like the Vanna Venturi House, the linear building appears symmetrical at first glance, yet this expectation is constantly subverted both without and within, as seen in the irregular window pattern and the overall proportions of the building. At the same time, the house has a strong presence and a monumentality that comes not from its scale but from the strength and clarity of the composition, which stands out against the backdrop of the woods beyond.

Inside, Kahn examined ideas about 'served' and 'servant' spaces, creating a double-height 'great room' at one end, complemented by a series of smaller, 'servant' spaces in the other portion of the building, which is arranged over two levels. One of the most striking elements of the house – which has been lovingly restored and furnished by new owners – is the level of craftsmanship seen in the joinery throughout, with the character of the wooden floors, bookcases and other integrated elements creating a constant feeling of warmth. The bespoke kitchen, made by Margaret's uncle Wharton Esherick, who was a good friend of Kahn's, is a particular delight, combining artisanal craftsmanship with space-saving ingenuity. There are echoes of this upstairs, where the only bedroom suite offers fitted features such as a window seat and storage cupboards, while the bathroom alongside has a secret bathtub hidden under a push-in, pull-out sofa positioned by a fireplace.

Designed according to Margaret Esherick's needs, while connecting vividly with the woods and gardens, the house is thoughtful as well as original. It seems tragic that Esherick herself had so little time to enjoy her new home, succumbing to pneumonia just a year after the house was finished. On a happier note, it is reassuring to see how well the house has endured, in every sense, and how it brings such pleasure to its current occupants.

Twists and turns in the Gwathmey Residence and Studio

During the Sixties many younger architects began to question both conventional pitch-roofed traditionalism and the linear precision of the International Style (see page 122). Prominent among these were a handful of contemporaries labelled the 'New York Five' by curators and critics. They were initially described as Modernists, but each one developed a very distinctive variant upon Modernism.

The 'New York Five' included Michael Graves, who embraced Post-Modernism wholeheartedly, and the architect Peter Eisenman, who became a radical Deconstructivist and sought to challenge conventional concepts of architectural space in a bid to 'reconceptualize architecture'. Of the others, Richard Meier is best known for the purity of his crisp, white compositions, while John Hejduk moved into academia and established himself as a respected theorist with a strong interest in symbolic forms. The fifth was Charles Gwathmey.

Gwathmey's first project, a house for his parents on Long Island, which was completed in 1965, was arguably his most fascinating and original piece of architecture (see page 6). In his own way, Gwathmey challenged preconceived ideas of what a house should look like and how it should be ordered, creating a home composed of two separate, sculptural elements dancing upon an open meadow.

After studying architecture at the University of Pennsylvania and then at Yale, followed by his own European tour, Gwathmey started working in the New York office of architect Edward Larrabee Barnes. But then Gwathmey was offered a dream commission by his parents: his father, Robert, who was an artist, and his mother Rosalie, a documentary photographer turned textile designer. During the early Sixties, when the South Fork of Long Island was still the preserve of potato farmers and painters, Gwathmey's

Charles Gwathmey – Gwathmey Residence and Studio, Amagansett,
Long Island, New York, United States, 1965

parents managed to buy nearly 0.5 hectare (1 acre) of land, not far from the sea, near Amagansett. Having bought the site, they were left with a budget of around $35,000 to build a house. Charles Gwathmey explained how he managed to make that figure work:

> When I put the house out to local contractors the lowest price was $65,000. So I quit my job at Edward Larrabee Barnes, applied for a teaching position at the Pratt Institute and brought over three craftsmen from Brooklyn to East Hampton and I became the contractor. We built the house for $35,000.[7]

Rather like the house that Robert Venturi created for his mother in Chestnut Hill, Philadelphia, Gwathmey managed to concentrate a wealth of thinking into this one small building. He had originally hoped to build with concrete, but the budget wouldn't allow it, so he opted for timber instead and managed to create a house on three levels with constant shifts in volume and form. On the ground floor there's a guest bedroom and a small studio for Rosalie, as well as an external staircase leading to a deck alongside the great room at mid-level. This is a spacious double-height room, with a kitchen to one side plus a mezzanine level above holding the master bedroom, which – as the highest point in the house – offers glimpses of the ocean.

As well as the many volumetric twists and turns, there are constant experiments with geometry. Gwathmey subverts the box-like essence of the plan by cutting into it and grafting on the cylindrical forms that hold the internal and external stairways. At the top of the house, a periscope window and a spouting chimney question the clean, straight line of the roof. Rather like the Esherick House, the Gwathmey Residence is subversive, taking a familiar geometrical outline and playing with it. This playfulness carries on with little splashes of bright colour here and there that shine out against the grey timber.

There is also a sculptural level of abstraction to the house, which was accentuated when the architect's parents asked him, a year later, to add a companion building. Set a small distance away, across the lawn, Robert Gwathmey's studio is a smaller building but uses the same materials and ideas. The result is a kind of mother and child, each enriching the other. Charles Gwathney described how he saw the house:

I designed and built it in a 'naïve' spirit of being unencumbered, uncontaminated and committed to a modern ethic. The house is as compelling today as it was in 1965. There is an irrefutability about its integrity and sculptural presence, spatial variation, clarity and balance of solid and void.[8]

Gwathmey's commitment to the house was unwavering. Like a great first novel, it launched the architect's career and established him as an original voice. When his parents passed away, Gwathmey moved into the house himself, along with his wife, and lived there happily for many years.

Bofill and La Fábrica

In Barcelona, the pioneering Spanish Post-Modernist Ricardo Bofill launched his career at around the same time as Charles Gwathmey and the other members of the 'New York Five'. Bofill began with a series of apartment buildings during the early to mid-Sixties and rapidly established a reputation not just for innovative fusions of aesthetic influences and points of inspiration but also for, like Louis Kahn, an ability to work on projects of extraordinary scale and complexity.

Bofill studied architecture in his native city of Barcelona and in Geneva before founding his practice, Taller de Arquitectura, in 1963. His 1968 apartment building at Sitges, near Barcelona, known as Kafka's Castle, resembles a surreal collection of interconnected cubes, stacked like a vast pyramid, but interlaced with courtyards and balconies. His Xanadú apartment on Spain's Costa Blanca (1971) was another sculptural tower of inter-connected forms rather like a great amalgamation of houses pushed together and painted in moss green. Both projects drew inspiration from the idea of a 'Plug-In City', first promoted by the English practice Archigram, providing a community in miniature formed of modular units attached to a central structural framework (not unlike Eduardo Longo's conceptual framework for his Casa Bola apartment blocks, see page 182).

In these projects and others that followed, Bofill was able to combine avant-garde concepts with vernacular references, classical elements and sometimes local materials, as seen in the Meritxell Sanctuary in Andorra (1976), constructed with local slate. Other projects, such as the Muralla

Ricardo Bofill – La Fábrica, Barcelona, Spain, 1975

Roja apartment block on the Costa Blanca (1973), referenced ancient citadels and fortresses, while adding plenty of Barragán-esque pink paintwork (see page 207). Such work takes into account the playful and the experimental but also contextual concerns. By the Eighties, Bofill was exploring more explicit neo-classical and historical references, particularly within his French mass housing schemes. One of his most ambitious Spanish social housing projects, Walden 7 (1975), also known as the 'kasbah', fuses the idea of a Mediterranean citadel with utopian ideals of a futuristic city-state drawn from science fiction.

Ricardo Bofill's own home and studio, on the outskirts of Barcelona, is another prime example of unfettered imagination applied on a monumental scale. In 1973, the architect began the ambitious process of transforming a former cement factory into a space for both living and working. Like many of Bofill's projects, La Fábrica has the feeling of a dreamscape and a cinematic sense of impossibility. The decision to purchase a factory of over

31,000 sq m (330,000 sq ft) with the idea of turning it into a home seems, in itself, a fantasy. Bofill explained his motivation:

> In the Renaissance and Baroque periods, somebody would turn up and add a new bit to an existing building that remained in place. I wanted to repeat this experience, only not with a normal building, but the most complicated one, a cement factory. Seduced by the contradictions and the ambiguity of the space, I decided quickly to retain the factory and, modifying its original brutality, sculpt it like a work of art.[9]

The project, which was completed in 1975, saw Bofill and his team carving into the concrete silos and spaces of the factory, within a process of sculpting and editing, which included demolishing a significant proportion of the factory. But, at the same time, there were also occasional anachronistic additions, such as the stumps of neo-classical columns used to frame one of the entrances to the complex. Also, Bofill relied on nature to help him soften the harsh, industrial character of La Fábrica with trees and planting, courtyards and terraces. Bofill recounts:

> We first occupied the silos as both private and work spaces, but the need of additional space for the studio made me reconsider the convenience of separating my private life and my professional activity. I then decided to move my home to the building at La Fábrica.[10]

The heart of the atelier is 'The Cathedral': an epic central hall or atrium, complete with a supersized meeting table; a grand piano sits at the far end and yet appears dwarfed within the space. Many remnants of the factory's industrial processes still remain, including vast hoppers and gantries. Bofill's own private quarters balance open space with more intimate areas carved into the factory; the dining room, for instance, features a band of arched windows and dining room furniture by Charles Rennie Mackintosh (see page 29). As Bofill has said, La Fábrica represents a radical fusion of different styles and aesthetics: 'minimalism, romanticism, historicism, classicism and high tech'. This is, in itself, a useful definition of Post-Modernism.

At its most successful, Post-Modern architecture was not about designing without rules but rather was a movement built on a thoughtful and disciplined referencing of aesthetic styles and structural solutions drawn from many centuries of historical precedent. But things did start to go wrong when some Po-Mo architects and designers began to think that anything goes and veered off into pastiche. The thoughtful designer has an answer to every question concerning the how and why of any aesthetic decision, but as time went by this was undermined by architects who simply began to plunder the archives of architectural history with little or no rationale.

Corporate Post-Modernism was especially troubling, with companies and institutions adopting mash-up styles simply because they thought it showed they were progressive and interesting. In the entire history of architecture, however, nothing has dated quite so quickly as the Po-Mo office building, hotel or bank. The playful qualities of the Post-Modern style did not sit well with such serious-minded businesses and, within the space of 20 years, a poorly conceived Post-Modern office block or chain hotel looked little more than ridiculous.

Arguably, Post-Modernism was at its best when it came to house and home. Po-Mo architects and designers showed us that there was not a single way of doing things, nor a single aesthetic style to chain ourselves to. Venturi, Scott Brown and others reminded us that eclecticism was good, not bad. They reassured us that it was okay to keep our grandmother's favourite chair in our glass house, if that's what we wanted. In the sense that Po-Mo was pro-choice, they offered us the power to make our own decisions.

High-Tech
The New Wave

16   Future Systems – Malator, Druidston, Pembrokeshire, Wales, 1998

Richard Rogers
Rogers House
Wimbledon, London,
England, 1969

Jan Benthem
Benthem House
Almere, Netherlands,
1984

Michael and Patty Hopkins
Hopkins House
Hampstead, London,
England, 1976

Future Systems
Malator
Druidston, Pembrokeshire,
Wales, 1998

Scott Tallon Walker
Goulding House
Enniskerry, Ireland, 1972

During the late Sixties and early Seventies a new kind of architecture began to emerge, focused initially on Britain and Europe. There was a strong sense of diverging paths around this time, with one signpost pointing towards Post-Modernism (see page 250) and another suggesting a very different direction, marked 'high-tech'. While the Post-Modernists embraced the idea that 'less is a bore' and drew upon a broad range of influences and points of inspiration, the advocates of high-tech built primarily upon the lessons of innovative post-war Modernists, particularly the North American pioneers of lightweight, steel-framed houses and buildings.

Many high-tech architects looked to the examples of Mies van der Rohe's American masterpieces, such as the Farnsworth House of 1951 (see page 140), with its exposed steel framework and glass walls, but also referenced the work of a number of Californian mid-century innovators (see page 102). The Case Study House Program, especially, and its architects were a key source of ideas when it came to the challenge of creating houses that were open and adaptable. Case Study Houses by Charles and Ray Eames, Pierre Koenig and Craig Ellwood – published in the pages of *Arts & Architecture* magazine, which promoted these buildings as exemplars – featured lightweight but superstrong skeletal steel frames. With the entire structural weight of the house carried by this framework, the curtain walls, free of any load-bearing function, could be filled with glass, drawing in light and creating a vivid indoor–outdoor relationship.

British high-tech architects, such as Richard Rogers, Norman Foster and Michael and Patty Hopkins, were well aware of the possibilities offered by such finely engineered, lightweight buildings. Rogers and Foster first met at the Yale School of Architecture in 1962, where they were both architectural students with scholarships for post-graduate study, and spent some time travelling across the United States while looking and learning along the way. Yet the fame of both Mies van der Rohe's work and the growing influence of the Case Study House Program during the early Sixties meant that such buildings crossed the Atlantic in any case and made themselves known.

For this new wave of idealistic young architects, the high-tech approach offered many advantages, especially when it came to designing houses. The buildings themselves were highly adaptable, allowing their designers the ability to configure living spaces at will, unhindered by any concerns about navigating around internal load-bearing walls or pillars. Using industrially made and factory-produced steelwork meant that costs could also be reduced compared with building in brick, stone or even concrete, which made good architecture potentially more accessible.

Together with flexibility and affordability, British and European high-tech architects and designers also added some ideas of their own to the mix. To enhance the malleability of the open space within their buildings, high-tech architects began taking elements like piping and vents to the exterior and adding them to the envelope, particularly on large-scale projects such as Rogers's and Renzo Piano's Pompidou Centre in Paris (1977). Rogers, Michael Hopkins and others were also tempted to lighten the semi-industrial character of their buildings with bold splashes of colour, as seen at the Pompidou.

High-tech, one-off houses offered architects the equivalent of laboratory space, enabling them to experiment with these ideas on a relatively small scale. Yet the tectonic systems and principles initially applied to a number of pioneering houses could then be radically scaled up to create super-sheds such as Norman Foster's Sainsbury Centre for Visual Arts in Norwich, England (1978), or Michael and Patty Hopkins's Greene King Brewery Draught Beer Cellars in Suffolk, England (1980). These used similar combinations of steel superstructures and 'structural expressionism', as high-tech was sometimes called, where the engineering and mechanics of the building were openly exposed and purposefully expressed. In this way, high-tech offers a prime example of the way in which innovative ideas that were explored within residential architecture affected not only the evolution of the home itself, but also other kinds of architectural typologies such as galleries and supersized service centres.

Rogers House, built from off-the-shelf elements

After Richard Rogers and Norman Foster returned from America, they formed a short-lived practice with Su Brumwell and Wendy Cheesman known as Team 4. One of the firm's most famous projects was Creek Vean (1966), a house in Cornwall for Su Brumwell's parents. Built on a hillside, largely using concrete blockwork, the house took three years to complete. Soon after that, in 1967, the practice was dissolved.

Richard Rogers – Rogers House, Wimbledon, London, England, 1969

Having established his own practice in the late Sixties, one of Richard Rogers's first solo commissions was for another house and, this time, it was for his own parents. Dr Nino and Dada Rogers had emigrated from Italy to England in 1939, settling in Surrey, but eventually decided that they would like to build a single-storey home of their own, which would also be suitable for their retirement years. Having found a leafy setting in suburban south London, they asked their son to design a house for the two of them that would also have enough space for a consulting room for Dr Rogers and a pottery studio for the architect's mother. Richard Rogers describes the background to the commission:

They were pretty clear about what they wanted. It was their last house and they moved in when they were in their sixties. They wanted single storey, so there wouldn't be any stairs to go up and down and they wanted to be within easy walking distance of Wimbledon village centre and the Common, as well as having somewhere where they could do some gardening. They also had some magnificent Thirties furniture from Italy, which was strongly influenced by the Bauhaus.[1]

Richard Rogers designed Rogers House, also known as 22 Parkside, in two distinct parts while making the most of the narrow infill site, which used to be part of the garden belonging to a neighbouring house. Towards the nearby road, he created a small steel-framed pavilion with space enough for both a small studio and a flexible area that could serve as either a consulting room or a guest bedroom. Rogers positioned the main house further back on the site, beyond a courtyard, but using the same architectural language. Here, again, the house is steel-framed with a flat roof and floor-to-ceiling glass windows to the garden, while the side walls are largely closed. This arrangement, with the studio pavilion acting as a kind of buffer between the main house and the public realm, helped to enhance the sense of seclusion. In addition, it offered an outdoor room in the form of a semi-sheltered courtyard, complemented by a larger rear garden. The positioning of the two elements also meant that Rogers could make the most of the transparency and light offered by the big banks of glass without worrying about questions of privacy.

As well as creating an open sense of connection with the gardens through the glass curtain wall, the steel framework created fluid internal space. At the heart of the house was an open-plan living area, with room enough for dining and seating zones. A run of half-height units helped shelter a compact galley kitchen to one side of this space, while to the other side two separate bedrooms shared a bathroom sitting between them. The exposed steel framework of both the house and the pavilion was picked out in vivid yellow paint, singing out against the greenery of the garden while underlining the clear, lucid structural system. Rogers explains:

It's an open frame made up of elements that could be bought 'over the counter', with standard steel joints and prefabricated panels made with very high insulation levels. It was built with components that were ready made and very much a prototype. You can make a direct link from the Wimbledon house to the Pompidou Centre. It's all there: the exposed steel frame, the bright colours and it's about flexibility and adaptability. The idea was that the house could easily grow as well as change.[2]

This has certainly proved to be the case. After serving Dr and Mrs Rogers, the house was then a home for the architect's son, designer Ab Rogers, and his young family. Having been gifted by the family to the Harvard Graduate School of Design, the fully restored building now hosts students as part of a residency programme. Each transition has been a natural process, helped by the versatility of the original design.

The infinitely versatile Hopkins House

Versatility was also at the heart of the plan for another influential high-tech London house, completed in 1976. Situated on a north London street dominated by traditional period houses, Michael and Patty Hopkins's house is quite easy to miss, even if it is one of the most innovative, modern buildings of its time. Given the topography of Hampstead, which slopes down towards Belsize Park, the site itself is lower than the street it sits upon, so even though the building is two-storey, only one of the storeys is visible from the road, and even this is tucked away behind a hedge and planting. Despite its distinctive, uncompromising character, the Hopkins House also manages to be very discreet.

The project came at an important moment for the Hopkins family and the evolution of Michael and Patty Hopkins's own architectural practice. Michael Hopkins had been working in partnership with Norman Foster, and collaborating on the design of another influential high-tech building, the Willis Building, headquarters of Willis Faber & Dumas in Ipswich, completed in 1975. The next year, Michael and Patty Hopkins decided to launch Hopkins Architects together. Around the same time, the couple, who had three children by this point, found that they were bursting out of the family home in Highgate, north London, and needed more space. The solution was to design and build a flexible home that would also offer enough space for the new architectural practice. Patty Hopkins explains the background:

Michael and Patty Hopkins – Hopkins House, Hampstead, London, England, 1976

In the mid-Seventies there was a property slump and you could buy sites in places like Hampstead, which was a dream. The site we found was a former garden plot, which used to have a studio and garage linked to the house next door, and a pair of brick houses had already been designed so we bought the site with that permission in place. And we definitely wanted to build a steel-framed house – that came very early on. We were keen on things like the Eames House and the Farnsworth House, so those things were in our minds. It all fell into place.[3]

Having sold their house in Highgate to buy the land, the two architects were left with a small budget to build with. They went back to the local planners with an idea for a lightweight, steel-framed building, which would be closed to the sides but would open up to the rear garden especially, with banks of floor-to-ceiling glass on both levels. Patty Hopkins continues:

We decided to expose the frame and create a grid. It's not a very big house and we wanted it to flow, so we only designed a few solid partitions and blinds that we used as partitions, as we wanted to see how it would work. It was very open plan.[4]

The architects placed the practice in an open studio on the upper level, which also holds the main entrance, accessed from the street by a small steel bridge. The family spaces were originally all downstairs, including the kitchen, living areas, bedrooms and shower rooms, while this part of the building feeds out to a terrace and the back garden. Michael and Patty Hopkins managed the project themselves, reducing the number of component parts as far as possible and keeping the costs down, with the steel frame and glass walls costing around £20,000. The flat roof was in standard asphalt, while elements such as the spiral staircase were prefabricated and then installed on site. Teflon coating was used on the metal panels at the side of the house and Melamine internally, helping to ensure that the house would be low maintenance.

Malleability was at the heart of the Hopkinses' thinking, with the ability to easily alter the function and use of various parts of the building simply by adjusting the partitions within the grid. Initially, the house was a valuable base for the practice and a showcase for Hopkins Architects' high-tech design approach. But, as the firm began to grow, the practice moved to custom-designed offices and the family was able to reclaim the upper portion of the house. Later still, as the children grew up, the house adjusted again to accommodate the needs of a couple living on their own, which Patty Hopkins feels it does well:

> The flexibility of it was very successful, but also the transparency. When I'm here on a nice day, it is really exciting to have that sense of connection to the outside and a great garden. All our early buildings were actually steel-framed, including more rural buildings like the Greene King Brewery.[5]

Scott Tallon Walker and Goulding House

This sense of malleability was a vital element in the growing appeal of high-tech, grid-based buildings like the Hopkins House. Superstrong but relatively light, steel-framed buildings were suited to a whole range of contexts and situations. At the same time, the simplicity of these skeleton structures and the openness of the internal areas within them created all kinds of opportunities to shape space at will.

One of the most dramatic examples of a high-tech home in a rural setting is the Goulding House in County Wicklow, Ireland, which is a versatile building in every respect. Completed in 1972, this steel-framed, linear pavilion cantilevers outwards over the rustling waters of the River Dargle but, anchored on the elevated bank of the river, also sits among the tree canopy. Surrounded by the shifting colours of the leaves and woods, framed by banks of glass, the pavilion has the feeling of a tree house immersed in nature.

This summer pavilion was commissioned by the Irish businessman Sir Basil Goulding as an addition to his country estate near Enniskerry. A keen cricketer, art collector and one of the founders of the Contemporary Irish Art Society, Goulding made his fortune in the family fertilizer business. He met his aristocratic English-born wife, Valerie Monckton, at the Fairyhouse Races in County Meath, and she went on to devote much of her working life to developing remedial clinics for polio victims.

The Gouldings wanted to build a summerhouse on their estate, yet at the same time they were worried about doing anything that might detract from the beauty of their gardens, which were a source of pride and joy. Their architect, Ronald Tallon, came up with a solution that took the pavilion away from the gardens and instead suspended it over the river, as he explained:

> They wanted a retreat from the rain, a place to confer and to party but without taking a single inch away from the gardens. To achieve this, the only site was over the gorge, so as not to disturb the banks of the glen or the river below.[6]

Ronald Tallon, one of the partners at the famous Irish practice Scott Tallon Walker, was another great admirer of Mies van der Rohe and especially the Farnsworth House. The architect's own Tallon House (1970), at Foxrock, a suburb of Dublin, was a single-storey, steel-framed pavilion with a long band of windows leading to a verandah and the garden. The Scott Tallon Walker practice also had form when it came to the idea of elevation, with

Scott Tallon Walker – Goulding House, Enniskerry, Ireland, 1972

another partner, Robin Walker, responsible for a concrete-framed house known as the O'Flaherty House (1965), which floats on stilts over a steep hillside above the River Bandon and Kinsale Harbour. The Goulding House can be seen as an agile fusion of the Miesian Tallon House and the floating form of the O'Flaherty House.

With assistance from the structural engineers Ove Arup & Partners, the single-storey Goulding summerhouse was designed to incorporate five bays, with the first two of these positioned landward, where the pavilion was accessed from the garden. Further along, two steel legs anchored to the bedrock helped to support the cantilever, as the other three bays headed out into the void over the sloping bank and the water below. Cross-bracing helps strengthen the building, which was partially covered in cedar panels to the sides. A service core near the entrance holds a kitchenette and bathroom but also acts as a kind of buffer zone, which enhances the sense of anticipation as you then walk around it towards the *pièce de résistance*: the open-plan living area hovering over the River Dargle, with floor-to-ceiling glass supported by the exposed skeletal steel providing a panorama over the treetops. Ronald Tallon described the structure:

> When the steel structure was being erected, the clients got excited and requested a glass floor so they could see the river below. But after consultation it was agreed that it would detract from the original concept. On the opening night, we danced on the outer space of the cantilever and I was surprised how well sprung the floor was.[7]

The Goulding summerhouse, which was later restored by the practice for new owners, was the ultimate high-tech belvedere, sitting lightly on the land while enhancing the experiential pleasure of seeing the seasons turn and enjoying the changing colours of the leaves, along with the way that the light and shadows gently drift over the course of the year. It proved that high-tech was not just an urban phenomenon.

Jan Benthem's Fantasie House

Many high-tech architects saw a significant overlap between their own interest in innovative structural building systems and the subject of prefabrication. Their architectural heroes were prefab pioneers such as Richard Buckminster Fuller and Jean Prouvé (see pages 171 and 175), while many high-tech projects involved certain key ingredients that were factory made, including steel frames that were bolted together on site like jigsaw puzzles, but also elements such as insulated wall panels and staircases, as seen in the Hopkins House. High-tech prefabs offered the possibility of building well-designed homes more cheaply and, therefore, making them more affordable for a wider audience.

Jan Benthem – Benthem House, Almere, Netherlands, 1984

In the Netherlands, architect Jan Benthem designed an experimental house for himself and his family that explored this crossover between high-tech construction and the ambition of creating homes that could potentially be replicated and mass-produced. Having graduated from Delft University of Technology in 1978, he had co-founded an architectural practice in Amsterdam the next year and had entered an 'Unusual Homes' competition known as De Fantasie, looking for prototypical and progressive homes that could, in theory, be rolled out across large-scale housing schemes. The winning architects would each be granted a parcel of land within the new city of Almere, built on reclaimed land near Amsterdam. The catch was that the land would be lent rather than given, meaning that the houses had to be temporary and easy to dismantle. In other words, after a period of five years they would have to either be moved to another site or be recycled, meaning that they needed to touch the canal-side setting as lightly as possible. On the other hand, the temporary nature of the buildings meant that they were free of the usual planning regulations. Benthem explains the parameters:

I wanted to design the most simple house that I could think of. The first idea was to make it light and strong, given that normal piling foundations were not allowed, and leave out everything that was unnecessary not only in the plan but also in the materials and detailing.[8]

Fittingly for a waterside setting, the house that Benthem designed has something of the look and feel of a futuristic houseboat, lightly anchored to the ground by a lattice of interconnected steel struts that lift the entire single-storey home upwards by around eight steps, or 1.8m (6ft). Elevating the building like this enhances the sense of lightness, while also helping to protect against flood risk.

Completed in 1984, Benthem House (also sometimes called Almere House or House De Fantasie) was prefabricated using a light steel frame plus a system of tension cables for added strength and support. Simple gantry-style ladders, of the kind that might be used to board a ship, reach up to the main body of the house, which features a band of floor-to-ceiling reinforced glass towards the front, overlooking the canal but also connecting with a simple balcony. The rear portion of the residence is more enclosed, and here the building is coated in panels made up of layers of plywood and insulating foam. These are painted a vivid green, allowing the house to sit discreetly among the trees. 'The house was prefabricated because that was the best means of getting the lightest and strongest materials and to be able to build it myself in a very short time,' Jan Benthem says.[9]

Inside, the semi-marine theme continues. The front portion of the house is fully open-plan, with zones for work, sitting, eating and sleeping only defined by the position of the furniture, which can easily be moved. Towards the rear, there is a bulkhead punctuated by rounded ship-style doorways leading to compartments, which hold the compact kitchen and bathroom plus two cabins for the children.

For Benthem himself, the project was a way of focusing his own high-tech architectural approach, even though the house was neither replicated nor rolled out. But, after five years, Benthem's family home was given a happy reprieve: all the prizewinning houses were given permission to stay.

Over the intervening years, nature had taken hold of the reclaimed land around them, which had transformed into green parkland intersected with waterways, enhancing the pleasure of living there.

Malator, aka the 'Teletubby House'

The legacy of high-tech remains strong. Steel-framed structures are now standard practice for many kinds of buildings, especially super-sheds such as warehouses and airport buildings. But lightweight steel skeletons continue to be used for houses as well, adding another option to the list of more familiar materials such as brick, stone, timber and concrete. The combination of versatility and transparency makes high-tech structures a tempting choice for residential architects and designers, especially when it comes to challenging or unusual locations.

Jan Kaplicky and Amanda Levete, the principals of the highly original practice Future Systems, fused their grounding in high-tech architecture with an open-minded and experimental approach to form, as seen, for instance, in their sculpted Selfridges Building (2003) in Birmingham, England. Both Kaplicky and Levete had worked with Richard Rogers before Future Systems, while Kaplicky had also spent time in Norman Foster's office.

During the mid-Nineties the practice was approached by the barrister, author and politician Bob Marshall-Andrews with an almost impossible task. For many years Marshall-Andrews and his wife had owned a simple timber cabin on the Pembrokeshire coast in Wales, within the National Park. The cabin, which was a former army barracks, was beginning to deteriorate and the couple wanted to replace it with a new house. But given the beauty and sensitivity of the landscape, both the architects and their clients realized that an inventive solution would be needed that would make the least possible impact upon the site.

Kaplicky and Levete's answer was to partially submerge the house in the undulating clifftop topography and then run a grass roof over the top of it so that it would be almost invisible. Yet the home also needed to open up to the views. So, Future Systems created a relatively modest glass entrance to the rear and then a larger steel-framed glass lens, like a giant's eye, facing the sea. This oculus is dotted with smaller porthole windows, which can be opened to bring in fresh air.

Inside, the central portion of the house is open, with a semicircular seating area arranged around a circular wood-burning stove. Two prefabricated curving pods sit to either side of this central space, holding the bathrooms and also a kitchenette, while partitioning off the two bedrooms, which are at opposite ends of the house, where the building tucks into the hillside.

Malator (see page 264) was completed in 1998. Nicknamed the 'Teletubby house' (referencing the BBC children's television series popular in the late Nineties), it brilliantly balanced a process of sensitive submersion with the need for light and transparency. The key materials were steel, glass and concrete yet the earth itself became the fourth material, used to both insulate and disguise the house. Malator took high-tech in a new direction, while also exploring a fresh way of building within the landscape that offered an alternative to the idea of the gentle, floating touch followed by Jan Benthem, Scott Tallon Walker and others.

Maximalism versus Minimalism
God is in the Detail

17   John Pawson and Claudio Silvestrin – Neuendorf House, Mallorca, Spain, 1989

Tony Duquette
Dawnridge
Beverly Hills, California,
United States, 1949

Piero Fornasetti
Casa Fornasetti
Milan, Italy, 1955

David Hicks
The Grove
Brightwell Baldwin,
Oxfordshire, England, 1979

John Pawson
and Claudio Silvestrin
Neuendorf House
Mallorca, Spain, 1989

John Pawson
Life House
Llanbister, Wales, 2016

Vincent Van Duysen
Van Duysen Residence
Antwerp, Belgium, 2003

The history of 20th-century residential design could be described as a grand battle between the forces of maximalism and minimalism. At various times and moments, one or the other of these armies has been in the ascendant within a constant process of advance and retreat. Modernist architects, in particular, took to their hearts the idea that 'ornament is crime', first professed by Adolf Loos (see page 66), and began chipping away at what they saw as elements of excess. Their rooms and houses were designed around the Miesian ideal of 'less is more', and there was undoubtedly a sense of reserve and restraint to early Modernist houses of the Thirties, in particular, which we tend to think of as crisp white cubes and rectangles, with finely detailed, pared-down interiors.

But there has always been a countercurrent to the idea of 'less is more', which the American designer Tony Duquette summed up suitably as 'more is more'. Designers such as Duquette, Piero Fornasetti and David Hicks preferred a more expressive approach to the home, which they layered and layered again with colour, pattern and personal treasures. They saw house and home as a place of theatre, full of drama, rather than 'a machine for living in', as Le Corbusier famously put it. Like fellow designers and contemporaries Oliver Messel and Lorenzo 'Renzo' Mongiardino, Duquette was working as a set designer, for both film and theatre, and treated the home as a stage for living. It was a stage that he filled to the max, as he described:

> Until I was an adult and then for nearly fifty happy years with my artist wife I have gone on accumulating, like a fascinated magpie, enough beautiful things, ugly things, curious things, from deer's antlers to Siamese figures of gilded wood, to fill boxes and boxes, baskets and baskets, houses and houses.[1]

For Duquette and like-minded people, such a house did not have to be packed full of precious art or fine period furniture. He was more concerned about creating a home with character and, famously, would design lights, mirrors and other installations using salvaged items such as car hubcaps and shells. He was a master of illusion, using not only mirrors but also trompe l'oeil techniques to trick the eye and intrigue the viewer, all adding to the theatrical quality of his spaces.

The great, multidisciplinary Italian designer Piero Fornasetti, similarly, was not only a maximalist but also a great dramatist. His heroine, whose black-and-white eyes stared out from many of his ceramics, was Lina Cavalieri, the famous Italian opera singer and great star of the stage. Like Duquette, Fornasetti was a master of illusion and infused his furniture and interiors with a highly playful personality. His escapist spaces had the ability to transport you to another time and place, imbued with an original sense of fantasy. This was especially true of his many pictorial references to the classical world, seen in his wallpapers and applied to his furniture, while his mesmerizing Nuvole wallpaper design carries you up into the clouds.

In the United Kingdom, David Hicks became one of the most influential interior designers of his generation through his houses, interiors, textiles and books. His spaces were so multilayered, with a range of references both old and new, that sometimes the mix feels almost Post-Modern (see page 250). In his books, Hicks set out the key principles of interior design as he saw them, but then invited his readers to experiment and to begin to break the rules, as he wrote in his book, *Style and Design*:

Many of the most successful schemes derive their impact from a startling combination of colours or a novel combination of patterns which fly in the face of accepted practice. Rules give structure, but often at the expense of vitality.[2]

Rule-breaking was part of the maximalist ethos, which helped set them apart from the minimalists for whom discipline was everything. During the Eighties, especially, the pendulum began swinging back the other way, towards a more pared-down aesthetic, partly as a reflection of the times but also perhaps as a reaction to the liberal interiors of the Sixties and Seventies, as well as the wilder incarnations of Post-Modernism. Architects and designers such as Claudio Silvestrin, John Pawson and Vincent Van Duysen developed a fresh take on minimalism, with an emphasis upon order and purity, as well as key design values such as proportion, scale, light, materiality and texture. They created spaces that were calm and contemplative, where the intrinsic beauty of crafted materials and finishes sang out very clearly, unencumbered by visual distraction. John Pawson explains:

It's very complex to make something simple. If you make it simple, if you make it visually clear and unornamented, without decoration, then all the lines have to be straighter. Primarily, I want to provide spaces in which people feel good.[3]

Tony Duquette, maximalism and celebrating excess at Dawnridge

Back in the late Forties and early Fifties, the key maximalists were able to tie themselves to the post-war push towards modern houses and interiors that were more playful, optimistic and layered. There was an intriguing strand of mid-century design that went way beyond the constraints of Modernism and the International Style and developed an approach emphasizing the importance of colour, pattern, texture and delight.

Chief among the American maximalists was Tony Duquette, who remains a key point of reference for those who prefer homes that are full of life, with rich strata of interest. Following his graduation from the Chouinard Art Institute in Los Angeles (where he had been awarded a scholarship), Duquette worked with the Hollywood actor turned interior designer William Haines. He went on to gain the attention of another famous designer, Elsie de Wolfe, who began commissioning him to design pieces of furniture while also championing his work. By 1951, when still in his 30s, Tony Duquette was the first American artist to be honoured with a one-man show in Paris at the Pavilion de Marsan, part of the Louvre.

In the early Forties, Tony Duquette had opened his own design studio and had begun balancing his work on interiors, furniture and jewellery with a second thriving career as a set designer. Among his films was the 1945 musical comedy *Yolanda and the Thief*, starring Fred Astaire, while his residential client list included film actress Mary Pickford, as well as the heiress and philanthropist Doris Duke and the billionaire J Paul Getty.

Duquette's own homes were, of course, places where he could let his imagination run riot. On his 70-hectare (175-acre) Malibu ranch, Duquette created a house called Sortilegium, filled with his own designs along with architectural salvage and his eclectic collections. Sortilegium was destroyed in a devastating fire in Malibu in 1993, which was four years after his Duquette Pavilion of Saint Francis in San Francisco had

Tony Duquette – Dawnridge, Beverly Hills, California, United States, 1949

burned down. It was fitting that Duquette liked to compare himself to a phoenix rising from the flames, but he was also enchanted by the combination of nature and magic that the fabled bird represented, which was referenced repeatedly in his work.

There was another magical Duquette home and this one not only survives but is still well cared for, by Duquette's business partner. Dawnridge in Beverly Hills was a collaboration with the German-born architect Caspar Ehmcke, who settled in Los Angeles during the Thirties, and also Duquette's wife, the artist Elizabeth Johnstone, who was known by her nickname, 'Beegle' (a combination of a busy bee and a soaring eagle). Johnstone contributed a number of murals that add to the feeling of a fantastical world at Dawnridge, including the figure of an 18th-century footman on the back of the front door.

Duquette used pieces of architectural salvage throughout the house, along with mirrored panels, which enhance the flow of light as well as the feeling of space and depth in what was a modestly scaled one-bedroom building; Duquette described it as carrying 'real space into dream space'. This idea was helped even further by a whole collection of inside–outside spaces: halfway zones and verandahs between the interiors and the gardens. The gardens themselves became an extension of the home and included a guesthouse, a painting studio for Beegle and a number of pavilions and pagodas. In terms of colour, emerald green was a particular favourite, with a number of walls papered in a signature marbled malachite pattern. Hutton Wilkinson, Duquette's friend, business partner, owner of Dawnridge and head of the ongoing Duquette Studio, describes the palette:

> He loved clear, bright, jewel colours: peridot, amethyst, coral. He also 'painted' his rooms using throw pillows and preferred fabric stretched on the walls because he could get greater depth of colour that way. And then there was gold, gold, gold, on walls and ceilings and anywhere else he could put it. But in Tony's hands it was never gaudy, just gold.[4]

Wilkinson has lovingly restored and revitalized Dawnridge, adding a number of pieces from the Duquette archives: a warehouse full of a magpie's treasures. It is a house that celebrates excess and excitement in the manner of a true maximalist.

Casa Fornasetti, a dazzling spectacle

The Italian mid-century designer Piero Fornasetti was not only a maximalist but a masterful storyteller with an eye for the surreal, the surprising and the unexpected. Many of Fornasetti's designs, including his wallpapers, ceramics and furniture, are still very much in demand, partly because they possess the charm of an enchanting narrative, whether explicit or only hinted at or suggested.

Even within the extraordinarily vibrant context of Fifties and Sixties Milan, Fornasetti stood out as a truly original voice. He began his career in design as a protégé of the great Italian architect and designer Gio Ponti, who was another of the most inspirational multidisciplinary talents, balancing buildings, furniture design, magazine editing and much more besides. Fornasetti followed the same model of 'anything is possible', with projects including not only his many collections of home and interior products, but also commissions for the design of houses, casinos, restaurants and even an ocean liner, the *Andrea Doria* (1951).

Gio Ponti said of Fornasetti that 'he makes objects speak'. The designer achieved this, in part, through his use of a portfolio of familiar motifs and symbols, including Lina Cavalieri's beautiful eyes, fish, the sun and the illustrated façades or details of classical buildings. These were applied to a whole range of pieces, including chairs, tables, screens and particularly cupboards, cabinets and bureaus, which often took on the appearance of miniature buildings and frequently unfolded to reveal further scenes and surprises within.

These 'speaking objects' were often layered within Fornasetti's interiors to create a more rounded narrative. This was very much the case at Casa Fornasetti in Milan, which is still in the hands of his family, and has been likened to a *wunderkammer*, or 'cabinet of curiosities'. The three-storey, 19th-century house was built by Piero Fornasetti's father, but the L-shaped house was then extended and enlarged by the designer during the Fifties. This included a design studio and office space, creating a fusion between work and home.

Piero Fornasetti – Casa Fornasetti, Milan, Italy, 1955

Usually Fornasetti used black-and-white images to decorate his products, yet the rooms of Casa Fornasetti are layered with rich colours. The walls of the sitting room, for instance, are painted a vivid emerald green while one of Fornasetti's striking *architettura* ('architectural') cabinets is flanked by fitted bookshelves and a collection of mirrors, creating a dazzling spectacle. One of the bedrooms is ruby red and another a vivid Prussian blue, which feels like the sky, particularly in combination with a wall in Fornasetti's cloud paper. Whereas Tony Duquette talked of 'dream space', Piero Fornasetti has been called the 'designer of dreams' and his home has the feel of a multilayered dreamscape.

Eclecticism at Britwell House and The Grove

The British maximalist David Hicks first came to fame in 1954, after the British magazine *House & Garden* published the interiors of his home at 22 South Eaton Place, in London's Belgravia. His first career was in advertising, working with the agency J Walter Thompson, but he soon launched his own interior design studio following the interest generated by the story.

By the early Sixties, Hicks was much in demand and working on restaurants, nightclubs and private houses, with a client list that included Vidal Sassoon and Helena Rubinstein. Before long, the designer's reputation had spread internationally and he began launching collections of textiles, carpets, wallpapers and other homeware designs.

With a deep-rooted love of colour and pattern, Hicks's work was perfectly suited to the Sixties. There was a boldness to it, with a love of geometry that fed into the mid-century predilection for playful patterns and Op Art-style abstraction. Early on, Hicks relied on fabrics bought from theatrical suppliers but then began creating his own pattern designs, which became a key element of the distinctive David Hicks look.

Many of the designer's clients, like Hicks himself, owned period houses in town or country, but he was able to transform the interiors into something new through his use of colour and an eclectic blend of period pieces, modern and contemporary art, together with some mid-century furniture and lighting. This eclecticism might sound dangerous, yet in David Hicks's confident hands the ingredients came together and the recipe was more than a success. His son Ashley Hicks, who is a designer himself as well as an author, writes:

David Hicks – The Grove, Brightwell Baldwin, Oxfordshire, England, 1979

Much of his aesthetic, unlike most modern designers at the time, was deeply rooted in an encyclopaedic knowledge of historical styles. Everywhere was symmetry and classical proportion. His colour palette, however wild and bizarre it occasionally seemed, was in fact tightly controlled, always playing on a narrow range of carefully balanced colour combinations that he gleaned from historical sources of every era, from portraits, fabric swatches or bits of old pottery. The result is that these rooms, while having a crisp modernity, are pervaded with an easy classicism that makes them ideal settings for antiques.[5]

Hicks's approach was very well encapsulated within the interiors of his own country houses in Oxfordshire. The first of these was a large 18th-century neo-classical villa called Britwell House, in the village of Britwell Salome, which became, as Hicks put it, 'a catalogue of the versatility and catholicity of my taste and my outlook on the treatment of rooms'.[6] Hicks described the house, pictures of which were published around the world, as one of the greatest showcases of his work.

Britwell House was followed, in the late Seventies, by The Grove, on the same estate, in the nearby village of Brightwell Baldwin. This was a period farmhouse that had been reinvented and extended during the 1790s to create an elegant home set in parkland and gardens. The Grove became another key calling card, with its photogenic mix of styles within one carefully considered aesthetic. Perhaps the most dramatic space in the house was the drawing room where the walls were covered in a rose-pink cotton fabric layered with 18th-century paintings by the renowned English portrait artist George Romney, which came from the family of David Hicks's wife, Lady Pamela Mountbatten, daughter of Earl Mountbatten, the last Viceroy of India. One of Hicks's own geometric carpet designs offered pattern and texture, while the choice of furniture blended old and new.

There was a library, with the feel of a gentleman's club, with bursts of colour provided by an Indian-style rug and curtains in papal purple. The backdrop in the dining room was a series of painted wall panels that had once graced Lady Pamela's study at Britwell House. The bedrooms were also full of colour while these spaces were softened with fabric canopies over the beds in the style of a half-tester. In Hicks's own bedroom he slotted a bath into an alcove, blurring the distinction between bedroom and bathroom in a relaxed and informal way that was eventually taken up as a point of inspiration by hotel designers in particular. But it was also the gesture of a maximalist, expressing his own particular take on eclecticism.

Hicks lived at The Grove until his death in 1998. He had written the instructions for his own funeral and placed them by his bed, in which he passed away peacefully and from where he had a picture-perfect view of his beloved garden from a window surrounded by bookshelves and books.

Neuendorf House, mixing geometry and earthiness

For every maximalist such as David Hicks, Piero Fornasetti or Tony Duquette there is also a minimalist. It is an aesthetic approach led principally and understandably by architects rather than interiors designers – especially those architects who prioritize key principles such as symmetry, proportion, scale and rhythm. They enjoy the clarity of clean lines and uncluttered spaces that allow the beauty and texture of materials and finishes to shine out. During the late Eighties and Nineties, there was a fresh wave of architectural minimalism, which saw the evolution of particular hotspots of purity and restraint.

Japan, for instance, is often associated with a minimalist aesthetic and a focus on characterful materiality, as seen in the work of Tadao Ando and his close contemporaries (see page 245). Mexican architects such as Luis Barragán (see page 205) and Ricardo Legorreta are also associated with a relatively minimal and pared-down approach, although used in combination with planes and surfaces of vivid colour.

In Europe, two of the most influential minimalist architects are the Italian-born but London-based architect Claudio Silvestrin and the English architect John Pawson. They both established their reputations during the late Eighties and briefly joined forces to work in partnership. One of the most enticing fruits of this brief creative union was a house in Mallorca for the German art dealer Hans Neuendorf and his family (see page 280).

The Neuendorfs wanted to go well beyond the rustic traditional style associated with the Balearics at the time and do something that was decidedly modern and different. Navigating their way carefully around the planning rules, Silvestrin and Pawson laced their minimalist aesthetic with vernacular references, including the use of an internal courtyard, as well as a choice of patios and terraces. The result was, typically, a process in which the design of the house was reduced down to its essential elements, giving it a nearly abstract purity of form. The outline of the house became a punctured cube, with the high walls featuring an ochre pigment mixed into the render, creating an almost Barragán-esque wash of colour. Windows, doors and other apertures formed neat linear incisions, including the entrance to the secret courtyard at the end of a long, processional pathway running parallel to a suitably pure swimming pool. Silvestrin explains their aim:

We wanted to express the life elements: water, earth, fire, air. And to express solidity, abstractness, earthiness, rigorous geometry, fortress-like introspectiveness, calmness, naturalness, timelessness, innovation and the play of light and shadows and the Mediterranean aura of the location.[7]

Inside, the house is also uncompromising in its commitment to a minimalist ethos. Walls are painted white and unadorned. The focus is on the lines of the spaces and materials like the stone floors, while in these settings pieces of furniture assume heightened importance, like sculptures in an art gallery. In the dining room, for instance, the stone table and a set of Hans Wegner Wishbone chairs are the only pieces to express themselves. Each carefully selected piece therefore has a powerful resonance.

'The absence of visual noise gives the house a wonderful calmness and serenity,' says Hans Neuendorf, 'while at the same time allowing for the dramatic play of the light. It is a spiritual house and never mundane.'[8]

The monastic Pawson House

During the Nineties and beyond, as John Pawson's star ascended, there was a growing preoccupation with how one might live comfortably with pure minimalism. There has always been a monastic quality to the Pawson houses and projects, which happen also to include the Novy Dvur Monastery in the Czech Republic (2004).

Pawson House (1999), the architect's family home in London, has been featured in many publications, along with much speculation on how easy or difficult it might be to live in such an ordered, disciplined world. Behind the façade of a 19th-century terraced house, Pawson created a new home, stripping away both the original floor plan of the house and any remaining ornamental detail. He placed a new staircase to one side of the house, while creating generous living spaces within the four-storey building.

The lower ground level holds a combined kitchen and dining area, with banks of cupboards to either side hiding away the usual clutter of daily living, and a long run of worktop, which was even extended outwards through a wall of glass into the rear garden, which is also neatly ordered. In the sitting room the walls are in a quiet white and the fireplace has been edited down to a rectangular slot in one wall, without a surround. Here, too, the textural beauty and grain of the Scandinavian furniture can shine through. 'What I am trying to achieve is a series of private and calm spaces,' says Pawson. 'I want an empty room, with just a bed in it. I want to be able to walk into a room that is only a shell.'[9]

Pawson's wife, Catherine, has talked of the soothing quality of the house, which she has compared to the relaxation of a perpetual massage. Pawson himself is clearly a perfectionist, a fact reflected in the quality of every detail. 'Some people ask, quite aggressively, "how can you live like this?"' he says. 'But I find it easier to think in a plain space.'[10]

In some ways, the questioning of the practicalities of minimalist living echoed the concerns expressed by Dr Edith Farnsworth, after taking up residence in her Illinois home designed by Ludwig Mies van der Rohe back in the early Fifties (see page 140). In other words, the adjustment to a pared-down space with a reduction of 'visual noise' necessitates a change of mind-set, which would certainly be daunting for any dedicated maximalist.

Life House, a contemplative space

John Pawson has now provided a kind of litmus test in the form of the Life House (2016) in the Welsh countryside, which can be rented for weekends and holidays through Living Architecture. Founded by the philosopher and author Alain de Botton, Living Architecture provides opportunities to enjoy spending time in one-off, architect-designed modern homes by architects such as Michael Hopkins (see page 270) and Pawson. Most of these homes are in escapist coastal or rural settings such as Wales.

Working in conjunction with de Botton, Pawson designed the Life House as a true escape, with a focus on calm serenity combined with the idea of connecting with nature and the open landscape. Here, Pawson was able to take the idea of contemplative space to a new level of sophistication, with the ambition of escapism threaded into every bit of it. Made of characterful Danish brick, combined with Douglas fir for the joinery, kitchen and fitted furniture, the six-bedroom house features a large, open-plan kitchen, dining and living room, where an L-shaped sofa faces a wood-burning stove and sits alongside a big corner window framing the view of the

John Pawson – Life House, Llanbister, Wales, 2016

valley. One of the bedrooms features a large bath next to the window, while another takes the form of a book-lined library and a third is devoted to music.

Alongside the house John Pawson also added a 'contemplation chamber', tucked into the hillside itself. This is minimalism at its most extreme and, arguably, at its most refreshing, where the space is reduced to a kind of architectural cave. Within this intellectual spa, free of any distraction, the aim is to 'train the mind on true essentials'.

Silent beauty at the Van Duysen Residence

The work of the influential Belgian architect Vincent Van Duysen has also been described as 'visually silent'.[11] His work combines a love of simplicity, materials, fine craftsmanship and character; and, for his clients, a sense of calm is – again – a truly vital ingredient of home space. In a busy, complex world, the idea of calm does have extraordinary appeal for many people, especially when it comes to the personal realm of the home. Writing in a monograph on Van Duysen's work, architecture critic Marc Dubois says:

> It is a search for intense simplicity to counterbalance the visual violence in the world. This quest for noble simplicity has nothing to do with laziness: it is the result of a conviction that human beings need harmonious spaces. It is much more a petition for a return to an approach in which silence can claim its place.[12]

The influences playing on Van Duysen's work overlap in many ways with Pawson's. There's the influence of Mies van der Rohe and his belief in the importance of detail, the crafted elegance of Japanese architecture and fashion design, along with an ingrained respect for the innate beauty of materials. As a young man, Van Duysen was also inspired by a Belgian monastery: Roosenberg Abbey in Waasmunster, designed in the 1970s by the Benedictine monk and architect Dom Hans van der Laan.

Van Duysen studied architecture in Ghent and founded his own practice in 1990 in Antwerp. As with Pawson, many of his earliest projects were retail stores, particularly for fashion houses, but increasingly he began working on residential commissions from the mid-Nineties onwards. His apartment in Antwerp was picked up and published by Ilse Crawford when she was editing the magazine *ELLE Decoration*, adding to the growing interest in Van Duysen's work. Crawford reports:

> His own place at the time was a conversion of an old Antwerp apartment, and it included such traditional elements as oak floors, painted brick, linen half-curtains, and classic upholstery in a crisp, modern plan. Van Duysen's apartment not only looked good, it was functional and felt good, too. Here was a designer with a sound grasp of materiality, someone who could take materials that were not in the lexicon of 'modern' and make them new.[13]

In 2003 Van Duysen created a new home for himself in Antwerp, which conveyed his ethos of silent beauty even more succinctly. The Van Duysen Residence was a late 19th-century townhouse, a typology that the architect knows well from many similar commissions in Belgium. Behind the original façade, the architect created a fresh home with unadorned plaster walls throughout and timber floors. Here, again, there was a reduction or editing, with the original staircase retained but the detailing purified while a skylight above draws in sunlight and brings out the texture of the wooden steps.

Through high walls of glass, the kitchen, hall and dining area look into an internal courtyard and lightwell graced with a single tree. The living room is a large, open space that leads through to a rear garden with a reflecting pool. Upstairs, nearly every bedroom and the media room look down into one of these contemplative gardens, further enhancing the sense of calm.

Architects such as Van Duysen and John Pawson have succeeded in elevating the importance of calm, peacefulness and serenity. Such virtues are not to be underestimated, particularly in today's world. There is an undoubted allure to minimalism, embraced by many home owners and devotees of hotels and spas that offer such similar virtues. Minimalism and maximalism are, in many ways, chalk and cheese, yet they both speak of the wide range of aesthetic open to us even within the medium of modernity.

Fashion Houses
Seduced by Style

18   Terence Conran – Barton Court, Kintbury, Berkshire, England, 1971

Andrée Putman
Putman Apartment
Paris, France, 1976

Terence Conran
Barton Court
Kintbury, Berkshire,
England, 1971

Philippe Starck
YOO residential projects
various locations worldwide,
from 1999

Giorgio Armani
Armani House
Saint-Tropez, France,
1996/2009

The relationship between our own homes and the world of fashion is both fascinating and complicated. Like a turbulent love affair, it's a union that can sometimes be intense but can also begin to fracture and fail at other times in our lives. Sometimes there is true passion, yet the constant demands of fashion can also be wearing and even a little overwhelming.

Some argue that our houses should be beyond fashion and that instead they should be essentially 'timeless'. This notion of the 'timeless home' is something that resurfaces constantly within the world of design itself, offering a tempting intellectual position that removes us from any great concern or worry about what's happening in the world of fashion. Timeless interiors tend to be grounded in familiar architectural and design principles, taking a relatively traditional approach to proportion, symmetry and scale while allowing for a degree of eclecticism and some scope for layers of personality. This is, in itself, rather reassuring.

Yet a counterargument suggests that there is no such thing as a truly timeless home. Our homes are generally, in one way or another, a mirror of our times, as well as expressions of our characters and preoccupations. Our houses, apartments and the way we live today are all radically different to how our families would have lived a hundred years ago. Over the past century we have seen major shifts and changes in design and aesthetics, from Arts & Crafts to Art Nouveau to Art Deco to Modernism, Post-Modernism and beyond. We call these shifts 'movements', yet if we take a long view they could be described as fashions that step beyond seasons to become something more profound and influential.

Over the last few decades, the relationship between home and fashion has become increasingly intertwined. Gradually, homeware brands have evolved along a model not unlike fashion labels, and some have begun to launch not just annual but seasonal collections. At the same time, fashion labels have moved into homeware while applying a very similar ethos to ranges and lines that are regularly updated. We can then factor in the rise of a certain layer of interiors magazines and newspaper supplements that also treat the home as an extension of fashion, promoting the idea of regular, cyclical change.

We still have the power of choice, of course, about the extent to which we embrace or deny the idea of the 'fashionable' home. But some of the influences upon us can be quite subtle. One powerful example of this is hotel design, which has played a key part in communicating major design trends, which have then filtered back into the home. For instance, the idea of placing your bathtub within a bedroom was taken up by luxury hotels and then adopted by residential architects and interior designers. The luxuriousness of hotel bathrooms, with their walk-in showers and double sinks, has also played into the aspirations of homeowners looking to create a spa-like experience for themselves. High-end hotels, on the other hand, have become increasingly residential in some respects, aiming to offer a level of comfort and individuality that we might expect in a thoughtfully designed and beautifully appointed house or apartment.

Putman Apartment, pioneering loft living

In terms of style-setting, one of the most influential designers of the Seventies and Eighties was the French designer Andrée Putman. Part of her message about modern living was conveyed through her work on seminal hotels around the world, which purposefully broke away from the kind of snobbery associated with grand, traditional luxury hotels and created an atmosphere and an aesthetic that was more informal, relaxed and yet still decidedly glamorous and even avant-garde.

Putman designed New York's first boutique hotel, Morgans Hotel (1984), for hotelier Ian Schrager, as well as Hotel Le Lac (1989) at the foot of Mount Fuji in Kawaguchi, Japan, and the Hotel im Wasserturm (1990) situated in a former water tower in Cologne. She possessed the talent of a fortune-teller, able to predict the mind-set changes that would see her audience begin to look for something new and original. She explained her approach:

> If you are asked to design a hotel, which will have nothing to do with what we've seen before and will break all the rules, you know which rules you want to break. Maybe by intuition and a little thinking, you have a feeling of what tomorrow people want to experience, what the traces are of dust and boredom from a past that you never want to see again, what is simply habit that is finished.[1]

This enticing ability to identify the needs and desires of the 'tomorrow people' made Andrée Putman unique. She managed to combine the lessons of Modernism with the adventurous spirit of the Twenties and then add a touch of futurism, which meant that her hotels, residences and high-end shop interiors felt a little ahead of their time. In this way, Putman was always in the vanguard of design.

As a child, Putman thought she might pursue a career in music when she grew up. Her mother was a musician, while her father was a writer, and she exhibited a talent for music at an early age. But when she was told that to be a composer would cost her at least ten years of quiet study, Putman began looking in different directions. She began her career in design working for magazines as a consultant on the subject of interiors and furniture, while settling into an apartment in Place Saint-Germain-des-Prés:

> I just had one or two pieces in my room: a Miró poster, a Barcelona chair by Mies van der Rohe, and for a young girl at the time it was extremely daring. I was shocking for my milieu and thought to be annoying and problematic.[2]

Putman began working on new collections for the French homeware store Prisunic and designing her first houses. Then, in 1978, she founded Ecart, a furniture company that championed the work of Modernist designers such as Eileen Gray and Pierre Chareau (see pages 60 and 72), as well as selling her own work. Increasingly, she also began to design residential interiors and hotels, and in 1997 she set up the Studio Putman.

Andrée Putman moved into a loft apartment in Paris in 1976, at a time before 'loft-style' living had caught on. She described people's reactions:

> At the time I received condolences. 'Poor André,' people would say, 'when do you think you will be able to find a real apartment?' I did it all too early to be respected as someone who had taken a good decision.[3]

The loft apartment was a former printing workshop within a semi-industrial building dating from the 1890s. She was drawn to the generous proportions and volume of the space, with its big windows and slim steel supporting columns. Tempted by the luxury of open space, Putman wanted to preserve this feeling as much as possible in her design, while adding skylights to bring

Andrée Putman – Putman Apartment, Paris, France, 1976

in more sunlight and floors of poured concrete with added resin to create a semi-reflective surface. Apart from a separate bathroom in one corner, the loft was kept open and zoned with areas for working and dining, while her bedroom was only divided from the rest of the space by sliding screens made of grey gauze. At roof level, Putman designed a kitchen within a glasshouse connected to a roof terrace.

Within the loft, every piece of furniture that Putman chose had some kind of special story behind it. There was a pair of carved wooden arm-chairs designed for the actress Sarah Bernhardt, for instance, along with Art Deco dining chairs by Émile-Jacques (aka Jacques-Émile) Ruhlmann and a dining table by Paul Dupré Lafon, as well as a grandfather clock that Putman fell in love with and chased around Parisian antique shops until a grateful client managed to buy it and presented it to her as a gift.

Yet, despite pioneering ideas such as loft living and the new breed of modern hotel interior, Putman herself still thought of her work as something different to or beyond fashion. Interior and residential design, she argued, were not seasonal and did not demand a new beginning every six months. She insisted:

There is a word to me, which is unbearable. It is *tendance*. It means a hyped trend, the top idea for today. This is to me a nightmare. I start to be almost mean when I hear people say I am fashionable or *tendance*, because I'm the opposite. It cuts me off from a certain world, but it's excellent for me not to belong to that world.[4]

Conran's Barton Court, a model for modern living

In terms of their overall impression upon the world of design and the home, one might compare Andrée Putman with the British design leader Terence Conran. It's hard to think of another single designer or entrepreneur who has had quite such a profound impact on the way England lives and eats as Conran. Like Putman, Conran communicated his lifestyle messages through multiple means. There were his many landmark restaurants, including Bibendum, Quaglino's and Bluebird in London, as well as his multiple books on the home and modern living, including *The Essential House Book* (1994). As a retailer, in 1964 Conran launched Habitat, which introduced two or three generations to affordable, modern homeware, and he followed this ten years later with the Conran Shop.

After studying at the Central School of Arts and Crafts, Conran began his long career by working on designs for the Festival of Britain in 1951, and a year later he started his own design studio. During the Fifties, he expanded his interests rapidly, opening his first restaurant and then the Conran Design Group in 1956. Later, Conran was involved in London's Butler's Wharf development (1990), near Tower Bridge, a hugely ambitious urban regeneration project that included converting warehouses into apartment buildings, the creation of the Pont de la Tour restaurant and 'gastrodome', and the establishment of London's Design Museum. Conran moved into an apartment here, showcasing open-plan riverside living.

Like Andrée Putman, Terence Conran has always been someone who follows his own passions and adopts the same style of life that he promotes to a design-world audience. His work was transformative and avant-garde, helping to encourage modern ways of living rather than simply following fashion.

Like his London loft by the Thames, Conran's own country house in Berkshire, Barton Court (see page 298), helped set a model for modern living in a period home. In 1971, Conran came across Barton Court, an 18th-century house in Berkshire, which had served time as a boys' school but was then left empty, falling into a state of semi-dereliction. The roof had started collapsing inwards and the windows had been smashed, but Conran saw the innate beauty of the building and its great potential as a family home:

> As soon as I saw it I fell in love with it, primarily because it's Georgian and I love the symmetry and restraint of the period, as well as the generous proportions, I could see how I could make it simple and modern and how the proportions would make a perfect 20th-century home.[5]

Many period details had already been lost, but Conran was keen to preserve and protect what he could, including the staircase and the flagstone floors. Yet the fact that the house was in such poor condition also created a degree of latitude within Conran's resuscitation and renovation plan for the house. One of the designer's most radical moves was to take out two internal walls around the central entrance hallway at the front of the building to create one large, multilayered living space that is around 24m (80ft) long in total. This became a dramatic, modern room, almost like a loft in itself, with different zones for sitting and relaxing. Walls are painted white, the flooring is largely timber and the space hosts Conran's curated mix of furniture, art and personal treasures, as he explains:

> I have always thought that a mixture of old and new works well if done tastefully. Easy living is what I have tried to achieve at Barton Court. It's this sort of unpretentious informality which makes a comfortable modern home.[6]

As an exemplar of easy living, Conran's country home had a powerful resonance. By opening up the key living spaces, Conran created a more fluid, generous, informal and welcoming setting, full of sunlight and personality. This was a truly modern, multipurpose space within a period home. As such, it connects with so many historical houses and conversions where the traditional pattern of compartmentalized spaces has been questioned and found wanting.As with Barton Court, the solution is so often to open up the internal living spaces to create a more open way of easy living.

Just as important was Conran's message about character. His spaces were always designed with a sense of restraint and order, but they were also infused with personality and layers of interest. Barton Court is the home of a Modernist, yet it is also full of the fruits of years of collecting and gathering. Circulation spaces, such as hallways and landings, become galleries for these collections, including an assembly of Bugatti toy racing cars, all in blue, which are hung upon the walls of a rear hallway like the mounted moths or butterflies collected by a Victorian lepidopterist. Some rooms, like Conran's study, are layered with books, models and points of inspiration while others – such as the master bedroom – have a much calmer feeling that allows the sense of space, volume and light to come to the fore. In this way, there is an important sense of rhythm and contrast within the house, which is rewarding in itself.

Conran's house serves as a kind of masterclass in many ways, with lessons about the art of display, the mixing of old and new, the importance of a large communal kitchen and dining zone, the value of a generous, escapist bathroom and so on. But, as well as being a kind of design laboratory, Barton Court also has the feeling of a much loved family home, which helps to make it even more inspirational. 'It is as crucial to my happiness,' says Conran, 'as a glass of wine, a cup of coffee or a fine cigar.'[7]

The global reach of Philippe Starck and YOO

Terence Conran was one of the first designers to develop a brand around himself, his work and his books. The French *créateur* Philippe Starck took this ambition onto a truly global level, as his work gradually expanded into a broad portfolio of different disciplines, including hotels, homeware and the home itself. While many architects and designers before him have attained renown and respect, Starck also achieved celebrity, becoming as close as the design world can offer to a household name.

The son of an aeronautical engineer, Starck studied at the Ecole Camondo in Paris before starting work with creative brands like Pierre Cardin. Within a few years he had founded his own studio, concentrating initially on product and furniture design. Like the great multifaceted designers of the mid-century, such as Alvar Aalto, Charles and Ray Eames or Arne Jacobsen (see pages 97, 109 and 155), Starck saw no boundaries between the various disciplines and began to expand in many different

Philippe Starck (in cooperation with Moore Yaski Sivan Architects and the Habas Group) – Yoo Tel Aviv 'vertical village', Tel Aviv, Israel, 2007

directions, ranging from everyday products to bathroom furniture through to motorbikes, superyachts and an habitation module for private space tourism.

Increasingly, Starck began working on large-scale architectural and interiors projects, including many restaurants and a series of hotels around the world, such as St Martins Lane in London and the Faena Hotel in Buenos Aires, which became magazine favourites and deeply *tendance*, as Andrée Putman might have put it. Hotels such as the Faena offered an aesthetic that was colourful, characterful, playful, luxurious, modern and even irreverent, with grand statements and touches of theatre. They were like stage sets for the 'tomorrow people', full of promise, and they soon became destinations in themselves. They also helped to build the demand for homes and apartment buildings that took a similarly dramatic and distinctive aesthetic approach, which was chanelled into a new company co-founded by developer John Hitchcox and Philippe Starck known as 'Yoo'. Today YOO has its own team of in-house and contributing designers, while often also playing the part of developer or working in partnership with other developers across a range of residential projects and hotels. Starck described the background to it:

> We could see a strong opportunity to create spaces that would reflect the happiness of the people who live in them, forgetting the old and obsolete idea of 'home'. We began spending our days dreaming up a sort of utopia, where all our friends could harmoniously co-exist.[8]

From the start, there was a menu of choices around YOO's residential buildings in both town and country. This included a set of aesthetic styles directed at the 'YOO tribe', as Starck described it, as well as opportunities to tailor the size and specification of the apartment. There was a degree of flexibility, as well as a level of contexuality to the architecture and interiors, depending on the location and setting. Later, as the business expanded globally, YOO enlisted other designers to enhance the portfolio of available choices.

Starck and Hitchcox also developed the idea of 'vertical villages': communities of like-minded people, often in urban settings, looking for a place not just to live but to socialize, exercise, perhaps to eat, drink and entertain. YOO developments typically offer the kind of amenities one expects from designer hotels, including gyms, pools, libraries, cinemas and other services, as well as grand entrance lobbies and concierge services. In this way, these villages are not just about creating private space but also about supporting an entire lifestyle, which revolves around connecting with like-minded residents. Starck explains:

> We are living in a society that has become more and more divided. That's why it's very important to bring people together and, yes, the way that you make a building definitely can help in this. It's simple. First, you have to make a building that is very personal. This way people feel at ease; they feel that they share the same place and the same values with the other people who live in the building. So if you make a gym, a library, a big table, some sort of place where people can meet and have a birthday party for their children or watch a movie together, then it definitely helps. To make a village you need communal spaces.[9]

The idea of a vertical village addressed the need to create a more meaningful sense of community, especially within large urban centres, which can feel very anonymous and even alienating. But just as crucially, or even more so, Philippe Starck and YOO began to stretch the definition of 'home' itself. The word no longer meant a purely private space, but also expanded to include communal amenities and shared social areas. Such thinking has become more and more common within 21st-century high-rises and residential developments as clients begin to expect the facilities and luxuries that were once the preserve of fine hotels.

Armani House and the Armani aesthetic

Over the course of the late Nineties and the early decades of the 21st century, the relationship between home and fashion has become increasingly intimate. Just as the grand, international fashion houses have been tempted into the hotel industry, the same is true of their expansion into homeware. Younger brands have grown up exploring the synergy between the two spheres in retail concepts that actively blur the distinctions, while presenting clothing and homeware alongside one another, as though they were two sides of the same coin. This fusion of fashion and home owes much to the example of the entrepreneurial Italian maestro, Giorgio Armani, and his global empire.

Born in northern Italy, Armani studied medicine at the University of Milan before embarking on a career in the design world. He began working as a window-dresser for a Milanese department store in the late Fifties and then transferred into menswear. By the mid-Sixties, Armani was creating menswear for Nino Cerruti and was soon designing on a freelance basis for a number of Italian fashion houses. Launching his own label in 1975, Giorgio Armani started expanding rapidly from menswear into womenswear and diffusion lines, actively targeting the United States as well as Europe. The business began to fly during the Nineties, with Armani paying close attention to every aspect of the design and marketing process, especially the look, atmosphere and feel of his stores. Perhaps more than any of his contemporaries, Armani recognized the importance of store interiors. The company commissioned the best architects and designers to create elegant and finely detailed stores, while keeping a tight hold of the image that they wanted these environments to convey. This was good business

Giorgio Armani – Armani House, Saint-Tropez, France, 1996/2009

and marketing sense, but also reflected Giorgio Armani's own personal interest in architecture and design, as this comment from him reveals:

> For both fashion and design, the underlying philosophy is the same. My ideas are born from the appreciation of pure forms, artisanal craftsmanship, and understated luxury. For me, design consists of creating objects, spaces and clothing that wield enduring charm and help enhance the personality of those who choose them.[10]

Perhaps it was inevitable that he would launch, in 2000, Armani/Casa, with its own collections of furniture, textiles and lighting. There's also an Armani interior design studio, founded in 2004, so you can commission a villa or yacht interior within the Armani aesthetic, plus partnerships that offer the opportunity to buy an Armani kitchen or bathroom. Two Armani hotels, in Milan and Dubai, offer the chance to experience the 'pure elegance, simplicity and sophisticated comfort that embody the designer's signature style and aesthetic'.

All of these elements, like the stores, are crisply tailored using beautifully crafted materials and refined finishes. The Armani aesthetic carries across all of these different mediums in a carefully controlled and considered way, yet they do reflect the tastes of the designer himself, for whom house and home is a central concern and an ongoing preoccupation.

Famously, Giorgio Armani has created a personal portfolio of houses that includes not only his pivotal home in Milan, but also a home in St Moritz, one on the Sicilian island of Pantelleria, one in Antigua (where he sometimes spends Christmas) and one in Saint-Tropez. Published in the pages of American *Architectural Digest* in 2015, the Saint-Tropez house was bought in 1996 and renovated in 2009 by Armani, who also added a swimming pool, loggia and guesthouse.

The façade of the house is traditional Provençal, while the interiors have that sense of restraint that one might associate with Armani but also warmth and colour, much of it derived from natural materials. The large living room, for instance, features teak floors and ceilings and a wall of bookcases that bring an organic character to the space, while the books and furniture, arranged around the stone fireplace, add personality. There are many pieces in the house from Armani/Casa but also flea-market finds and personal treasures that introduce more in the way of colour, texture and pattern than one might first expect. On the subject of ambience, Armani says:

> People always ask me how I have fun. I have fun with my homes, which have been my greatest investments. I don't buy Picassos; I buy houses. This is a passion I've had since I was young – creating ambiences that make you want to stay.[11]

They are ambiences that might be heartfelt, yet they also add to the aspirations of those who wish to translate the Armani aesthetic into their own homes. There is undoubtedly a glamour to these spaces, representing a kind of dream world. Some might welcome the idea of a fashion house to the full, while others just have a taster of it in an Armani store or hotel. Again, it's all about the choices we make and the extent to which we wish to adopt such a ready-made aesthetic or carve out a space for ourselves that might be more eclectic and expressive in terms of reflecting our own individual passions.

Living Lightly
21st-Century Vernacular

19

Patterson Architects – Scrubby Bay House, Banks Peninsula,
New Zealand, 2013

Glenn Murcutt
Marie Short House
Kempsey, New South Wales,
Australia, 1975

Todd Saunders
Fogo Island Arts Studios
Fogo Island, Newfoundland,
Canada, 2015

John Wardle
Shearers Quarters
Bruny Island, Tasmania,
Australia, 2011

Lily Jencks
Ruins Studio
Dumfries, Scotland, 2016

Patterson Architects
Scrubby Bay House
Banks Peninsula,
New Zealand, 2013

D uring the early years of the 21st century, we began to think about the idea of 'home' in a different way. At last, we began to wake up to the vulnerable beauty of the Earth around us and our shared responsibility to look after it. This realization connected with the idea of a shared home, which architect and inventor Richard Buckminster Fuller (see page 171) called 'Spaceship Earth'. Typically prescient, Fuller used the term back in the Sixties as a way of talking about the importance of sustainability on a global level, while trying to encourage thinking about the use of new technologies and systems to help us address the challenge of balancing modern living with a care plan for the planet.

More recently, similar language around climate change has focused attention upon both environmental responsibility and the importance of sustainable ways of living, especially at home. When we talk about climate emergency we now say, thanks to Greta Thunberg and others, that 'our house is on fire'. Like Fuller's 'Spaceship Earth' or James Lovelock's 'Gaia theory' of global environmental synergy, Thunberg's phrase reminds us that we are all living in one shared and precious space and that we need to look after it.

Like the rest of us, architects and designers have been slow to realize that 'our house is on fire'. But the design community is now starting to address questions of sustainability and greener ways of living, within a concerted push towards reducing carbon footprints and energy consumption. This is especially true of the houses that we live in, given their considerable energy use, both during the process of building them and in the ongoing need to keep them running smoothly with electricity, heating, cooling and water.

Increasingly, design innovations have helped us to conserve energy. During the Nineties, for instance, architects began pioneering the idea of 'passive houses', also known by the German term Passivhaus, as a lot of the early thinking came from Germany. The concept of passive houses revolves around buildings that are made to be as energy-efficient as possible, with the very highest standards of insulation and window glazing to create a tight envelope around the home.

Passive houses combine low-tech common sense with more sophisticated bits of kit for generating and holding onto energy. The careful positioning of these houses helps them to benefit from the warmth of the sun, known as 'solar gain', while at the same time making sure that they do not overheat during the summer. Using solar gain plus super-insulation plus airtightness reduces the overall energy needs for heating the home, while any heat that is generated is kept in the house through the use of heat-recovery ventilation systems, which also keep the air fresh and clean. Using passive house principles, a home can be kept warm even during the winter with just the occasional use of small radiators or underfloor heating. Factoring in low-energy lighting using LED bulbs, as well as ultra-efficient appliances, helps to reduce the overall carbon footprint in quite simple ways and without any dramatic compromises on lifestyle choices or aesthetics. Such thinking is becoming more and more commonplace, as we give greater thought to our own impact upon 'Spaceship Earth'.

Sustainable architecture and the Marie Short House

One of the most inspirational figureheads in terms of environmentally aware homes is the Australian architect Glenn Murcutt. For an architect who has continued to work as a solo practitioner, based in the Sydney suburb of Mosman, Murcutt's global influence has been extraordinary. Resisting the temptation to increase the size of his practice, or take on large-scale commissions in other countries, Murcutt has focused his attention upon a small number of clients while keeping a list of those prepared to wait patiently until some of his valuable time becomes available. Even so, Murcutt's design philosophy has still travelled the world, sometimes through lectures and masterclasses, but more often through his buildings as they are published and pored over by other architects and students; he has also been awarded the Pritzker Prize for Architecture.

Murcutt's work reflects not only the significance of local contexts, but just as importantly the principle of 'touching the earth lightly'. An Aboriginal phrase, it speaks of the need to always adopt a respectful sensitivity to the landscape, while also accepting the relatively temporary nature of our place within it compared with the story of the land. The architect has always recognized that we are part of nature, rather than simply observers, and that as soon as we start to distance ourselves from the natural world, then the more we make excuses for damaging it. 'If our populations consumed and polluted the earth's resources in balance with the ability of nature to renew, then we'd be sustainable,' says Murcutt. 'But we're not sustainable. We destroy.'[1]

Murcutt's buildings work in synergy with nature rather than imposing themselves upon it. He has compared them to sensitive instruments rather than machines, instruments that respond to changes in light and temperature by opening or closing as needed. The buildings use natural heating and cooling techniques, including long eaves to help hold off the high summer sun, natural cross breezes, and vents that spill hot air from the roof as needed. His houses often catch rainwater, which can be used not only to supply the home but to water the garden and potentially, when it's held in storage tanks or ponds, to help fight forest fires.

Threaded throughout Murcutt's work is a particular respect for the value of natural resources and materials, especially timber. This fuses with an appreciation of the intrinsic beauty of the materials themselves and of true craftsmanship, as well as a respect for vernacular ideas and references, whether they are borrowed from farmhouses or barns. With a focus upon craft and beauty, as well as modernity, Murcutt has managed to elevate 'sustainable architecture' above the outmoded idea of green design as 'alternative' and begin to translate it into something that is not just desirable but aspirational.

One of the most important early examples of Glenn Murcutt's 'climate-responsive architecture' is the Marie Short House, dating back to 1975. Marie Short had bought a farm not far from the coast near Kempsey, in New South Wales, around five hours' drive from Sydney, with the aim of raising cattle there. Originally, Short asked the architect to convert and update an existing farmhouse. But after visiting the farm and getting some costings, Murcutt realized that he could build a new house for the same budget and so Short encouraged him to go ahead. Like so much of Murcutt's work, the design of the new building was a sensitive response to the site and setting, while it also needed to be simple enough to be put together by local builders. Murcutt explains his approach:

> I knew exactly what to do here. It released within me ideas that I'd been working on for a long time. Here, all of a sudden, was an opportunity to fulfill a lot of thinking. It was my first country house and it was a turning point.[2]

Short had also raised the idea of perhaps moving the house one day, if she wanted to build something new and put the house elsewhere on the farm for her son. So Murcutt realized that the timber building would need to have a temporary quality, with the ability to unbolt the whole thing and relocate it. 'That made me realize that this was a really important issue in the debate on ecology – how you put something together in a way that can be changed comparatively easily,' Murcutt says. 'So it was a fantastic experiment for me.'[3]

Murcutt created two single-storey elements sitting alongside one another in a parallel formation, with gently rounded pitched rooflines. The house managed to fuse the elegance of a Modernist villa with the vernacular character of a wool shed, while the decision to raise the building slightly above the ground plane – helping to protect it from floods and animal life – enhances the sense of lightness. There's also the influence of boat-building, which is a local tradition here, with one of the construction team trained in the craft, and the house almost resembling two upturned boats, sitting side by side.

The building itself was pivotal in Murcutt's development as an architect. But Marie Short found that while the house suited her, cattle farming did

Glenn Murcutt – Marie Short House, Kempsey, New South Wales, Australia, 1975

not, and she eventually sold up. In 1980, Murcutt heard that the house and farm were for sale again and decided to buy it. Given that the building had been designed with adaptability in mind, he was able to easily extend each portion of the twin-hulled house and adapt it to his needs and those of his own family. One wing features a large, open-plan kitchen and dining room, with a verandah at one end and the master bedroom suite at the other. The second wing alongside holds the sitting room, two bedrooms and another verandah, while the wooden floors and hoop-pine ceilings and walls give the house an organic warmth. Murcutt says of his country escape:

> It felt very easy for us moving into the building. Unless we design houses that are appropriate for our clients but equally appropriate for ourselves then we are missing the point. It's important that you give the best of yourself and, of course, that should be something that you would like yourself.[4]

Just as importantly, Murcutt has invested a good deal of time in restoring the landscape here, while looking to help regenerate the local wetlands. The conservation programme included burying the power cables to the house to help preserve the natural character of the landscape. Looking after the land is a key part of the responsibility here, as Mercutt says:

> On any one day we have up to fifteen or twenty kangaroos around the house and eight or nine wallabies. And we have a beautiful lake, fed by springs, which is laden with water lilies. That's to the north-east of the house and in the summer you get the perfume of the water lilies carried over the breeze.[5]

Shearers Quarters, a return to Australian vernacular

Australian and Australasian architects have long been at the forefront of the push towards greater environmental consciousness when it comes to house and home. Perhaps this is partly connected with the influence of Glenn Murcutt, but it might be more to do with the undeniable natural beauty of the region, combined with a growing awareness of the vulnerability of key habitats such as the Great Barrier Reef, the eucalyptus forests and the

John Wardle – Shearers Quarters, Bruny Island, Tasmania, Australia, 2011

epic coastline of Australia. The landscape itself serves as a key source of inspiration for architects and designers looking for fresh ways of balancing the desire to build and the need to protect the land and sea.

One of the most striking examples of this is architect John Wardle's home on Bruny Island, which floats off the coast of Tasmania. There is something very special about Bruny, which feels remote but beautiful, rather like a haven at the end of the world; as you drive off the small ferry onto the shore, you are told that you are now on 'Bruny time'. There are sheep farms and forests, along with important populations of bird life, such as short-tailed shearwater, sea eagles and black-faced cormorants.

Wardle, whose practice is based in Melbourne, first visited Bruny Island as a child and it made a lasting impression. Thirty years later, the island resurfaced in his life when he and his wife saw that a farm called Waterview had come up for sale. They had been looking for a place out in the country, and the farm offered an ideal opportunity and a challenge.

At around 485 hectares (1,200 acres), the farmland was in poor condition when the Wardles first took it on, requiring a sensitive restoration process. This included revitalizing the pastures for the Merino sheep and lambs on the farm, but also conservation work on the forestry here and a nature reserve. Waterview came with barns and a farmhouse overlooking the sea, but naturally Wardle began thinking about what else he might do, as he says:

> The original house was built by Captain James Kelly and so it was built by a mariner, not a farmer. We were going to restore and enlarge the farmhouse but we thought it would be a slow project, so my wife Susan suggested that we build this companion building for the shearers, as well as for friends and family, so that we could also use it while restoring the old house.[6]

The new building, called Shearers Quarters, is a distinctly modern but thoughtful take on a vernacular farmstead building. Carefully positioned alongside the farmhouse and to frame the views of the sea, it's a single-storey structure with a sculptural tin roof and tin walls, plus banks of glass that connect with a terrace to one side. There's an open-plan living, dining and kitchen area at one end, with a wood-burning stove and crafted interiors with timber floors and ceilings. Down the long axial corridor there are two family bedrooms and then a bunkroom, with adjustable louvres over the window that control the amount of light, heat and fresh air coming into the space.

In keeping with the focus on sustainability that runs through the farm, Shearers Quarters uses natural cross-ventilation with heat coming from the wood-burner, while water is sourced and harvested on site. The only connection back to the grid is for electricity, which comes from locally generated hydropower. Wardle also used some recycled materials for the interiors of the building, including old apple-storage boxes, which were repurposed to serve as wall panelling.

For John Wardle and his family, Waterview is a long-term commitment that carries a particular sense of responsibility along with the wish to protect and preserve an extraordinary landscape, as Wardle explains:

> We do have a plan that we will build another smaller house on the property and a barn/studio. Then, importantly, there will be landscape elements that will link all the buildings together and we have invested greatly in the farm itself: the paddocks, water reticulation and fencing. it's now very much a working sheep farm.[7]

A dialogue with the landscape at Scrubby Bay House

In Auckland, New Zealand, across the Tasman Sea from Bruny Island, architect Andrew Patterson has developed an approach to architecture that is, similarly, deeply rooted in the landscape. He studied architecture at the University of Auckland and founded his own practice, Patterson Associates, in 1986. There have been urban projects and cultural projects, but Patterson is best known for his houses, which he describes as a collaboration between the architect, the client and the site itself:

> New Zealand's natural beauty is admired worldwide, but beautiful buildings have been few and far between. What we have in abundance are elements such as the grand natural amphitheatres on the North Island's volcanic plateau, forest plazas encircled by pillars of wood

deeply carpeted by ferns, and beautiful underwater rooms corniced in reefs and floored in white sand, with castles of rock punching out of the sea towards the sky.[8]

Many of the practice's houses sit within highly picturesque locations by the coast or up in the hills. There's a range of responses, depending on the setting and situation, but what the houses have in common is the wish to form a respectful dialogue with the landscape. Within this dialogue, the wish to leave the landscape unchanged is not just an ambition but often an explicit part of the brief. Patterson's buildings do take a light touch to the land and coast, yet he also talks of the importance of longevity: 'To be truly sustainable a building has to endure, and for it to endure it needs to be attractive to future generations.'[9]

The emphasis on longevity and adaptability can be seen as a reaction to the disposable and careless character of so much contemporary design, including the impossible trend towards short-life buildings that might be replaced after little more than 20–30 years rather than passing down the generations. Any definition of sustainable architecture has to include the ability of a building to not only last and endure, but to accommodate the evolving needs of its owners as circumstances change and the ages and stages of family members shift over time.

One of the prime examples of a house that sits lightly on the land yet is also built to last is Patterson Associates' Scrubby Bay House (see page 312), located on a sheep and cattle station upon the Banks Peninsula, which is on the eastern coast of New Zealand's South Island. Sited within a natural bowl in the hills and close to the shore of a gentle coastal inlet, Scrubby Bay House sits within an almost pristine natural landscape that can only be accessed down a long farm track or by boat or helicopter. Here, again, a key part of the pleasure of being here is the remoteness and isolation, yet this carries a responsibility in terms of caring for the land itself.

A modern timber-built farmhouse, not unlike Glenn Murcutt's Marie Short House, Scrubby Bay sits very gently upon its site with minimal disturbance. It's composed of two parallel elements, one pulled beyond the other to form a staggered formation. A key aspect of this 'home base' retreat was that it would require little maintenance and could be shut down when not in use, with timber storm shutters that could be used to help protect the banks of glass. Yet, when in use, the house opens up to the outside and to the views. Inside, a spacious 'great room' revolves around a central stone fireplace and chimney that underlines the continuing importance of the hearth. Scrubby Bay House is a tempting and crafted retreat, yet in the summer months, when the grass is almost the same colour as the wood used to build the cabin, it almost disappears into the landscape.

Fogo Island Studios, where nature comes first

The whole notion of 'touching the earth lightly' encompasses a delicate balancing act between longevity and transience. On the one hand, a house should endure and willingly adapt to changing needs and patterns of living. On the other, architects need to remember their sense of responsibility to the environment and landscape, recognizing that even if a building lasts for hundreds of years, the land will still be there long after the building has gone.

This sense of our own place within nature and time is something felt very keenly by architects such as Todd Saunders, whose work is concentrated in the precious northern landscapes of Norway and Canada. Saunders grew up in Gander, Newfoundland, and studied architecture in Montreal. He first began investigating ecological approaches to architecture as a masters student as well as travelling widely in Europe and beyond to research his thesis. Having settled in Bergen, Saunders established his own practice in 1998 in Norway, while increasingly working between Scandinavia and Canada, which have much in common in terms of their northern landscapes and climates.

For Saunders, one of his most important and rewarding projects was a multilayered commission to design a series of buildings on Fogo Island, off the northeastern coast of Newfoundland. Around 24km (15 miles) long, Fogo Island sits to the north of Gander, and the project represented something of a homecoming for the architect. This fishing community had witnessed a gradual drift of younger generations back to the mainland, until entrepreneur and philanthropist Zita Cobb, who also grew up there, decided to try and do something to halt this slow process of decline.

Cobb and her family's Shorefast Foundation asked Saunders to build a new hotel, the Fogo Island Inn, on the island. But this was just one part of a wider and more ambitious community project that also involved rescuing and restoring original saltbox buildings and cottages, as well as creating a collection of artists' studios and retreats around the island. These 'punctuation marks' upon the landscape are sculptural and modern, yet use traditional materials and construction techniques, while referencing the local vernacular. Just as importantly, each of the studios is fully off-grid and self-sufficient in terms of heating, power and water. Saunders explains the priorities:

> One of the things that we looked out for was to put nature first and architecture second. When we did the Inn, for example, we put a wooden platform all the way around the construction site to help protect the land and when we were finished we took it away and it looked as though the building had always been there, with the ecosystem of plants and lichens all maintained. With the Studios because they are 100 per cent off the grid we didn't have an umbilical line of power cables coming into them or an umbilical line of sewage pipes going out. They are self-contained.[10]

Rather like traditional fishermen's huts and houses, the Fogo Island Studios are all small buildings that can be heated quickly and easily with wood-burning stoves. There's rainwater harvesting, composting toilets and solar panels for electricity, which is stored in batteries. These hybrids of home and studio spaces are fully independent entities with very modest footprints, while each one is focused like a camera lens on a specific aspect of the Fogo landscape. Saunders describes the risks inherent in the project:

> The thing about this landscape is that it's sub-Arctic, so it's not so forgiving if you destroy it. If you damage a landscape in southern England, then maybe in a year and a half it might repair itself. But if you destroy a landscape in Newfoundland, it could take hundreds of years to get back to where it was, so even though it is a very strong landscape we have to be careful. It is an ancient landscape and if we build here it won't last that long – maybe a hundred years or two or three hundred. In five hundred years the architecture will be gone, but the landscape will still be there, so we need to respect that and not alter it in a way that would impact upon it for ever.[11]

Todd Saunders – Fogo Island Arts Studios, Fogo Island,
Newfoundland, Canada, 2015

Going off-grid at the Ruins Studio

A combination of tried-and-tested low-tech solutions and newer technologies means that building off-the-grid or net-zero homes is now more than possible. Because of technology like ground-source heat pumps and solar thermal and photovoltaic panels, along with the kind of insulation that you might expect from a passive house (see page 314), we can be increasingly self-sufficient without giving up anything in terms of aesthetics or comfort.

British architect Lily Jencks drew upon a carefully curated portfolio of such solutions when she was designing her own family retreat in a rural region of Dumfries in Scotland. The Ruins Studio, as Jencks and her family call the house, features passive strategies and micro-energy generation to achieve self-sufficiency. More than this, the new studio sits within the remnants of the stone walls of a 17th-century farmhouse set among fields and pasture. The repurposed stone walls form a partial

Lily Jencks – Ruins Studio, Dumfries, Scotland, 2016

protective outer layer around the fresh building, which is very well insulated and glazed to a high specification. Jencks, who designed the house in association with architect Nathanael Dorent, describes what living there is like:

> Being one small cottage in a remote landscape feels wild and sometimes a little desolate. But there is great pleasure in the feeling of independence and self-sustainability that gives us. When we are at the house, we are in tune with the rhythms of the day and really notice the changing dynamics of the light and weather.[12]

Completed in 2016, the Ruins Studio runs on electricity from a photovoltaic solar array with battery storage, plus two wood-burning stoves. If needed, there's a back-up gas-powered generator, while water is sourced from a nearby farm, and waste water is treated on site. Jencks sums it up:

There's not one solution for going off-grid, but many different ways to make the off-grid lifestyle easier and more enjoyable. We used a whole collection of technologies but because the house is so light in the day and the long summer evenings, we hardly turn the lights on then, and during the winter we like to use the fire and candles.[13]

Subtly, the modern home is being reinvented once again. We all understand the green imperative and the essential need to protect and preserve the natural environment. Inevitably, our houses will change and evolve over the coming years to reduce our carbon footprint and help in the great effort to combat climate change. But this should not frighten us at all, given that our homes and the way that we live within them will be protected by these gentle changes in design and technology. In some ways it might feel that we are going backwards, but actually we are stepping very firmly forwards, as Lily Jencks says:

One hundred and fifty years ago we were all off-grid. We have just become so comfortable being connected to the grids that it seems difficult to separate ourselves now. But I hope that as clean technologies become more affordable, and people are able to produce their own energy and clean water, there may be a time when switching off grid is as easy as turning off data roaming.[14]

So many micro-generation and energy-conservation solutions will become standard within the next few years and feature in all of our homes. It's quite possible that we will barely notice the difference in the way that we enjoy our patterns of living at home, while our houses and apartments will remain our most precious and golden spaces. And yet, along with everything else that they have done for us over the years, our homes will also play an important part in saving the world.

Glossary

Art Deco

With a name derived from an influential 1925 exhibition in Paris, the Exposition Internationale des Arts Décoratifs et Industriels Modernes ('International Exhibition of Modern Decorative and Industrial Arts'), Art Deco was a loose movement of architects, artists and designers from around the world looking for a modern aesthetic that would hold up a mirror to the Twenties. In terms of architecture and design, there was a strong interest in new materials, streamlined forms and dynamic machine age influences. There was a significant overlap with the preoccupations and concerns of many early Modernists, yet there were also key differences. Art Deco was an opulent aesthetic, which spliced a love of Futurism and modernity with rich materials, a passion for the bespoke and high levels of craftsmanship, as well as an openness to both natural and new industrially produced materials such as chromium and Bakelite. Increasingly, as the Thirties progressed, Modernist architects began to reject the more lavish aspects of Art Deco design, searching instead for a more functional, democratic and pared down 'less is more' design philosophy.

Art Nouveau

Flourishing during the late 19th and early 20th centuries, Art Nouveau was a fresh aesthetic movement that sought to combine a version of modernity with a passion for artisanal craftsmanship and a love of nature and natural forms. In this respect, it can be seen as an evolution of the Arts & Crafts movement, with a shared concern for craft and a suspicion of machine age production. Yet Art Nouveau designers went far beyond the quiet reserve and simplicity of the Arts & Crafts movement, embracing a highly ornate style with references to organic, natural forms such as flowers, trees, branches, leaves and tendrils that were woven into buildings, furniture, jewellery, posters and graphics. While Art Nouveau can be seen as an international movement, there were many distinct variants upon it, including the Vienna Secession, Jugendstil in Germany, Stile Liberty in Italy and Modernisme in Spain. The emphasis upon applied ornament, pattern and colour set Art Nouveau apart from Art Deco and Modernism, which rejected such ornamental excess and flamboyance.

Arts & Crafts

The term 'Arts & Crafts' first came into currency in the United Kingdom around 1888, named after the Arts and Crafts Exhibition Society. The Society and its members promoted artisanal craftsmanship and handmade production while reacting against the threat, as they saw it, of industrial mass manufacturing. Grounded in the work and writings of John Ruskin and William Morris, in particular, Arts & Crafts architects and designers found inspiration in pre-industrial ways of working while seeking a revival of traditional skills. They referenced the architecture and design of the Middle Ages, and the strong craft tradition in countries such as Japan, but combined this with an aesthetic that was relatively simple and unadorned in comparison with the multilayered interiors of the Victorian period. There was an emphasis on the beauty of natural materials, especially wood, and honestly expressed ways of making, as seen in the exposed joints and junctions of

Arts & Crafts furniture or the plain plaster or brick walls within residential projects. Although Arts & Crafts architects looked to the past, there were also early stirrings of modernity in the way that their houses explored – or reinterpreted – the multipurpose 'great room', for instance, and adopted a more fluid approach to spatial planning, while also stressing the need for greater synergy between house and garden.

atrium

An atrium is essentially a courtyard within a building, which can be either open or covered with a skylight. The concept dates back to the classical idea of a Roman courtyard house but was also adopted within, for example, traditional Moorish and Arabic architecture. Architects of the 20th and 21st centuries have been drawn to modern interpretations of atria, given how effectively they can help introduce light and air to the heart of a building. Such private, secluded outdoor rooms have particular benefits in built-up urban areas, but also have advantages in more exposed rural or coastal settings, where such sheltered spaces offer a retreat from the wind or sun.

Brutalism

A sub-movement of Modernist architecture, Brutalism emerged during the post-war period and was at its height during the Sixties and Seventies. The term 'New Brutalism' is associated, in particular, with the work of architects Alison and Peter Smithson and critic Reyner Banham, who was one of the first to explore the importance of the movement. Brutalism denotes an uncompromising and robust approach to materials and form, usually expressed in concrete, combined with a sometimes semi-sculptural approach. Initially associated with the tower blocks and high-rises of the United Kingdom and Europe, Brutalism was also explored in many other parts of the world, including Brazil, Mexico and elsewhere

in Latin America, where architects such as Félix Candela used concrete shells in a more expressive way.

Case Study House Program

The Case Study House Program was an influential initiative launched by John Entenza, the editor of *Arts & Architecture*, in 1945. Focused on California, the programme championed the design of innovative houses invented by architects such as Craig Ellwood, Richard Neutra, Charles and Ray Eames, Eero Saarinen, Pierre Koenig and others. The houses in the series were privately commissioned but then promoted by the magazine as key exemplars of modern architecture. Many of these houses were steel-framed, lightweight buildings with a strong relationship between indoor and outdoor space, while a number were relatively modest in scale and intended to be relatively affordable prototypical homes.

Congrès International d'Architecture Moderne (CIAM)

An international forum for Modernist architects and designers, CIAM was founded in 1928 by an influential collective that included Le Corbusier, Pierre Chareau and Gerrit Rietveld. Members met for a number of thematic annual conferences, while CIAM sub-branches sprang up in many affiliated countries. The conferences were interrupted by World War II, and, with CIAM having reached its zenith during the Thirties, its relevance waned, until the group broke up during the late Fifties.

curtain wall

A non-supporting wall with no structural, load-bearing function. While brick or stone walls in traditional period houses play a key part in supporting the weight of the building, pioneering Modernist architects developed an alternative structural approach where reinforced concrete frames or steel skeletons supported the building. This freed the external walls, which could be filled with ribbon windows or banks of glass, allowing a stronger relationship between the interiors and exteriors. Glass houses by Mies van der Rohe, Philip Johnson and others took the idea of curtain walls to a new extreme, using steel frames and banks of floor-to-ceiling glazing to create transparent or semi-transparent buildings.

Desert Modernism

Focused upon California and neighbouring States during the post-war period, Desert Modernism was a sub-movement within Modernism. Desert Modernists such as Richard Neutra, Craig Ellwood and Albert Frey pioneered an approach that maximized connectivity between inside and outside space, including the desert landscape, while seeking to mitigate the impact of the sun. Steel-framed buildings, curtain walls, banks of glass and outdoor rooms were common features.

Five Points of Architecture

Le Corbusier's Five Points represent a Modernist manifesto in miniature. Expressed in his writings and buildings of the Thirties, the Five Points were: the use of piloti, or supporting pillars, made from reinforced concrete, which supported the building and could lift it above the ground plane; ribbon windows; a free façade, or curtain wall, enabled by the liberation of the external walls from their structural load-bearing role; internal open plans, also known as 'free plans' or 'universal spaces'; and, lastly, the use of roof gardens or terraces. Many key early Modernist houses of the Thirties adopted some or all of the Five Points.

genius loci

A classical concept referring to the 'spirit of a place', the *genius loci* remains particularly important to architects and designers committed to a contextual and site-specific approach.

Organic architecture, for example, places a strong emphasis on the *genius loci*, while many contemporary architects connect it to a renewed focus on sustainable design and how it responds to particular local conditions.

high-tech

High-tech architecture emerged during the Seventies, particularly in the United Kingdom and Europe, with a focus on lightweight and steel-framed buildings that allowed for the provision of open space internally and strong connections to outside space via curtain walls. Pioneering high-tech architects such as Richard Rogers, Norman Foster and Michael Hopkins drew inspiration from, among others, the work of West Coast Modernists such as Craig Ellwood, Pierre Koenig and Charles & Ray Eames, who worked with steel-framed structures.

International Style

Coined by curator-turned-architect Philip Johnson and his colleague Henry-Russell Hitchcock, the term International Style emerged from the key 1932 *Modern Architecture: International Exhibition* at the Museum of Modern Art in New York and the associated book (*The International Style: Architecture Since 1922*). Both the exhibition and the book featured work by early Modernist architects including Le Corbusier, Walter Gropius, Richard Neutra and Ludwig Mies van der Rohe. The term carried over to the post-war period and is associated with a transatlantic aesthetic focused on geometrical purity, linear precision, functional order and modern materials. The term came to worry some Modernists, including Gropius, as it seemed to neglect the importance of regional variation and context.

maximalism

The antithesis of minimalism, maximalism promotes creative self-expression, layered spaces and a liberated approach to colour, pattern, texture and materials. Maximalism is not associated with any one period of design, yet Art Nouveau could be regarded as a semi-maximalist movement, while the Sixties and Seventies can be seen as hot spots; Post-Modernism could also be regarded as a maximalist aesthetic style. Maximalism has periodically resurfaced throughout the 20th and 21st centuries, largely promoted by aficionados within the interior design community more than architects.

mid-century Modernism

This post-war movement was characterized by its commitment to Modernist principles fused with an approach that was more characterful, expressive and sometimes playful than was usually the case during the pre-war years. A global movement with regional variations, mid-century Modernism encompassed the Fifties, when the focus was upon more natural materials and themes, as well as the Sixties, when the movement was influenced by Pop Art, Op Art and design experiments with a new generation of plastics.

minimalism

Minimalist design is pared down, refined, disciplined and ordered, with a focus on the character, detailing and finish of materials. Generally seen as Modernist in spirit, minimalism rejects ornament and pattern in favour of texture and light.

Modernism

Emerging during the Twenties and carrying through to the post-war period and far beyond, Modernism was the defining architectural and design movement of the 20th century. Early pioneers such as Le Corbusier and Ludwig Mies van der Rohe promoted buildings that were linear, geometric, rational, functional and precisely ordered, while embracing reinforced concrete construction, piloti and open-plan living spaces. At the same time, applied ornament and aesthetic excess were largely rejected. By the post-war period, steel-framed buildings and curtain walls were common, allowing the creation of universal spaces within and banks of glass that connected inside and outside space. Yet Modernism was a broad umbrella movement that allowed for many different approaches and variations linked to the push for a more modern way of living. These included organic architecture, mid-century Modernism, Desert Modernism and Regional Modernism; architecture of the International Style is often regarded as the purest and most disciplined expression of core Modernist principles.

neo-classicism

Rooted in the Renaissance period, neo-classical architecture offered a reinterpretation of design principles established during the ascendancy of the Greek and Roman civilizations. Such classical principles included a commitment to symmetry, proportion and scale, along with a vocabulary of pillars, porticos and pediments that was revived during the 16th and 17th centuries. Neo-classical buildings were not always urban or ecclesiastical, as seen in the Palladian farmhouses of northern Italy. Neo-classicism has remained a highly important and influential strand of architecture ever since, enjoying periodic phases of popularity and relevance around the world. Modernists were largely suspicious of neo-classicism, while taking note of its key lessons. Post-Modernists such as Robert Venturi and Denise Scott Brown saw neo-classicism as an essential point of reference, while also drawing on many other influences.

organic architecture

Promoted by Frank Lloyd Wright and his many followers, organic architecture argued in favour of highly contextual buildings that were a considered response to a particular site and setting. Such houses and buildings appeared to 'grow' from the landscape rather than imposing themselves upon it, while making use of local materials, as well as 'modern' materials such as reinforced concrete. Organic architecture is regarded as a sub-movement of Modernism, but with a focus on connectivity with the landscape and the natural world.

piano nobile

Meaning the 'noble floor', the term *piano nobile* originates in neo-classical and Palladian architecture, where it denotes the principal level of a building, which sits above a subservient ground or lower ground floor (usually devoted to ancillary and service spaces). The use of an elevated *piano nobile* for key living spaces and reception rooms helped to promote greater connectivity with the surroundings and often improve the flow of light. Many early Modernist architects, including Le Corbusier, borrowed the idea of a piano nobile while supporting it with structural piloti, or pillars, which created an undercroft that could be used for garaging and service spaces, as well as an entry sequence. Others adopted 'upside-down' plans, where the bedrooms were on the lower level while the main living spaces were hosted by the *piano nobile* above.

piloti

Supporting pillars or columns, usually made of reinforced concrete. Favoured and promoted by Le Corbusier in particular, piloti featured in his mini-Modernist manifesto known as the Five Points of Architecture. They were often used, during the Thirties especially, to elevate the principal living spaces above the ground plane to create a *piano nobile*.

Post-Modernism

Associated with the 'less is a bore' philosophy advocated by architects and designers Robert Venturi and Denise Scott Brown, Post-Modernism evolved during the Seventies as a reaction to the perceived limitations of Modernism. Post-Modern architects around the world embraced a multitude of influences, including neo-classicism, Modernism and references from popular culture. While the best Post-Modern design retained a logic, discipline and order of its own, the movement started to suffer when it began to move into the mainstream, where its countercultural leanings were lost on its corporate sponsors. Architecturally, Post-Modernism flourished in the United States, the United Kingdom and Europe. The legacy of Post-Modernism lies in its acceptance of eclecticism and even maximalism.

prefabrication

The idea of a prefabricated, factory-made home or other building was a key preoccupation for a number of Modernist designers in particular, such as Richard Buckminster Fuller. The goal of a more affordable, readily available house gained traction during the post-war years when architects such as Jean Prouvé developed prefabricated structures in response to the need for urban reconstruction, especially in France and other parts of Europe. Prefabrication has remained a subject of fascination within the architectural community, with an increased interest in the way that ready-made component parts might help in the drive towards more sustainable buildings featuring high levels of insulation and reduced construction times, which should equal a smaller carbon footprint during the building process.

promenade architecturale

A concept associated with Le Corbusier, the *promenade architecturale* refers to the journey towards and through a house or building. For him, and many other architects, this journey or pathway is a key process within the discovery and enjoyment of a building. Le Corbusier favoured not only a gradual unfolding of a building, which heightened the sense of anticipation and delight, but also the provision of alternative circulation routes such as the choice between a staircase and a ramp, as seen at his Villa Savoye (1931). This focus on the importance of the *promenade architecturale* remains one of Le Corbusier's most lasting legacies.

regional Modernism

As a broad church, Modernism made space for regional variations and sub-branches around the world, generated by a particular response to climate and weather patterns. These sub-movements included Desert Modernism and Tropical Modernism, while Scandinavia, Latin America, Asia, India, Africa and other parts of the world developed their own unique versions of Modernist architecture and design, influenced not only by the climate but also the availability of local materials and vernacular traditions.

'soft' Modernism

'Soft' Modernism, or 'warm' Modernism, is another sub-branch of Modernist architecture and design. Mid-century Scandinavian architecture and design provides the strongest expression of soft Modernism, with its focus on natural materials, organic architecture and a playful attitude to colour, texture, pattern and form. Other parts of the world, such as Latin America, also developed a softer, warmer take on Modernism when compared with the geometric rigour and precision of the International Style.

streamlining

Streamlining first evolved during the Art Deco period when architects and designers took inspiration from the rounded forms of cars, planes, trains and liners and applied them to buildings, furniture and products. This machine age aesthetic then carried through into various strands of early Modernist design, with houses and apartment buildings adopting rounded decks, terraces and detailing. During the post-war period, streamlining experienced a renaissance as it was widely applied within the car industry and also within new generations of appliances and products that embraced futuristic and sinuous curves suggesting speed and dynamism.

vernacular architecture

The vernacular refers to a traditional form of architecture rooted in a particular sense of place. This has generally been influenced by the availability of local materials and the development of local crafts, but also by the climate and topography of a region, as well as its social and cultural traditions. Familiar vernacular buildings such as farmsteads, barns, courtyard houses and so on have influenced many 20th- and 21st-century architects.

Vienna Secession

Closely affiliated with the Art Nouveau movement, the Vienna Secession was a grouping of architects and artists who broke away from the prevailing Vienna Academy of Arts in 1897. Key figures such as Otto Wagner and Gustav Klimt argued for synergy between artistic disciplines and a design philosophy more in tune with the times. While the movement largely rejected tradition and historicism, its aesthetic was still expressive and ornate in the manner of Art Nouveau. By 1903, the movement began to splinter, with the creation of the Wiener Werkstätte, yet the Secessionists later regrouped. While Secession architects such as Wagner and Josef Hoffmann are seen as proto-Modernists, their work became a target for criticism from another highly influential Viennese architect, Adolf Loos. He pulled away from the Secessionists and began to argue for a more reserved, pared-down aesthetic while rejecting what he saw as ornamental excess within architecture and the applied arts.

Chronology & Gazetteer

NOTE – Please respect the privacy of privately-owned properties and ensure that you check the visiting arrangements for any houses that might be open to the public before making any plans to travel.

1860 – Philip Webb and William Morris – Red House, Bexleyheath, Kent, England
www.nationaltrust.org.uk/red-house

1886 – Otto Wagner – Villa Wagner I, Vienna, Austria
www.ernstfuchsmuseum.at

1903 – Charles Rennie Mackintosh – Hill House, Helensburgh, Argyll and Bute, Scotland
www.nts.org.uk/visit/places/the-hill-house

1905 – Charles Voysey – The Homestead, Frinton-on-Sea, Essex, England
Privately Owned

1905 – Edward Prior – Voewood, Holt, Norfolk, England
www.voewood.com

1908 – Greene & Greene – Gamble House, Pasadena, California, United States
gamblehouse.org

1909 – Frank Lloyd Wright – Robie House, Chicago, Illinois, United States
www.flwright.org/visit/robiehouse

1910 – Adolf Loos – Steiner House, Vienna, Austria
Privately Owned

1911 – Josef Hoffmann – Palais Stoclet, Brussels, Belgium
Privately Owned

1912 – Otto Wagner – Villa Wagner II, Vienna, Austria
Privately Owned

1921 – Frank Lloyd Wright – Hollyhock House, Los Angeles, California, United States
barnsdall.org

1922 – Rudolph Schindler – Schindler House, Los Angeles, California, United States
makcenter.org/visit/

1924 – Gerrit Rietveld – Schröder House, Utrecht, Netherlands
www.rietveldschroderhuis.nl/en/rietveld-schroder-house

1928 – Ludwig Wittgenstein and Paul Engelmann – Haus Wittgenstein, Vienna, Austria
www.haus-wittgenstein.at

1929 – Eileen Gray – E-1027, Roquebrune-Cap-Martin, France
capmoderne.com

1930 – Edwin Lutyens – Castle Drogo, Drewsteignton, Devon, England
www.nationaltrust.org.uk/castle-drogo

1930 – Eliel Saarinen – Saarinen House, Bloomfield Hills, Michigan, United States
Cranbrookart.edu

1930 – Ludwig Mies van der Rohe – Villa Tugendhat, Brno, Czech Republic
www.tugendhat.eu/en/

1931 – Cedric Gibbons – Del Río House, Santa Monica, California, United States
Privately Owned

1931 – Le Corbusier – Villa Savoye, Poissy, Paris, France
www.villa-savoye.fr

1932 – Pierre Chareau – Maison de Verre, Paris, France
Privately Owned

1933 – Robert Mallet-Stevens – Villa Noailles, Hyères, France
Villanoailles-hyeres.com

1934 – Wells Coates – Isokon, London, England
www.isokongallery.co.uk

1935 – Berthold Lubetkin – Highpoint I, London, England
Privately Owned

1936 – Seely & Paget – Eltham Palace, Eltham, London, England
www.english-heritage.org.uk/visit/places/eltham-palace-and-gardens

1936 – Alden B Dow – Alden B Dow Home and Studio, Midland, Michigan, United States
www.abdow.org

1937 – Frank Lloyd Wright – Fallingwater, Bear Run, Pennsylvania, United States
Fallingwater.org

1938 – Berthold Lubetkin – Highpoint II, London, England
Privately Owned

1938 – Patrick Gwynne – The Homewood, Esher, Surrey, England
www.nationaltrust.org.uk/the-homewood

1938 – Walter Gropius – Gropius House, Lincoln, Massachusetts, United States
www.historicnewengland.org/property/gropius-house/

1939 – Alvar Aalto – Villa Mairea, Noormarkku, Finland
maisonlouiscarre.fr/mlc/en/visits-and-booking/

1940s–1960s – Joseph Eichler – Eichler Homes, California, United States
Privately Owned

1945 – Richard Buckminster Fuller – Dymaxion House, various locations, United States
www.thehenryford.org/visit/henry-ford-museum/exhibits/dymaxion-house/

1947 – Richard Neutra – Kaufmann House, Palm Springs, California, United States
Privately Owned

1947 – Jean-François Zevaco – Villa Sami Suissa, Casablanca, Morocco
www.iconichouses.org/houses/villa-suissa-villa-zevaco

1949 – Charles and Ray Eames – Eames House, Pacific Palisades, California, United States
eamesfoundation.org/visit/how-to-visit/

1949 – Philip Johnson – Glass House, New Canaan, Connecticut, United States
theglasshouse.org

1949 – Tony Duquette – Dawnridge, Beverly Hills, California, United States
Privately Owned

1950 – Harry Seidler – Rose Seidler House, Sydney, New South Wales, Australia
Privately Owned

1950s–1960s – Eric Lyons – Span Houses, various locations, England
Privately Owned

1951 – Ludwig Mies van der Rohe – Farnsworth House, Plano, Illinois, United States
farnsworthhouse.org

1951 – Lina Bo Bardi – Casa de Vidro, São Paulo, Brazil
Institutobobardi.com.br

1951 – Ludwig Mies van der Rohe – Lake Shore Drive Apartments, Chicago, Illinois, United States
Privately Owned

1952 – Jørn Utzon – Utzon House, Hellebaek, Helsingør, Denmark
Privately Owned

1952 – Le Corbusier – Unité d'Habitation, Marseille, France
www.marseille-tourisme.com/en/discover-marseille/the-essentials/cite-radieuse-le-corbusier/

1953 – Oscar Niemeyer – Casa das Canoas, Rio de Janeiro, Brazil
www.niemeyer.org.br/fundacao/locais/cas-das-canoas

1954 – Jean Prouvé – Prouvé House, Nancy, France
www.nancy-tourisme.fr/en/offers/maison-jean-prouve-nancy-en-2036927/

1955 – Piero Fornasetti – Fornasetti House, Milan, Italy
Privately Owned

1957 – Eero Saarinen – Miller House, Columbus, Indiana, United States
columbus.in.us/miller-house-and-garden-tour/

1957 – Arne Jacobsen – Round House, Zealand, Denmark
Privately Owned

1958 – Josep Lluís Sert – Sert Residence, Cambridge, Massachusetts, United States
Privately Owned

1958 – Jakob Halldor Gunnløgsson – Gunnløgsson House, Øresund Strait, Denmark
Privately Owned

1959 – Alvar Aalto – Maison Louis Carré, Bazoches-sur-Guyonne, France
maisonlouiscarre.fr/mlc/en/visits-and-booking/

1960 – Pierre Koenig – Case Study House #22, Los Angeles, California, United States
Privately Owned

1961 – Louis Kahn – Esherick House, Philadelphia, Pennsylvania, United States
Privately Owned

1962 – Hanne and Poul Kjaerholm – Kjaerholm House, Rungsted, Hørsholm, Denmark
Privately Owned

1962 – Alison & Peter Smithson – Upper Lawn, Tisbury, Wiltshire, England
Privately Owned

1963 – Antonio Bonet Castellana – La Ricarda, Barcelona, Spain
Privately Owned

1964 – Robert Venturi – Vanna Venturi House, Philadelphia, Pennsylvania, United States
Privately Owned

1965 – Charles Deaton – Sculptured House, Genesee Mountain, Colorado, United States
Privately Owned

1965 – Charles Gwathmey – Gwathmey Residence and Studio, Amagansett, Long Island, United States
Privately Owned

1968 – John Lautner – Elrod House, Palm Springs, California, United States
Privately Owned

1968 – Matti Suuronen – Futuro House, various locations, Finland
www.futurohouse.co.uk

1968 – Richard Foster –
The Round House, Wilton,
Connecticut, United States
Privately Owned

1968 – Luis Barragán –
San Cristóbal, Los Clubes,
Mexico City, Mexico
Privately Owned

1969 – Craig Ellwood –
Palevsky House, Palm Springs,
California, United States
Privately Owned

1969 – Geoffrey Bawa –
Lunuganga, Bentota,
Sri Lanka
Geoffreybawa.com/lunuganga

1969 – Staffan Berglund –
Villa Spies, Torö, Finland
Privately Owned

1969 – Richard Rogers –
Rogers House, Wimbledon,
London, England
Privately Owned

1970 – Paulo Mendes da Rocha
– Millán House,
São Paulo, Brazil
Privately Owned

1970 – Agustín Hernández –
Casa Hernández,
Mexico City, Mexico
Privately Owned

1971 – Terence Conran –
Barton Court, Kintbury,
Berkshire, England
Privately Owned

1972 – Robert Venturi
and Denise Scott Brown –
Venturi–Scott Brown House,
Philadelphia, Pennsylvania,
United States
Privately Owned

1972 – Scott Tallon Walker –
Goulding House,
Enniskerry, Ireland
Privately Owned

1973 – Mario Botta –
House at Riva San Vitale,
Ticino, Switzerland
Privately Owned

1975 – Ricardo Bofill –
La Fábrica, Barcelona,
Spain
Privately Owned

1975 – Glenn Murcutt –
Marie Short House,
Kempsey, New South Wales,
Australia
Privately Owned

1976 – Michael and Patty
Hopkins – Hopkins House,
Hampstead, London, England
Privately Owned

1976 – Chamberlin, Powell
& Bon – Barbican Estate,
London, England
Privately Owned

1976 – Andrée Putman –
Putman Apartment, Paris,
France
Privately Owned

1979 – Eduardo Longo –
Casa Bola, São Paulo, Brazil
Privately Owned

1979 – David Hicks –
Britwell House, Britwell
Salome, Oxfordshire,
England
Privately Owned

1984 – Tadao Ando –
Koshino House, Kobe, Japan
Privately Owned

1984 – Jan Benthem –
Benthem House, Almere,
Netherlands
Privately Owned

1988 – Charles Correa –
House at Koramangala,
Bangalore, India
Privately Owned

1989 – Antti Lovag –
Palais Bulles, Théoule-sur-Mer,
Nice, France
Privately Owned

1989 – John Pawson
and Claudio Silvestrin –
Neuendorf House,
Mallorca, Spain
Privately Owned

1998 – Future Systems
– Malator, Druidston,
Pembrokeshire, Wales
Privately Owned

1999 – Philippe Starck –
YOO residential projects,
various locations worldwide
Privately Owned

2003 – Vincent Van Duysen
– Van Duysen Residence,
Antwerp, Belgium
Privately Owned

2009 – Giorgio Armani –
Armani House, Saint-Tropez,
France
Privately Owned

2011 – John Wardle –
Shearers Quarters,
Bruny Island, Tasmania,
Australia
Privately Owned

2013 – Patterson Architects –
Scrubby Bay House,
Banks Peninsula,
New Zealand
Privately Owned

2015 – Todd Saunders –
Fogo Island Arts Studios,
Fogo Island, Newfoundland,
Canada
www.fogoislandarts.ca

2016 – John Pawson – Life
House, Llanbister, Wales
www.livingarchitecture.co.uk/
the-houses/life-house

2016 – Lily Jencks – Ruins
Studio, Dumfries, Scotland
Privately Owned

Endnotes

INTRODUCTION

1   Gaston Bachelard, *The Poetics of Space*, London: Penguin Classics, 2014 (originally published 1964)
2   Le Corbusier, *Towards A New Architecture*, New York: Dover Publications, 1986 (originally published 1931)
3   Bachelard, *The Poetics of Space*
4   Henry David Thoreau, *Walden and Civil Disobedience*, London: Penguin American Library, 1983 (originally published 1854)
5   Quoted in Adam Sharr, *Heidegger's Hut*, Cambridge, Massachusetts: MIT Press, 2017
6   Witold Rybczynski, *Home: A Short History of an Idea*, London: Penguin, 1987

CHAPTER 1

1   William Morris, 'The Lesser Arts', *News from Nowhere and Other Writings*, London: Penguin, 1993
2   Hugh Casson, 'Foreword', in Edward Hollamby, *Philip Webb: Red House*, London: Phaidon, 1991
3   Quoted in Hollamby, *Philip Webb: Red House*
4   Nikolaus Pevsner, *Pioneers of Modern Design*, New Haven and London: Yale University Press, 2005 (first published 1936)
5   Morris, 'The Lesser Arts'
6   Quoted in Wendy Hitchmough, *C F A Voysey*, London: Phaidon, 1995
7   Quoted in Linda G Arntzenius, *The Gamble House*, Los Angeles: University of Southern California School of Architecture, 2000

CHAPTER 2

1   Quoted in August Sarnitz, *Otto Wagner*, Cologne: Taschen, 2007
2   Ibid.
3   Quoted in August Sarnitz, *Josef Hoffmann*, Cologne: Taschen, 2007
4   Adolf Loos, 'Ornament and Crime', in *Ornament and Crime*, London: Penguin, 2019
5   Ibid.
6   Ibid.
7   Adolf Loos, 'Learn a New Way of Dwelling!', in *Ornament and Crime*
8   Quoted in Nana Last, *Wittgenstein's House*, New York: Fordham University Press, 2008
9   Ibid.
10 Quoted in Ray Monk, *Wittgenstein: The Duty of Genius*, London: Jonathan Cape, 1990

CHAPTER 3

1   Quoted in Jean-François Pinchon (ed.), *Rob Mallet-Stevens: Architecture, Furniture, Interior Design*, Cambridge, Massachusetts: MIT Press, 1990
2   Quoted in Peter Adam, *Eileen Gray: Architect/Designer*, New York: Harry N Abrams, 1987
3   From *L'Architecture Moderne*, Winter 1929, reproduced in Simon Unwin, *Twenty-Five Buildings Every Architect Should Understand*, London: Routledge, 2014

CHAPTER 4

1   Adolf Loos, *Ornament and Crime*, London: Penguin Classics, 2009
2   Ibid.
3   Louis Sullivan, 'The Tall Office Building Artistically Considered', *Lippincott's Magazine*, 1896
4   Le Corbusier, *L'Almanach d'Architecture Moderne*, quoted in Jean Jenger, *Le Corbusier: Architect of a New Age*, London: Thames & Hudson, 1993
5   Dominique Vellay and François Halard, *La Maison de Verre: Pierre Chareau's Modernist Masterwork*, London: Thames & Hudson, 2007
6   Quoted in Bertus Mulder and Ida van Zijl, *Rietveld Schröder House*, New York: Princeton Architectural Press, 1999
7   Quoted on the Villa Tugendhat website, www.tugendhat.eu/en/ (accessed 7 November 2019)
8   Ibid.

CHAPTER 5

1   Quoted in Robert McCarter, *Frank Lloyd Wright: Architect*, London: Phaidon, 1997
2   Quoted in Neil Levine, *The Architecture of Frank Lloyd Wright*, Princeton: Princeton University Press, 1996
3   Quoted in Bruce Brooks Pfeiffer, *Frank Lloyd Wright*, Cologne: Taschen, 2006
4   Frank Lloyd Wright, 'In the Nature of Materials', reprinted in Robert McCarter (ed.), *On and By Frank Lloyd Wright*, London: Phaidon, 2005
5   Ibid.
6   Quoted in Patrick J Meehan (ed.), *The Master Architect: Conversations with Frank Lloyd Wright*, Hoboken: Wiley-Interscience, 1984

7   Quoted in Diane Maddex, *Alden B. Dow: Midwestern Modern*, Midland: Alden B. Dow Home & Studio/W W Norton & Company, 2007

CHAPTER 6

1   Quoted in Kathryn Smith, *Schindler House*, New York: Harry N Abrams, 2001
2   Quoted in Gloria Koenig, *Charles & Ray Eames*, Cologne: Taschen, 2005
3   Ibid.
4   Esther McCoy, *Case Study Houses: 1945–1962*, Santa Monica: Hennessy & Ingalls, 1977
5   Quoted in Neil Jackson, *Pierre Koenig*, Cologne: Taschen, 2007
6   Ibid.

CHAPTER 7

1   Henry-Russell Hitchcock and Philip Johnson, MOMA exhibition catalogue for *Modern Architecture: International Exhibition*, quoted in Kenneth Frampton, *Modern Architecture: A Critical History*, London: Thames & Hudson, 1980
2   Ati Gropius Johansen, *Historic New England*, Fall 2003
3   Walter Gropius, *Scope of Total Architecture*, London: Allen & Unwin, 1956
4   Quoted in Josep M Rovira (ed.), *Sert 1928–1979 Complete Work*, Barcelona: Fundació Joan Miró, 2006
5   Quoted by Luis Ridao in 'To the Letter', *The World of Interiors*, August 2010
6   Quoted in Kenneth Frampton and Philip Drew, *Harry Seidler: Four Decades of Architecture*, London: Thames & Hudson, 1992

CHAPTER 8

1   Quoted in Clare Zimmerman, *Mies van der Rohe*, Cologne: Taschen, 2006
2   Quoted in Maritz Vandenberg, *The Farnsworth House*, London: Phaidon, 2003
3   Quoted in Olivia de Oliveira, *Subtle Substances: The Architecture of Lina Bo Bardi*, Barcelona: Gustavo Gili, 2006

CHAPTER 9

1   Quoted in Esa Laaksonen and Ásdís Ólafsdóttir (eds.), *Alvar Aalto Architect: Maison Louis Carré, 1956–63*, Helsinki: Alvar Aalto Foundation, 2008
2   Ibid.

CHAPTER 10

1   Quoted in Nils Peters's *Jean Prouvé*, Cologne: Taschen, 2006
2   Interview with the author, 9 September 2010

CHAPTER 11

1   Quoted in John Allan, *Berthold Lubetkin*, London: Merrell, 2002
2   Le Corbusier, *Towards a New Architecture*, New York: Dover Publications, 1986 (originally published in English in 1931)
3   Interview with the author, 6 October 2011

CHAPTER 12

1   Kenneth Frampton, *Modern Architecture: A Critical History*, London: Thames & Hudson, 2007
2   Quoted in Ruth Peltason and Grace Ong-Yan (eds.), *Architect: The Pritzker Prize Laureates in Their Own Words*, London: Thames & Hudson, 2010
3   Ibid.
4   Ibid.

5   Ibid.
6   Ibid.
7   Charles Correa, *Charles Correa*, London: Thames & Hudson, 1996

CHAPTER 13

1   Quoted in Kate Jacobs, 'Take Me Higher', *ELLE Decoration*, June 2004
2   Interview with the author, 24 June 2009
3   Ibid.
4   Quoted in 'Architect's Revolutionary Idea: Living in a House That Rotates', *New York Times*, 3 September 1968
5   Quoted in Emma O'Kelly, 'Simon Says', *Wallpaper**, January–February 1998
6   Quoted in Jonathan Wingfield, 'Double Bubble', *GQ*, September 2000
7   Quoted in Bruno de Laubadre, 'Vive La Différence', *Interior Design*, January 2002

CHAPTER 14

1   Reyner Banham, 'The New Brutalism', *Architectural Review*, December 1955
2   Quoted in Ruth Peltason and Grace Ong-Yan (eds.), *Architect: The Pritzker Prize Laureates in Their Own Words*, London: Thames & Hudson, 2010
3   Interview with the author, 4 September 2002
4   Ibid.
5   Coincidentally, Tadao Ando's later projects also included a 2003 concrete tower house, known as the 4x4 House, overlooking the waters of Japan's Inland Sea at Kobe, Hyogo.
6   Quoted in Peltason and Ong-Yan (eds.), *Architect: The Pritzker Prize Laureates in Their Own Words*
7   Ibid.
8   Ibid.

9   Tadao Ando, *Tadao Ando: Houses & Housing*, Toto Shuppan, Tokyo, 2007

CHAPTER 15

1   Denise Scott Brown, *Architecture Today*, August 2008
2   Interview with the author, 27 July 2010
3   Quoted in Ruth Peltason and Grace Ong-Yan (eds.), *Architect: The Pritzker Prize Laureates in Their Own Words*, London: Thames & Hudson, 2010
4   Robert Venturi, 'Vanna Venturi House in Philadelphia', www. storiesofhouses.blogspot.com (accessed 6 December 2019)
5   Ibid.
6   Quoted in Joseph Rosa, *Louis I. Kahn*, Cologne: Taschen, 2006
7   Interview with the author, 20 February 2008
8   Ibid.
9   Quoted in Robert Klanten et al (eds.), *Ricardo Bofill: Visions of Architecture*, Berlin: Gestalten, 2019
10   Interview with the author, 23 September 2011

CHAPTER 16

1   Interview with the author, 21 May 2009.
2   Ibid.
3   Interview with the author 19 March 2009.
4   Ibid.
5   Ibid.
6   Interview with the author, 28 February 2008.
7   Ibid.
8   Interview with the author, 18 February 2008.
9   Quoted in Alison Arieff and Bryan Burkhart, *Prefab*, New York: Gibbs Smith, 2002

CHAPTER 17

1   Tony Duquette in a lecture entitled 'The Enchanted Vision', in Hutton

Wilkinson, *More is More: Tony Duquette*, New York: Harry N Abrams, 2009
2   David Hicks, *Style and Design*, London: Viking, 1987
3   Interview with Sheryl Garratt, *Sunday Telegraph*, 4 September 2010
4   Interview with the author, 7 February 2011
5   Ashley Hicks, 'Forever Hicks', *World of Interiors*, March 2003
6   David Hicks, *Living With Design*, London: Weidenfeld & Nicolson, 1979
7   Interview with the author, 19 November 2008.
8   Ibid.
9   Quoted in Deyan Sudjic, *John Pawson: Works*, London: Phaidon, 2005
10   Quoted in Elfreda Pownall, 'Perfectly Plain', *Sunday Telegraph*, 19 September 2010
11   Marc Dubois, 'Nobilis Simplicitas', in Vincent van Duysen, *Complete Works*, London: Thames & Hudson, 2010
12   Marc Dubois, introduction to Vincent van Duysen, *Complete Works*
13   Ilse Crawford, foreword to Vincent van Duysen, *Complete Works*

CHAPTER 18

1   Interview with the author, 5 July 2000
2   Ibid.
3   Ibid.
4   Ibid.
5   Interview with the author, 22 March 2011
6   Ibid.
7   Ibid.
8   Quoted in Dominic Bradbury and John Hitchcox, *Vertical Living: Interior Experiences by Yoo*, London: Thames & Hudson, 2014
9   Ibid.

10   Quoted in Carly Olson, 'Caffè Society', *Architectural Digest*, May 2019
11   Quoted in J J Martin, 'Riviera Retreat', *Architectural Digest*, September 2015

CHAPTER 19

1   Quoted in Ruth Paltason and Grace Ong-Yan (eds.), *Architect: The Pritzker Price Laureates in Their Own Words*, London: Thames & Hudson, 2010
2   Interview with the author, March 2009
3   Ibid.
4   Ibid.
5   Ibid.
6   Interview with the author on 24 November 2014
7   Ibid.
8   Andrew Patterson writing in Patterson Associates, *Patterson: Houses of Aotearoa*, London: Thames & Hudson, 2018
9   Ibid.
10   Interview with the author, 27 March 2020
11   Ibid.
12   Interview with the author on 13 December 2018
13   Ibid.
14   Ibid.

Select Bibliography

ALVAR AALTO
Jetsonen, J. and Jetsonen, S.,
Alvar Aalto Houses, New York:
Princeton Architectural Press,
2011.

Laaksonen, E. and Ólafsdóttir, Á.
(eds.), *Alvar Aalto Architect: Maison
Louis Carré, 1956–63*, Helsinki:
Alvar Aalto Foundation, 2008.

Pallasmaa, J. (ed.), *Villa Mairea:
1938–39*, Helsinki: Alvar Aalto
Foundation, 1998.

Pallasmaa, J. and Sato, T. (eds.),
*Alvar Aalto Through the Eyes of
Shigeru Ban*, London:
Black Dog Publishing, 2007.

Weston, R., *Alvar Aalto: Villa
Mairea*, London: Phaidon, 2002.

TADAO ANDO
Ando, T., *Tadao Ando: Houses and
Housing*, Tokyo: Toto Shuppan,
2007.

Furuyama, M., *Tadao Ando*,
Cologne: Taschen, 2006.

Pare, R., *Tadao Ando: The Colours
of Light*, London: Phaidon, 1996.

LUIS BARRAGÁN
Barragán, L. and Burn, R.,
Luis Barragán, London:
Phaidon, 2000.

Zanco, F. (ed.), *Luis Barragán:
The Quiet Revolution*, Milan:
Skira, 2001.

GEOFFREY BAWA
Bon, G. et al, *Lunuganga*,
Singapore: Marshall Cavendish
Editions, 2007.

Robson, D., *Geoffrey Bawa:
The Complete Works*, London:
Thames & Hudson, 2002.

Robson, D., *Beyond Bawa: Modern
Masterworks of Monsoon Asia*,
London: Thames & Hudson,
2007.

Taylor, B. B., *Geoffrey Bawa*,
London: Thames & Hudson,
1986.

LINA BO BARDI
Bo Bardi, L. et al, *Lina Bo Bardi*,
São Paulo: Instituto Lina Bo e
P.M. Bardi/Edizioni Charta,
1994.

de Oliveira, O., *Subtle Substances:
The Architecture of Lina Bo Bardi*,
Barcelona: Gustavo Gili, 2006.

RICARDO BOFILL
Klanten, R. et al (eds.), *Ricardo
Bofill: Visions of Architecture*, Berlin:
Gestalten, 2019.

MARCEL BREUER
Cobbers, A., *Marcel Breuer*,
Cologne: Taschen, 2007.

Driller, J., *Breuer Houses*,
London: Phaidon, 2000.

**CHAMBERLIN,
POWELL & BON**
Orazi, S., *The Barbican Estate*,
London: Batsford, 2018.

PIERRE CHAREAU
Taylor, B. B., *Pierre Chareau:
Designer and Architect*, Cologne:
Taschen, 1992.

Vellay, D., *La Maison de Verre:
Pierre Chareau's Modernist
Masterwork*, London:
Thames & Hudson, 2007.

TERENCE CONRAN
Conran, T. and Cliff, S.,
Terence Conran's Inspiration,
London: Conran Octopus,
2008.

WELLS COATES
Cohn, L., *The Door to a Secret
Room: A Portrait of Wells Coates*,
Aldershot: Scolar Press, 1999.

Daybelge, L. & Englund, M.,
Isokon & the Bauhaus in Britain,
London: Batsford, 2019.

CHARLES CORREA
Correa, C., *Charles Correa*,
London: Thames & Hudson,
1996.

Correa, C., *Charles Correa:
Housing and Urbanisation*, London:
Thames & Hudson, 2000.

ALDEN B. DOW
Maddex, D., A*lden B. Dow:
Midwestern Modern*, Midland:
Alden B. Dow Home & Studio/
Norton & Company, 2007.

TONY DUQUETTE
Goodmand, W. and Wilkinson,
H., *Tony Duquette*, New York:
Harry N Abrams, 2007.

Wilkinson, H., *More is More: Tony
Duquette*, New York: Harry N
Abrams, 2009.

CHARLES & RAY EAMES
Koenig, G., *Charles & Ray Eames*,
Cologne: Taschen, 2005.

Neuhart, J. & Neuhart, M.,
Eames House, Hoboken: Ernst &
Sohn, 1994.

Steele, J., *Charles & Ray Eames:
Eames House*, London: Phaidon,
1994.

CRAIG ELLWOOD
Jackson, N., *Craig Ellwood*,
London: Laurence King, 2002.

McCoy, E., *Craig Ellwood:
Architecture*, Venice: Alfieri, 1968.

Vacchini, L. et al, *Craig Ellwood: 15 Houses*, Barcelona: 2G/ Gustavo Gili, 1999.

JOSEPH ESHERICK
Lyndon, D. and Alinder, J., *The Sea Ranch*, New York: Princeton Architectural Press, 2004.

PIERO FORNASETTI
Mauriès, P., *Fornasetti: Designer of Dreams*, London: Thames & Hudson, 1991.

RICHARD BUCKMINSTER FULLER
Gorman, M. J., *Buckminster Fuller: Designing for Mobility*, Milan: Skira, 2005.

Hays, K. M. and Miller, D. A., *Buckminster Fuller: Starting with the Universe*, New York: Whitney Museum of Art, 2008.

FUTURE SYSTEMS
Field, M., *Future Systems*, London: Phaidon, 1999.

Sudjic, D., *Future Systems*, London: Phaidon, 2006.

EILEEN GRAY
Adams, P., *Eileen Gray: Architect/ Designer*, New York: Harry N. Abrams, 1987.

Constant, C., *Eileen Gray*, London: Phaidon, 2000.

GREENE & GREENE
Arntzenius, L. G., *The Gamble House*, Los Angeles: University of Southern California School of Architecture, 2000.

Bosley, E. R., *Gamble House: Greene & Greene*, London: Phaidon, 1992.

Bosley, E. R., *Greene & Greene*, London: Phaidon, 2000.

Smith, B. and Vertihoff, A., *Greene & Greene*, London: Thames & Hudson, 1998.

WALTER GROPIUS
Gropius, W., *Scope of Total Architecture*, London: Allen & Unwin, 1956.

Lupfer, G. and Sigel, P., *Walter Gropius*, Cologne: Taschen, 2006.

MacCarthy, F., *Walter Gropius: Visionary Founder of the Bauhaus*, London: Faber & Faber, 2019.

CHARLES GWATHMEY
Breslow, K., *Charles Gwathmey & Robert Siegel: Residential Works, 1966–77*, New York: Architectural Book Publishing Company, 1977.

AGUSTÍN HERNÁNDEZ
Noelle Mereles, L. N., *Agustín Hernández*, Barcelona: Gustavo Gili, 1995.

DAVID HICKS
Hicks, A., *David Hicks: A Life of Design*, New York: Rizzoli, 2008.

Hicks, D., *Living With Design*, London: Weidenfeld & Nicholson, 1979.

Hicks, D., *Style and Design*, London: Viking, 1987.

JOSEF HOFFMANN
Sarnitz, A., *Josef Hoffman*, Cologne: Taschen, 2007.

STEVEN HOLL
Frampton, K. *Steven Holl: Architect*, Milan: Electa, 2002.

Garofalo, F., *Steven Holl*, London: Thames & Hudson, 2003.

MICHAEL HOPKINS
Davies, C., Hodgkinson, P., and Frampton, K., *Hopkins: The Work of Michael Hopkins & Partners*, London: Phaidon, 1995.

Donati, C., *Michael Hopkins*, Geneva: Skira, 2006.

ARNE JACOBSEN
Faber, T., *Arne Jacobsen*, London: Alec Tiranti, 1964.

Solaguren-Beascoa, F., *Arne Jacobsen: Approach to His Complete Works, 1926–1949*, Copenhagen: Danish Architectural Press, 2002.

Solaguren-Beascoa, F., *Arne Jacobsen: Works and Projects*, Barcelona: Gustavo Gili, 1989.

PHILIP JOHNSON
Dunn, D., *The Glass House*, New York: Assouline, 2008.

Fox, S., et al, *The Architecture of Philip Johnson*, Boston: Bulfinch, 2002.

Whitney, D. and Kipnis, J. (eds.), *Philip Johnson: The Glass House*, New York: Pantheon Books, 1993.

LOUIS KAHN
McCarter, R., *Louis Kahn*, London: Phaidon, 2005.

Rosa, J., *Louis I. Kahn*, Cologne: Taschen, 2006.

PIERRE KOENIG
Jackson, N., *Pierre Koenig*, Cologne: Taschen, 2007.

Steele, J. and Jenkins, D., *Pierre Koenig*, London: Phaidon, 1998.

KENGO KUMA
Alini, L., *Kengo Kuma: Works and Projects*, Milan: Electa, 2005.

Bognar, B., *Kengo Kuma: Selected Works*, New York: Princeton Architectural Press, 2005.

Casamonti, M. (ed.), *Kengo Kuma*, Milan: Motta Architettura, 2007.

CARL LARSSON
Af Segerstad, U. H., *Carl Larsson's Home*, Boston: Addison-Wesley, 1978.

Snodin, M. and Stavenhow-Hidemark, E. (eds.), *Carl and Karin Larsson: Creators of the Swedish Style*, London: V&A Publications, 1997.

JOHN LAUTNER
Campbell-Lange, B-A., *John Lautner*, Cologne: Taschen, 2005.

Escher, F., (ed.), *John Lautner: Architect*, New York: Princeton Architectural Press, 1998.

Hess, A., *The Architecture of John Lautner*, London: Thames & Hudson, 1999.

LE CORBUSIER
Cohen, J-L., *Le Corbusier*, Cologne: Taschen, 2006.

Jenger, J., *Le Corbusier: Architect of a New Age*, London: Thames & Hudson, 1996.

Kries, M. et al (eds.), *Le Corbusier – The Art of Architecture*, Weil am Rhein: Vitra Design Museum, 2007.

Sbriglio, J., *Le Corbusier: The Villa Savoye*, Basel: Birkhäuser, 2008.

ADOLF LOOS
Sarnitz, A., *Adolf Loos*, Cologne: Taschen, 2003.

BERTHOLD LUBETKIN
Allan, J., *Berthold Lubetkin*, London: Merrell, 2002.

Reading, M. & Coe, P., *Lubetkin and Tecton*, London: Triangle Architectural Publishing, 1992.

EDWIN LUTYENS
Edwards, B., *Sir Edwin Lutyens: Goddards*, London: Phaidon, 1996.

Stamp, G., *Edwin Lutyens Country Houses*, London: Aurum, 2001.

ERIC LYONS
Simms, B., *Eric Lyons & Span*, London: RIBA Publishing, 2018.

CHARLES RENNIE MACKINTOSH
Macaulay, J., *Charles Rennie Mackintosh: Hill House*, London: Phaidon, 1994.

ROBERT MALLET-STEVENS
Deshoulières, D. et al (eds.), *Rob Mallet-Stevens: Architecte*, Brussels: Archives d'Architecture Moderne, 1981.

Pinchon, J-F., (ed.), *Rob Mallet-Stevens: Architecture, Furniture, Interior Design*, Cambridge, Massachusetts: MIT Press, 1990.

LUDWIG MIES VAN DER ROHE
Mertens, D., *Mies*, London: Phaidon, 2014.

Vandenberg, M., *Farnsworth House: Mies van der Rohe*, London: Phaidon, 2003.

Zimmerman, C., *Mies van der Rohe*, Cologne: Taschen, 2006.

WILLIAM MORRIS & PHILIP WEBB
Hollamby, E., *Philip Webb: Red House*, London: Phaidon, 1991.

Morris, W. *News from Nowhere and Other Writings*, London: Penguin, 1993.

GLENN MURCUTT
Beck, H. & Cooper, J., *Glenn Murcutt: A Singular Architectural Practice*, Melbourne: Images Publishing Group, 2002.

Fromonot, F., *Glenn Murcutt: Buildings & Projects, 1962–2003*, London: Thames & Hudson, 2003.

RICHARD NEUTRA
Hines, T. S., *Richard Neutra and the Search for Modern Architecture*, New York: Rizzoli, 2005.

Lamprecht, B., *Richard Neutra*, Cologne: Taschen, 2006.

OSCAR NIEMEYER
Andreas, P. and Flagge, I., *Oscar Niemeyer: A Legend of Modernism*, Basel: Birkhauser, 2003.

Hess, A., *Oscar Niemeyer Houses*, New York: Rizzoli, 2006.

Niemeyer, O., *The Curves of Time: The Memoirs of Oscar Niemeyer*, London: Phaidon, 2000.

PATTERSON
Patterson Associates, *Patterson: Houses of Aotearoa*, London: Thames & Hudson, 2018.

JOHN PAWSON
Morris, A., *John Pawson: Plain Space*, London: Phaidon, 2010.

Pawson, J., *John Pawson*, Barcelona: Gustavo Gili, 1998.

JEAN PROUVÉ
Peters, N., *Jean Prouvé*, Cologne: Taschen, 2006.

Prouvé, C. & Coley, C., *Jean Prouvé*, Paris: Galerie Patrick Seguin, 2008.

von Vegstack, A., *Jean Prouvé: The Poetics of Technical Objects*, Weil am Rheim: Vitra Design Museum, 2004.

ANDREÉ PUTMAN
Tasma-Anargyos, S., *Andreé Putman*, London: Laurence King, 1993.

GERRIT RIETVELD
Mulder, B. and van Zijl, I., *Rietveld Schröder House*, New York: Princeton Architectural Press, 1999.

Overy, P. et al, *The Rietveld Schröder House*, Oxford: Butterworth, 1988.

van Zijl, I. and Kuper, M., *Gerrit Rietveld: The Complete Works*, Utrecht: Centraal Museum Utrecht, 1993.

RICHARD ROGERS
Powell, K., *Richard Rogers: Complete Works, Vols 1–3*, London: Phaidon, 1999–2006.

EERO SAARINEN
Merkel, J., *Eero Saarinen*, London: Phaidon, 2005.

Serraino, P., *Eero Saarinen*, Cologne: Taschen, 2006.

ELIEL SAARINEN
Hansen, M. et al, *Eliel Saarinen: Projects 1896–1923*, Helsinki: Otava Publishing, 1990.

Wittkopp, G. (ed.), *Saarinen House and Garden: A Total Work of Art*, New York: Harry N Abrams, 1995.

SCOTT TALLON WALKER
O'Regan, J. (ed.), *Scott Tallon Walker Architects: 100 Buildings and Projects, 1960–2005*, Kinsale: Gandon Editions, 2006.

TODD SAUNDERS
Stathaki, E. and Bell, J. (eds.), *Todd Saunders: Architecture in Northern Landscapes*, Basel: Birkhäuser, 2016.

RUDOLPH SCHINDLER
March, L. and Sheine, J. (eds.), *R.M. Schindler: Composition and Construction*, London: Academy Editions, 1993.

Noever, P., *Schindler by MAK*, Munich: Prestel, 2005.

Sheine, J., *R.M. Schindler*, London: Phaidon, 2001.

Smith, K., *Schindler House*, New York: Harry N. Abrams, 2001.

Steele, J., *R.M. Schindler*, Cologne: Taschen, 1999.

HARRY SEIDLER
Frampton, K. and Drew, P., *Harry Seidler: Four Decades of Architecture*, London: Thames & Hudson, 1992.

Seidler, H., *Harry Seidler, 1955–63 – Houses, Buildings and Projects*, Sydney: Horwitz Publications, 1964.

Sharp, D., *Harry Seidler: Selected and Current Works*, Melbourne: Images Publishing Group, 1997.

JOSEP LLUIS SERT
Rovira, J. M., *José Luis Sert, 1901–1983*, London: Phaidon, 2000.

Rovira, J. M. (ed.), *Sert: Complete Work, 1928–1979*, Barcelona: Fundació Joan Miro, 2005.

CLAUDIO SILVESTRIN
Silvestrin, C. et al, *Claudio Silvestrin*, Basel: Birkhäuser, 1999.

ALISON & PETER SMITHSON
Crinson, M., A*lison & Peter Smithson*, London: Historic England, 2018.

van den Heuvel, D. and Risselada, M., *Alison & Peter Smithson – From the House of the Future to a House of Today*, Rotterdam: 010 Publishers, 2004.

MATTI SUURONEN
Home, M. and Taanila, M., *Futuro: Tomorrow's House from Yesterday*, Helsinki: Desura, 2002.

JØRN UTZON
Pardey, J., *Jørn Utzon Logbook Vol. III: Two Houses on Majorca*, Copenhagen: Edition Bløndal, 2004.

Sten Møller, H. and Udsen, V., *Jørn Utzon Houses*, Copenhagen: Living Architecture Publishing, 2007.

VINCENT VAN DUYSEN
Van Duysen, V., *Complete Works*, London: Thames & Hudson, 2010.

ROBERT VENTURI
Schwartz, F. (ed.), *Mother's House: The Evolution of Vanna Venturi's House in Chestnut Hill*, New York: Rizzoli, 1992.

Venturi, R. and Scott Brown, D., *Learning from Las Vegas: The Forgotten Symbolism of Architectural Form*, Cambridge, Massachusetts: MIT Press, 1977.

CHARLES VOYSEY
Hitchmough, W., *C.F.A. Voysey*, London: Phaidon, 1995.

Hitchmough, W., *C.F.A. Voysey: The Homestead*, London: Phaidon, 1994.

OTTO WAGNER
Sarnitz, A., *Otto Wagner*, Cologne: Taschen, 2005.

LUDWIG WITTGENSTEIN
Last, N., *Wittgenstein's House*, New York: Fordham University Press, 2008.

FRANK LLOYD WRIGHT
Brooks Pfeiffer, B. B., *Frank Lloyd Wright*, Cologne: Taschen, 2000.

Levine, N., *The Architecture of Frank Lloyd Wright*, New York: Princeton University Press, 1996.

McCarter, R., *Frank Lloyd Wright: Architect*, London: Phaidon, 1997.

McCarter, R., *Frank Lloyd Wright: Fallingwater*, London: Phaidon, 1994.

McCarter, R. (ed.), *On and By Frank Lloyd Wright: A Primer of Architectural Principles*, London: Phaidon, 2005.

Meehan, P. J., (ed.), *The Master Architect: Conversations with Frank Lloyd Wright*, Hoboken, New Jersey: Wiley, 1984.

Weintraub, A., *Lloyd Wright: The Architecture of Frank Lloyd Wright Jr*, London: Thames & Hudson, 1998.

YOO
Bradbury, D. ans Hitchcox, J., *Vertical Living: Interior Experiences by Yoo*, London: Thames & Hudson, 2014.

Index

Numbers in italics = illustrations; g = glossary entries

Picture Credits

The publishers would like to acknowledge and thank the following for providing photographs for publication.

4, 6–7 Richard Powers; 16–17 Ivan Vdovin/Alamy Stock Photo; 20 Andrew Butler/National Trust/Alamy Stock Photo; 23, 25, 28 Richard Powers; 31 Dennis Gilbert/The National Trust Photo Library/Alamy Stock Photo; 32–33 Volkerpreusser/Alamy Stock Photo; 37 Azoor Photo Collection/Alamy Stock Photo; 40 Alan John Ainsworth/Heritage Image Partnership/Alamy Stock Photo; 44 Bildarchiv Monheim/Alamy Stock Photo; 47 Dietmar Rauscher/Alamy Stock Photo; 48–49 Steve Vidler/Mauritius Images/Alamy Stock Photo; 51 Santi Visalli/Getty Images; 54, 58, 62 Richard Powers; 64–65 Photo Schütze/Rodemann/Bildarchiv Monheim/Alamy Stock Photo © Fondation Le Corbusier/ADAGP, Paris and DACS, London 2021; 73 Collection Artedia/Bridgeman Images; 74 Stuart Cox/National Trust Images; 77 © Centraal Museum, Utrecht/photo Stijn Poelstra; 79 V Dorosz/Alamy Stock Photo © DACS 2021; 82–83 James Schaedig/Alamy Stock Photo; 86 Andrea Jemolo/akg-images; 89 Kayte Deioma/Alamy Live News; 94 Richard T Nowitz/Getty Images; 98 Richard Powers; 100–101 Tim Street-Porter/OTTO; 104 Peter Cook/VIEW/Alamy Stock Photo; 108 Slim Aarons/Getty Images; 111 Peter Stackpole/The LIFE Picture Collection via Getty Images; 116 Richard Powers/Donald Judd © Judd Foundation/ARS, NY and DACS, London 2021; 119, 120–21, 126 Richard Powers; 131 Marius Reynolds/Architectural Association Archives; 133, 135 Richard Powers; 138–39 Richard Powers © DACS 2021; 147 Richard Powers © Mies van der Rohe, DACS 2021; 150, 152–53 Richard Powers; 157 The Danish National Art Library/Royal Danish Library; 159 Laura Stamer; 162 FP Collection/Alamy Stock Photo; 165 Richard Powers; 168–69 Eric Lyons/Architectural Association Archives; 172 Courtesy The Estate of R Buckminster Fuller; 176 Richard Powers © ADAGP, Paris and DACS, London 2021; 181, 183 Richard Powers; 184–85 Silvan Bachmann/Shutterstock; 188 Nicholas Kane/Arcaid/Alamy Stock Photo; 191 Rachael Smith Photography; 194 Georgio Possenti, www.giorgiopossenti.com © DACS 2021; 197 Dino Fracchia/Alamy Stock Photo © Fondation Le Corbusier/ADAGP, Paris and DACS, London 2021; 202–203 Anna Bertho/CC BY-SA (https://creativecommons.org/licenses/by-sa/4.0) © Barragan Foundation/DACS 2021; 210 Richard Powers © Niemeyer, Oscar/DACS 2021; 212 Andy Martin Architecture; 215 Luca Tettoni/Alamy Stock Photo; 217 © Charles Correa Associates, courtesy Charles Correa Foundation; 218–19, 223, 225 Richard Powers; 226 Per-Erik Uddman/TT News Agency/Press Association Images; 231 Aleksandra Suzi/Shutterstock; 232–33, 237 Richard Powers; 241 Mark Luscombe-Whyte/TIA Digital Ltd; 243 Richard Powers; 248–49 Alpha Stock/Alamy Stock Photo; 255, 258, 261 Richard Powers; 264–65 Architecture UK/Alamy Stock Photo; 268, 271, 274 Richard Powers: 276 Richard Powers © Gerrit Rietveld, DACS 2021; 280–81, 285, 288 Richard Powers; 290 Fritz von der Schulenburg/TIA Digital Ltd; 295 © Gilbert McCarragher www.gilbertmccarragher.com; 297–98 Richard Powers; 303 Mark Luscombe Whyte/TIA Digital Ltd; 307 Michael Jacobs/Alamy Stock Photo; 310 Richard Powers; 312–13 Pattersons Associates; 317, 319 Richard Powers; 325 Shankar Adiseshan/Alamy Stock Photo; 326 © Sergio Pirrone.

Acknowledgements

The author would like to express his sincere thanks to Alison Starling, Ella Parsons, Ben Gardiner, Giulia Hetherington, Anna Kelsall and the rest of the team at Ilex and Octopus Publishing Group.

Thanks are also due to Danny Heller for the wonderful cover image, my agent Carrie Kania and to my much respected collaborators over the past twenty years of writing, travelling and freelancing: photographers Richard Powers, Mark Luscombe-Whyte and Rachael Smith.

My gratitude is also due to the many architects, designers and home owners who have tolerated my questions and interest over the last two decades. Without them this book would not have been possible.

Last, but not least, thank you to my patient family: Faith, Florence, Cecily, Noah and Elsie Bradbury.

First published in Great Britain
in 2021 by Ilex,
an imprint of Octopus
Publishing Group Ltd
Carmelite House
50 Victoria Embankment
London EC4Y 0DZ
www.octopusbooks.co.uk

An Hachette UK Company
www.hachette.co.uk

Text copyright © Dominic
Bradbury 2021
Design and layout copyright ©
Octopus Publishing Group Ltd
2021

Distributed in the US by
Hachette Book Group
1290 Avenue of the Americas
4th and 5th Floors
New York, NY 10104

Distributed in Canada by
Canadian Manda Group
664 Annette St.
Toronto, Ontario,
Canada M6S 2C8

ISBN 978-1-78157-761-5

A CIP catalogue record for this book
is available from the British Library.

Printed and bound in China

10 9 8 7 6 5 4 3 2 1

Publisher: Alison Starling
Editor: Ella Parsons
Art Director: Ben Gardiner
Picture Research Manager:
Giulia Hetherington
Picture Research: Claire Hamilton
Production Manager:
Caroline Alberti

Page 4: Craig Ellwood – Palevsky
House, Palm Springs, California,
United States, 1969